THE OVERWORKED AMERICAN

THE
OVERWORKED
AMERICAN

The Unexpected
Decline of Leisure

JULIET B. SCHOR

BasicBooks
A Division of HarperCollins*Publishers*

Library of Congress Cataloging-in-Publication Data

Schor, Juliet.

The overworked American : the unexpected decline of leisure / Juliet B. Schor.

p. cm.

Includes bibliographical references and index.

ISBN 0-465-05433-1

1. Leisure—United States.   2. Hours of labor—United
States.   I. Title.

HD4904.6.S36   1991

306.4′812′0973—dc20   91-70057
                                                            CIP

For Eleanor,
who always had time

Contents

Figures

Tables

Preface

I live in the fastest city in the country. According to a recent study which measured the speed of walking and talking, the length of working hours, and the prevalence of watch wearing and coronary heart disease, Boston outpaces even New York.[1] Until recently, I fitted right in. I hated wasting time, frequently hurried about, and subscribed to prevailing professionals' standards of working hours. A few years ago, I began to question my behavior. The influence of my husband, who has never had a modern American attitude toward time, was important. He helped me to see that much about the American "culture of time" is detrimental to our well-being. In the words of historian Edward Thompson, time has become a currency, which we "spend" instead of "pass." Many of us need to relax, to unwind, and, yes, to work less.[2]

The intellectual interests which led me to write *The Overworked American* have their origins in a new view of the labor market which, along with colleagues, I have been developing over the last decade. In contrast to the standard characterization, the new view emphasizes asymmetries between workers and their employers. A key asymmetry is the existence of a chronic shortage of jobs, which puts workers at a disadvantage in their dealings with employers. I

why e/rs
preter longer hours —

✳

identified a second asymmetry: namely, the preference of employers for long hours, which makes it difficult to translate productivity
increases into free time. With this insight, I began to scrutinize the
consensus view that capitalism has delivered increases in leisure.
And I found that far from raising leisure time, the development of
capitalism involved a tremendous expansion of human effort. People began to work longer and harder. In this new light, I reinterpre-
ted the postwar U.S. experience of stable and then rising hours.
This book is an attempt to understand that experience.

Since the research program associated with my ideas is just beginning, I offer this book in the hope not that it has settled difficult
questions, but rather that it will spur new lines of inquiry and new
debates. If nothing else, I hope to help revive the public discussion
on hours of work which died out fifty years ago.

I have incurred many debts over the last few years connected with
this work. Perhaps the largest is to Laura Leete-Guy, with whom I
jointly constructed the estimates of worktime which form the core
of the book. I am afraid that in the process Laura was turned into
an overworked American herself. I am very grateful for her collabo-
ration. I am also much indebted to a few friends and colleagues
who generously read nearly the entire manuscript: Sam Bowles,
Jerry Epstein, Laurie Sheridan, and my husband, Prasannan Par-
thasarathi. Individual chapters were read by Allen Steinberg, Nancy
Folbre, Jim Duesenberry, and Daniel Cantor. Each of these readers
gave me invaluable help and criticism. They proved to be a gold
mine of penetrating ideas. I have not done their comments justice,
but the book is certainly better as a result of their contributions. I
am grateful to all of them.

Many others have helped along the way, with comments on the
papers that led up to this book or discussions on the material. I
would like to thank Steve Marglin, Tibor Scitovsky, Paul Streeten,
Herb Gintis, Larry Mishel, Michele Naples, Tom Michl, David Gor-
don, Clair Brown, Robert Cilman, James Schor, Claudia Goldin,
Jong-il You, Shannon Stimson, and two anonymous journal review-
ers. I am also grateful for a steady stream of materials from friends:
Elaine Bernard, Sam Bowles, Daniel Cantor, Teresa Ghilarducci,
Steve Marglin, Larry Mishel, and Cheryl Passalaqua. I am especially
appreciative of Laurie Sheridan's willingness to share the transcript

of her interviews on worktime, which I found extremely useful. I would also like to thank others who provided papers or other material: namely, Benjamin Hunnicutt, Carmen Sirianni, Gary Cross, John Robinson, Frank Stafford, Nancy Folbre, Barbara Brandt, Elaine McCrate, Claudia Goldin, Gregory Clark, Joyce Manchester, and Randy Albelda. Thanks also to those who arranged interviews for me: Katherine Karlin, Elisabeth Karlin, and Bill Meyersen. I would like to thank my research assistants on this project: Deepak Bhargava, Alexandra Edsall, and Elora Shehabuddin. Steven Love, librarian at Harvard's Hilles Library, has been accommodating with computer searches. I would also like to thank my colleagues at Social Studies, who provided a welcoming place to write. I received financial assistance from the Economic Policy Institute and Harvard University. I am also grateful for the excellent work of Cheryl Passalaqua, whose province was the manuscript itself. Thanks also to Martin Kessler and Phoebe Hoss of Basic Books. My friends and family have been a tremendous help. To Prasannan, in keeping with tradition, I offer no thanks. I will only say that I look forward to doing for you what you have done for me.

My mother, Eleanor-Marie Schor, died a few months before I finished this book. I would like to dedicate it to her memory.

THE OVERWORKED AMERICAN

===== CHAPTER 1 =====

The Overworked American

since 1970s

In the last twenty years the amount of time Americans have spent at their jobs has risen steadily. Each year the change is small, amounting to about nine hours, or slightly more than one additional day of work. In any given year, such a small increment has probably been imperceptible. But the accumulated increase over two decades is substantial. When surveyed, Americans report that they have only sixteen and a half hours of leisure a week, after the obligations of job and household are taken care of. Working hours are already longer than they were forty years ago. If present trends continue, by the end of the century Americans will be spending as much time at their jobs as they did back in the nineteen twenties.*[1]

The rise of worktime was unexpected. For nearly a hundred years, hours had been declining. When this decline abruptly ended in the late 1940s, it marked the beginning of a new era in worktime. But the change was barely noticed. Equally surprising, but also hardly recognized, has been the deviation from Western Europe. After progressing in tandem for nearly a century, the United States

*In attempting to keep the main text simple, I have relegated detailed discussion of these estimates, discussions of sources and methods, and debates among scholars to the notes and the appendix.[1]

decline since 1850s

veered off into a trajectory of declining leisure, while in Europe work has been disappearing. Forty years later, the differences are large. U.S. manufacturing employees currently work 320 more hours—the equivalent of over two months—than their counterparts in West Germany or France.[2]

The decline in Americans' leisure time is in sharp contrast to the potential provided by the growth of productivity. Productivity measures the goods and services that result from each hour worked.[3] When productivity rises, a worker can either produce the current output in less time, or remain at work the same number of hours and produce more. Every time productivity increases, we are presented with the possibility of either more free time or more money. That's the productivity dividend. [4]

Since 1948, productivity has failed to rise in only five years. The level of productivity of the U.S. worker has more than doubled.[4] In other words, we could now produce our 1948 standard of living (measured in terms of marketed goods and services) in less than half the time it took in that year. We actually could have chosen the four-hour day. Or a working year of six months. Or, *every worker in the United States could now be taking every other year off from work—with pay*. Incredible as it may sound, this is just the simple arithmetic of productivity growth in operation.

But between 1948 and the present we did not use any of the productivity dividend to reduce hours. In the first two decades after 1948, productivity grew rapidly, at about 3 percent a year. During that period, worktime did not fall appreciably. Annual hours per labor force participant fell only slightly. And on a per-capita (rather than a labor force) basis, they even rose a bit. Since then, productivity growth has been lower, but still positive, averaging just over 1 percent a year. Yet hours have risen steadily for two decades. In 1990, the average American owns and consumes more than twice as much as he or she did in 1948, but also has less free time.[5]

How did this happen? Why has leisure been such a conspicuous casualty of prosperity? In part, the answer lies in the difference between the markets for consumer products and free time. Consider the former, the legendary American market. It is a veritable consumer's paradise, offering a dazzling array of products varying in style, design, quality, price, and country of origin. The consumer is treated to GM versus Toyota, Kenmore versus GE, Sony, or

Magnavox, the Apple versus the IBM. We've got Calvin Klein, Anne Klein, Liz Claiborne, and Levi-Strauss; McDonald's, Burger King, and Colonel Sanders. Marketing experts and advertisers spend vast sums of money to make these choices appealing—even irresistible. And they have been successful. In cross-country comparisons, Americans have been found to spend more time shopping than anyone else. They also spend a higher fraction of the money they earn.[6] And with the explosion of consumer debt, many are now spending what they haven't earned.

After four decades of this shopping spree, the American standard of living embodies a level of material comfort unprecedented in human history. The American home is more spacious and luxurious than the dwellings of any other nation. Food is cheap and abundant. The typical family owns a fantastic array of household and consumer appliances: we have machines to wash our clothes and dishes, mow our lawns, and blow away our snow. On a per-person basis, yearly income is nearly $22,000 a year—or sixty-five times the average income of half the world's population.[7]

On the other hand, the "market" for free time hardly even exists in America. With few exceptions, employers (the sellers) don't offer the chance to trade off income gains for a shorter work day or the occasional sabbatical. They just pass on income, in the form of annual pay raises or bonuses, or, if granting increased vacation or personal days, usually do so unilaterally.[8] Employees rarely have the chance to exercise an actual choice about how they will spend their productivity dividend. The closest substitute for a "market in leisure" is the travel and other leisure industries that advertise products to occupy our free time. But this indirect effect has been weak, as consumers crowd increasingly expensive leisure spending into smaller periods of time.

Nor has society provided a forum for deliberate choice. The growth of worktime did not occur as a result of public debate. There has been little attention from government, academia, or civic organizations. For the most part, the issue has been off the agenda, a nonchoice, a hidden trade off. It was not always so. As early as 1791, when Philadelphia carpenters went on strike for the ten-hour day, there was public awareness about hours of work. Throughout the nineteenth century, and well into the twentieth, the reduction of worktime was one of the nation's most pressing social issues.

Employers and workers fought about the length of the working day, social activists delivered lectures, academics wrote treatises, courts handed down decisions, and government legislated hours of work. Through the Depression, hours remained a major social preoccupation. Today these debates and conflicts are long forgotten. Since the 1930s, the choice between work and leisure has hardly been a choice at all, at least in any conscious sense.

Almost as paradoxical as the rise of worktime itself is the fact that it occurred on the heels of widespread predictions that work was disappearing. By the late 1950s, the problem of excessive working hours had been solved—at least in the minds of the experts. The four-day week was thought to "loom on the immediate horizon." It was projected that economic progress would yield steady reductions in working time. By today, it was estimated that we could have either a twenty-two-hour week, a six-month workyear, or a standard retirement age of thirty-eight.[9]

These prospects worried the experts. In 1959 the Harvard Business Review announced that "boredom, which used to bother only aristocrats, had become a common curse." What would ordinary Americans do with all that extra time? How would housewives cope with having their husbands around the house for three- or four-day weekends? The pending crisis of leisure came in for intensive scrutiny. Foundations funded research projects on it. The American Council of Churches met on the issue of spare time. Institutes and Departments of Leisure Studies cropped up as academia prepared for the onslaught of free time. There were many like Harvard sociologist David Riesman who wrote about "play" in the lonely crowd, and the "abyss" and "stultification" of mass leisure.[10]

The leisure scare died out as the abyss of free time failed to appear. Throughout the 1970s leisure was a non-issue. A few lone souls recognized that men's hours had not budged in over two decades. And there were those who argued that we should reduce hours in order to solve the worsening unemployment situation. But virtually no one realized that beginning in the late 1960s the United States had entered an era of rising worktime. Even as the 1980s were ending, the question of time eluded academics. An otherwise excellent and widely read study on the American standard of living by economist Frank Levy failed to broach the subject. Neither leisure nor working hours even appear in the index.[11]

One highly visible aspect of the increase in work finally did draw attention—the growing participation of women in the labor force. Sociologists began writing on "role overload" and the dual responsibilities of home and family. But rising work has been seen as a women's issue. That both women and men are working longer hours has still not been recognized. *Despite the fact that worktime has been increasing for twenty years, this is the first major study to explain or even acknowledge this trend.*[12]

In fact, prominent researchers are holding onto the conventional wisdom of declining worktime. In 1990, Brookings economist Gary Burtless wrote that "average time on the job has fallen more than five hours a week—roughly 13%—since 1950." Leading experts on how people use their time draw similar conclusions. According to John P. Robinson of the University of Maryland, Americans "have more free time today than ever before." But we should be skeptical of these claims. As I shall argue in chapter 2, my estimates indicate a major increase in working hours.[13]

Contrary to the views of some researchers, the rise of work is not confined to a few, selective groups, but has affected the great majority of working Americans. Hours have risen for men as well as women, for those in the working class as well as professionals. They have grown for all marital statuses and income groups. The increase also spans a wide range of industries.[14] Indeed, the shrinkage of leisure experienced by nearly all types of Americans has created a profound structural crisis of time.

While academics have missed the decline of leisure time, ordinary Americans have not. And the media provide mounting evidence of "time poverty," overwork, and a squeeze on time. Nationwide, people report their leisure time has declined by as much as one third since the early 1970s. Predictably, they are spending less time on the basics, like sleeping and eating. Parents are devoting less attention to their children. Stress is on the rise, partly owing to the "balancing act" of reconciling the demands of work and family life.[15]

The experts were unable to predict or even see these trends. I suspect they were blinded by the power of technology—seduced by futurist visions of automated factories effortlessly churning out products. After all, they say, if we can build robots to do humans' work, what sense is there in doing it ourselves? Appealing as this optimism may be, it misses a central point about technology: the context is all important. Machines can just as easily be used to harness human labor as to free it. To understand why forty years of increasing productivity have failed to liberate us from work, I found that I had to abandon a naïve faith in technological potential and analyze the social, economic, and political context in which technology is put to use. Only then was I able to see that the experts' vision of our economic system is both analytically mistaken, in ignoring powerful economic incentives to maintain long working hours, and historically inadequate, owing to a selective misreading of the past.

The experts' faith is based on their assumption that capitalism has already proved itself, by a hundred years of declining worktime. Before the market system, the majority of people are thought to have toiled from sunup to sundown, three hundred and sixty-five days a year. Today we are blessed with a forty-hour week, annual vacations, and extended years of schooling and retirement. The reigning conventional wisdom is that capitalism has created the world's first truly leisured societies.

Yet the claim that capitalism has delivered us from excessive toil can be sustained only if we take as our point of comparison eighteenth- and nineteenth-century Europe and America—a period that witnessed what were probably the longest and most arduous work schedules in the history of humankind. If we set our sights back a bit farther chronologically, as I do in chapter 3, the comparison underlying the conventional wisdom fails to hold up.

The first step to a realistic comparison is to reject the idea that the medieval economy entailed continuous toil. It is unlikely that the workday was much above the standards of today. The medieval economy also provided ample opportunities for leisure within the year. And the medieval period appears not to have been exceptional, at least in Western history.[16] Leisure time in Ancient Greece and Rome was also plentiful. Athenians had fifty to sixty holidays annually, while in Tarentum they apparently had half the year. In the old Roman calendar, 109 of 355 days were designated *nefasti,* or "unlawful for judicial and political business." By the mid-fourth century, the number of *feriae publicae* (public festival days) reached 175.[17]

The lives of ordinary people in the Middle Ages or Ancient

Greece and Rome may not have been easy, or even pleasant, but they certainly were leisurely. Initially, the growth of capitalism dramatically raised work effort. In the words of the anthropologist Marshall Sahlins, the market system handed down to human beings a sentence of "life at hard labor."[18]

Once we realize that capitalism entailed an expansion of working time, the mid-nineteenth-century turn toward leisure no longer appears as a structural imperative of the market system, as proponents of the conventional wisdom believe. It occurred because workers struggled mightily *against* the normal processes that determined the length of working hours. In this sense, leisure exists *in spite of* rather than as a result of capitalism.

In its starkest terms, my argument is this: Key incentive structures of capitalist economies contain biases toward long working hours. As a result of these incentives, the development of capitalism led to the growth of what I call "long hour jobs." The eventual recovery of leisure came about because trade unions and social reformers waged a protracted struggle for shorter hours. Some time between the Depression and the end of the Second World War, that struggle collapsed. As the inevitable pressures toward long hours reasserted themselves, U.S. workers experienced a new decline that now, at the century's end, has created a crisis of leisure time. I am aware that these are strong claims which overturn most of what we have been taught to believe about the way our economy works. To make my case that the market system tends to create work, I compare it with the medieval economy preceding it.

Ironically, the tendency of capitalism to expand work is often associated with a growth in joblessness. In recent years, as a majority have taken on the extra month of work, nearly one-fifth of all participants in the labor force are unable to secure as many hours as they want or need to make ends meet. While many employees are subjected to mandatory overtime and are suffering from overwork, their co-workers are put on involuntary part-time. In the context of my story, these irrationalities seem to make sense. The rational, and humane, solution—reducing hours to spread the work—has practically been ruled out of court.

In speaking of "long hour jobs" exclusively in terms of the capitalist marketplace, I do not mean to overlook those women who perform their labor in the privacy of their own homes. Until the late

What creates "long hour jobs"?

nineteenth century, large numbers of single and married women did participate in the market economy, either in farm labor or through various entrepreneurial activities (taking in boarders, sewing at home, and so on). By the twentieth century, however, a significant percentage of married women, particularly white women, spent all their time outside the market nexus, as full-time "domestic laborers," providing goods and, increasingly, services for their families. And they, too, have worked at "long hour jobs."

Studies of household labor beginning in the 1910s and continuing through to the 1970s show that the amount of time a full-time housewife devoted to her work remained virtually unchanged for over fifty years—despite dramatic changes in household technology. As homes, like factories, were "industrialized," refrigerators, laundry machines, vacuum cleaners, and microwaves took up residence in the American domicile. Ready-made clothes and processed food supplanted the home-produced variety. Yet with all these labor-saving innovations, no labor has been saved. Instead, housework expanded to fill the available time. Norms of cleanliness rose. Standards of mothering grew more rigorous. Cooking and baking became more complicated. At the same time, a variety of cheaper and more efficient ways of providing household services failed in the market, and housewives continued to do their own.

The stability of housewives' hours was due to a particular bias in the incentives of what we may term the "labor market for housewives." Just as the capitalist labor market contains structural biases toward long hours, so too has the housewife's situation. As I detail in chapter 4, there are strong analogies between the two cases. And in neither case has technology automatically saved labor. It has taken women's exodus from the home itself to reduce their household labor. As women entered paid employment, they cut back their hours of domestic work significantly—but not by enough to keep their total working time unchanged. According to my estimates, when a woman takes a paying job, her schedule expands by at least twenty hours a week. The overwork that plagues many Americans, especially married women, springs from a combination of full-time male jobs, the expansion of housework to fill the available hours, and the growth of employment among married women. The biases of the household and the labor market have been powerful impediments to shorter hours. Yet Western Europe also

What are these biases?

has both capitalist labor markets and full-time housewives and hours there have fallen substantially. A full explanation for longer hours in the United States involves specifically American factors. For one thing, trade unions are not as powerful here as they are in Europe, where they represent many more workers and have pushed hard for shorter hours. For another, there are the peculiarities of the American consumer.

Most economists regard the spending spree that Americans indulged in throughout the postwar decades as an unambiguous blessing, on the assumption that more is always better. And there is a certain sense in this approach. It's hard to imagine how having more of a desired good could make one worse off, especially since it is always possible to ignore the additional quantity. Relying on this little bit of common sense, economists have championed the closely related ideas that more goods yield more satisfaction, that desires are infinite, and that people act to satisfy those desires as fully as they can.

Now anyone with just a little bit of psychological sophistication (to go with this little bit of common sense) can spot the flaw in the economist's argument. Once our basic human needs are taken care of, the effect of consumption on well-being gets tricky. What if our desires keep pace with our incomes, so that getting richer doesn't make us more satisfied? Or what if satisfaction depends, not on absolute levels of consumption, but on one's level *relative* to others (such as the Joneses). Then no matter how much you possess, you won't feel well off if Jones next door possesses more.

How many of us thought the first car stereo a great luxury, and then, when it came time to buy a new car, considered it an absolute necessity? Or life before and after the microwave? And the fact that many of these commodities are bought on credit makes the cycle of income-consumption-more income-more consumption even more ominous. There is no doubt that some purchases permanently enhance our lives. But how much of what we consume merely keeps us moving on a stationary treadmill? The problem with the treadmill is not only that it is stationary, but also that we have to work long hours to stay on it. As I shall argue in chapter 5, the consumerist treadmill and long hour jobs have combined to form an insidious cycle of "work-and-spend." Employers ask for long hours. The pay creates a high level of consumption. People buy houses and go into debt; luxuries become necessities; Smiths keep up with Joneses. Each year, "progress," in the form of annual productivity increases, is doled out by employers as extra income rather than as time off. Work-and-spend has become a powerful dynamic keeping us from a more relaxed and leisured way of life.

Faith in progress is deep within our culture.[19] We have been taught to believe that our lives are better than those who came before us. The ideology of modern economics suggests that material progress has yielded enhanced satisfaction and well-being. But much of our confidence about our own well-being comes from the assumption that our lives are easier than those of earlier generations or other cultures. I have already disputed the notion that we work less than medieval European peasants, however poor they may have been. The field research of anthropologists gives another view of the conventional wisdom.

The lives of so-called primitive peoples are commonly thought to be harsh—their existence dominated by the "incessant quest for food." In fact, primitives do little work. By contemporary standards, we'd have to judge them extremely lazy. If the Kapauku of Papua work one day, they do no labor on the next. !Kung Bushmen put in only two and a half days per week and six hours per day. In the Sandwich Islands of Hawaii, men work only four hours per day. And Australian aborigines have similar schedules. The key to understanding why these "stone age peoples" fail to act like us— increasing their work effort to get more things—is that they have limited desires. In the race between wanting and having, they have kept their wanting low—and, in this way, ensure their own kind of satisfaction. They are materially poor by contemporary standards, but in at least one dimension—time—we have to count them richer.[20]

I do not raise these issues to imply that we would be better off as Polynesian natives or medieval peasants. Nor am I arguing that "progress" has made us worse off. I am, instead, making a much simpler point. We have paid a price for prosperity. Capitalism has brought a dramatically increased standard of living, but at the cost of a much more demanding worklife. We are eating more, but we are burning up those calories at work. We have color televisions and compact disc players, but we need them to unwind after a stressful day at the office. We take vacations, but we work so hard throughout the year that they become indispensible to our sanity. The conventional wisdom that economic progress has given us more things *as well as* more leisure is difficult to sustain.

However scarce academic research on the rising workload may be, what we do know suggests it has contributed to a variety of social problems. For example, work is implicated in the dramatic rise of "stress." Thirty percent of adults say that they experience high stress nearly every day; even higher numbers report high stress once or twice a week. A third of the population says that they are rushed to do the things they have to do—up from a quarter in 1965. Stress-related diseases have exploded, especially among women, and jobs are a major factor. Workers' compensation claims related to stress tripled during just the first half of the 1980s. Other evidence also suggests a rise in the demands placed on employees on the job. According to a recent review of existing findings, Americans are literally working themselves to death—as jobs contribute to heart disease, hypertension, gastric problems, depression, exhaustion, and a variety of other ailments. Surprisingly, the high-powered jobs are not the most dangerous. The most stressful workplaces are the "electronic sweatshops" and assembly lines where a demanding pace is coupled with virtually no individual discretion.[21]

Sleep has become another casualty of modern life. According to sleep researchers, studies point to a "sleep deficit" among Americans, a majority of whom are currently getting between 60 and 90 minutes less a night than they should for optimum health and performance. The number of people showing up at sleep disorder clinics with serious problems has skyrocketed in the last decade. Shiftwork, long working hours, the growth of a global economy (with its attendant continent-hopping and twenty-four-hour business culture), and the accelerating pace of life have all contributed to sleep deprivation. If you need an alarm clock, the experts warn, you're probably sleeping too little.[22]

The juggling act between job and family is another problem area. Half the population now says they have too little time for their families. The problem is particularly acute for women: in one study, half of all employed mothers reported it caused either "a lot" or an "extreme" level of stress. The same proportion feel that "when I'm at home I try to make up to my family for being away at work, and as a result I rarely have any time for myself." This stress has placed tremendous burdens on marriages. Two-earner couples have less time together, which researchers have found reduces the happiness and satisfaction of a marriage. These couples often just don't have enough time to talk to each other. And growing numbers of husbands and wives are like ships passing in the night, working sequential schedules to manage their child care. Among young parents, the prevalence of at least one partner working outside regular daytime hours is now close to one half. But this "solution" is hardly a happy one. According to one parent: "I work 11–7 to accommodate my family—to eliminate the need for babysitters. However, the stress on myself is tremendous."[23]

A decade of research by Berkeley sociologist Arlie Hochschild suggests that many marriages where women are doing the "second shift" are close to the breaking point. When job, children, and marriage have to be attended to, it's often the marriage that is neglected. The failure of many men to do their share at home creates further problems. A twenty-six-year-old legal secretary in California reports that her husband "does no cooking, no washing, no anything else. How do I feel? Furious. If our marriage ends, it will be on this issue. And it just might."[24]

Serious as these problems are, the most alarming development may be the effect of the work explosion on the care of children. According to economist Sylvia Hewlett, "child neglect has become endemic to our society." A major problem is that children are increasingly left alone, to fend for themselves while their parents are at work. Nationwide, estimates of children in "self"—or, more accurately, "no"—care range up to seven million. Local studies have found figures of up to one-third of children caring for themselves. At least half a million preschoolers are thought to be left at home part of each day. One 911 operator reports large numbers of frightened callers: "It's not uncommon to hear from a child of six or seven who has been left in charge of even younger siblings."[25]

Even when parents are at home, overwork may leave them with limited time, attention, or energy for their children. One working parent noted, "My child has severe emotional problems because I am too tired to listen to him. It is not quality time; it's bad quantity time that's destroying my family." Economist Victor Fuchs has found that between 1960 and 1986, the time parents actually had *why do we work as much as we do?*

available to be with children fell ten hours a week for whites and twelve for blacks. Hewlett links the "parenting deficit" to a variety of problems plaguing the country's youth: poor performance in school, mental problems, drug and alcohol use, and teen suicide. According to another expert, kids are being "cheated out of childhood. . . . There is a sense that adults don't care about them."[26]

Of course, there's more going on here than lack of time. Child neglect, marital distress, sleep deprivation, and stress-related illnesses all have other causes. But the growth of work has exacerbated each of these social ailments. Only by understanding why we work as much as we do, and how the demands of work affect family life, can we hope to solve these problems.

Our earlier discussion of primitive peoples raises a thorny issue—what exactly do we mean by work and leisure? Of the hundreds, perhaps thousands of pages that have been written in the attempt to define work and leisure, there are two basic approaches. One emphasizes the subjective. Work is unpleasant—what we have to do. Leisure, by contrast, is what we enjoy. Among "leisure studies" researchers, a variant of this definition is common: leisure comprises discretionary activities; work is mandatory.[27] The problem with this perspective is obvious: work, too, can be pleasurable; and leisure may or may not be. Similarly, "discretion" is not an adequate criterion. Those with plenty of money work by choice. So, too, do many who take second jobs or remain at the office longer than they have to. Upon reflection, the subjective approach turns out to be analytically suspect and operationally flawed.

The second approach, which I have chosen, is objective, and concentrates on defining work, rather than leisure. And here I have kept things simple, identifying two kinds of work. The first is hours of paid employment—a reasonably straightforward measure. The second is hours of household labor—a category whose major components are cleaning, cooking, and child care (see the appendix for a precise list). The combination of these two forms of work make "total working hours." Leisure is then defined as a residual. Throughout the book, my quantitative discussions tend to center on work, which I have been able to measure, rather than on leisure.

These demarcations are most tenable for the modern period and present relatively little problem for the postwar era. The identification of work with paid employment is standard practice. And for those who are uncomfortable calling household responsibilities "work," I have presented separate estimates throughout. Serious problems arise for comparisons farther back in history—in medieval Europe, for example. A wide body of opinion holds that before capitalism work and leisure were less distinct concepts than they are today. In historian Keith Thomas's words, "the recreational activities of the Middle Ages recall the old primitive confusion as to where work ended and leisure began." Indeed, the terms *leisure* and *free time* were not even in common usage in mid-nineteenth-century England. According to a widely held interpretation, it was the rise of capitalism itself which created today's sharp and identifiable distinction between work and leisure. The imposition of "labor discipline" and the growing instrumentality of work (as a means to a paycheck) combined to create the subjective disjuncture noted by leisure studies researchers. Work is what we dislike but are forced to do; leisure is what we choose. However, while it is plausible that capitalism did clarify what was at times a blurry line between work and leisure, it is important not to overstate the case. Especially among people who worked for others, the notion of labor as a chore was present even in medieval times. As Keith Thomas recognizes, labor services—owed by serfs to their lords— were "deeply unpopular with those who had to discharge them."[28]

In a sense, the historians' characterization of precapitalist societies may teach us most about our own dreams and imaginations. It is hard to avoid at least a touch of nostalgia for a world in which work was more integrated into family and social life, recreation less commercialized, and time more an easy background than a scarce commodity frenetically spent. And from this vision of the past, we are drawn to think about our future. Will the ranks of those who consider themselves "time poor" continue to grow? Or will we find it possible to reclaim the sense of work, time, and leisure we have lost? As I outline in chapter 6, this reclamation will require major, but not infeasible, transformations in attitudes of employers, economic incentive structures, and the culture of consumption.

The past forty years should provide a warning. They have brought us nothing in the way of leisure time and a saner pace of life. The bias of the system is strongly toward the status quo. But time poverty is straining the social fabric. Continued growth threatens environmental balance, and gender equality requires new work patterns. Despite these obstacles, I am hopeful. By understanding how we came to be caught up in the cycle of work-and-spend, perhaps we can regain a reasonable balance between work and leisure.

new work patterns —

Issue is not just shorter hours but breaking down the rigid distinctions between work and leisure —

Reasons for shorter work time
why time an issue?
gender equality
environmental
children —
work stress
more leisure.
training, high skill

CHAPTER 2

Time Squeeze: The Extra Month of Work

Time squeeze has become big news. In summer 1990, the première episode of Jane Pauley's television show, "Real Life," highlighted a single father whose computer job was so demanding that he found himself at 2:00 A.M. dragging his child into the office. A Boston-area documentary featured the fourteen- to sixteen-hour workdays of a growing army of moonlighters. CBS's "Forty-Eight Hours" warned of the accelerating pace of life for everyone from high-tech business executives (for whom there are only two types of people—"the quick and the dead") to assembly workers at Japanese-owned automobile factories (where a car comes by every sixty seconds). Employees at fast-food restaurants, who serve in twelve seconds, report that the horns start honking if the food hasn't arrived in fifteen. Nineteen-year-olds work seventy-hour weeks, children are "penciled" into their parents' schedules, and second-graders are given "half an hour a day to unwind" from the pressure to get good grades so they can get into a good college. By the beginning of the 1990s, the time squeeze had become a national focus of attention, appearing in almost all the nation's major media outlets.[1]

The shortage of time has also become a staple of women's

magazines and business publications. The subject is covered in major newspapers, such as the *New York Times,* the *Wall Street Journal,* and *USA Today,* as well as in the regional dailies. *Time* magazine devoted a cover story to the fact that "America has run out of time."[2] How-to books on time management have proliferated. Even Madison Avenue has discovered time poverty. In a 1990 commercial, statistics on the decline of leisure time flashed across the screen; then General Motors hawked its wares by promising to get the customer in and out of the showroom faster than the competition.

The time squeeze surfaced with the young urban professional. These high achievers had jobs that required sixty, eighty, even a hundred hours a week. On Wall Street, they would regularly stay at the office until midnight or go months without a single day off. Work consumed their lives. And if they weren't working, they were networking. They power-lunched, power-exercised, and power-married. As the pace of life accelerated, time became an ever-scarcer commodity, so they used their money to buy more of it. Cooking was replaced by gourmet frozen foods from upscale delis. Eventually the "meal" started disappearing, in favor of "grazing." Those who could afford it bought other people's time, hiring surrogates to shop, write their checks, or even just change a light bulb. They cut back on sleep and postponed having children. ("Can you carry a baby in a briefcase?" queried one Wall Street executive when she was asked about having kids.)[3]

High-powered people who spend long hours at their jobs are nothing new. Medical residents, top corporate management, and the self-employed have always had grueling schedules. But financiers used to keep bankers' hours, and lawyers had a leisured life. Now bankers work like doctors, and lawyers do the same. A former Bankers Trust executive remembers that "somebody would call an occasional meeting at 8 A.M. Then it became the regular 8 o'clock meeting. So there was the occasional 7 A.M. meeting. . . . It just kept spreading."[4] On Wall Street, economic warfare replaced the club-house atmosphere—and the pressure forced the hours up. As women and new ethnic groups were admitted into the industry, competition for the plum positions heightened—and the hours went along. Twenty-two-year-olds wear beepers as they squeeze in an hour for lunch or jogging at the health club.

What happened on Wall Street was replicated throughout the country in one high-income occupation after another. Associates in law firms competed over who could log more billable hours. Workaholics set new standards of survival. Even America's sleepiest corporations started waking up; and when they did, the corporate hierarchies found themselves coming in to work a little earlier and leaving for home a little later. As many companies laid off white-collar people during the 1980s, those who remained did more for their monthly paycheck. A study of "downsizings" in auto-related companies in the Midwest found that nearly half of the two thousand managers polled said they were working harder than two years earlier.[5]

At cutting-edge corporations, which emphasize commitment, initiative, and flexibility, the time demands are often the greatest. "People who work for me should have phones in their bathrooms," says the CEO from one aggressive American company. Recent research on managerial habits reveals that work has become positively absorbing. When a deadline approached in one corporation, "people who had been working twelve-hour days and Saturdays started to come in on Sunday, and instead of leaving at midnight, they would stay a few more hours. Some did not go home at all, and others had to look at their watches to remember what day it was." The recent growth in small businesses has also contributed to overwork. When Dolores Kordek started a dental insurance company, her strategy for survival was to work harder than the competition. So the office was open from 7 A.M. to 10 P.M. three hundred and sixty-five days a year. And she was virtually always in it.[6]

This combination of retrenchment, economic competition, and innovative business management has raised hours substantially. One poll of senior executives found that weekly hours rose during the 1980s, and vacation time fell. Other surveys have yielded similar results.[7] By the end of the decade, overwork at the upper echelons of the labor market had become endemic—and its scale was virtually unprecedented in living memory.

If the shortage of time had been confined to Wall Street or America's corporate boardrooms, it might have remained just a media curiosity. The number of people who work eighty hours a week and bring home—if they ever get there—a six-figure income is very small. But while the incomes of these rarefied individuals were out of reach, their schedules turned out to be downright common. As Wall Street waxed industrious, the longer schedules penetrated far down the corporate ladder, through middle management, into the secretarial pool, and even onto the factory floor itself.[8] Millions of ordinary Americans fell victim to the shortage of time.

The most visible group has been women, who are coping with a double load—the traditional duties associated with home and children and their growing responsibility for earning a paycheck. With nearly two-thirds of adult women now employed, and a comparable fraction of mothers on the job, it's no surprise that many American women find themselves operating in overdrive.[9] Many working mothers live a life of perpetual motion, effectively holding down two full-time jobs. They rise in the wee hours of the morning to begin the day with a few hours of laundry, cleaning, and other housework. Then they dress and feed the children and send them off to school. They themselves then travel to their jobs. The three-quarters of employed women with full-time positions then spend the next eight and a half hours in the workplace.

At the end of the official workday, it's back to the "second shift"—the duties of housewife and mother. Grocery shopping, picking up the children, and cooking dinner take up the next few hours. After dinner there's clean-up, possibly some additional housework, and, of course, more child care. Women describe themselves as "ragged," "bone-weary," "sinking in quicksand," and "busy every waking hour." For many, the workday rivals those for which the "satanic mills" of the Industrial Revolution grew justly infamous: twelve- or fourteen-hour stretches of labor. By the end of the decade, Ann Landers pronounced herself "awestruck at the number of women who work at their jobs and go home to another full-time job. . . . How do you do it?" she asked. Thousands of readers responded, with tales ranging from abandoned careers to near collapse. According to sociologist Arlie Hochschild of the University of California, working mothers are exhausted, even fixated on the topic of sleep. "They talked about how much they could 'get by on': . . . six and a half, seven, seven and a half, less, more . . . These women talked about sleep the way a hungry person talks about food."[10]

By my calculations, the total working time of employed mothers now averages about 65 hours a week. Of course, many do far more than the average—such as mothers with young children, women in professional positions, or those whose wages are so low that they must hold down two jobs just to scrape by. These women will be working 70 to 80 hours a week. And my figures are extremely conservative: they are the lowest among existing studies. A Boston study found that employed mothers *average* over 80 hours of housework, child care, and employment. Two nationwide studies of white, married couples are comparable: in the first, the average week was 87 hours; in the second, it ranged from 76 to 89, depending on the age of the oldest child.[11]

One might think that as women's working hours rose, husbands would compensate by spending less time on the job. But just the opposite has occurred. Men who work are also putting in longer hours. The 5:00 Dads of the 1950s and 1960s (those who were home for dinner and an evening with the family) are becoming an "endangered species." Thirty percent of men with children under fourteen report working fifty or more hours a week. And many of these 8:00 or 9:00 Dads aren't around on the weekends either. Thirty percent of them work Saturdays and/or Sundays at their regular employment. And many others use the weekends for taking on a second job.[12]

A twenty-eight-year-old Massachusetts factory worker explains the bind many fathers are in: "Either I can spend time with my family, or support them—not both." Overtime or a second job is financially compelling: "I can work 8–12 hours overtime a week at time and a half, and that's when the real money just starts to kick in. . . . If I don't work the OT my wife would have to work much longer hours to make up the difference, and our day care bill would double. . . . The trouble is, the little time I'm home I'm too tired to have any fun with them or be any real help around the house."[13] Among white-collar employees the problem isn't paid overtime, but the regular hours. To get ahead, or even just to hold on to a position, long days may be virtually mandatory.

Overwork is also rampant among the nation's poorly paid workers. At $5, $6, or even $7 an hour, annual earnings before taxes and deductions range from $10,000 to $14,000. Soaring rents alone have been enough to put many of these low earners in financial jeopardy. For the more than one-third of all workers now earning hourly wages of $7 and below, the pressure to lengthen hours has been inexorable. Valerie Connor, a nursing-home worker in Hartford, explains that "you just can't make it on one job." She and many of her co-workers have been led to work two eight-hour shifts a day. According to an official of the Service Employees International Union in New England, nearly one-third of their nursing-home employees now hold two full-time jobs. Changes in the low end of the labor market have also played a role. There is less full-time, stable employment. "Twenty hours here, thirty hours there, and twenty hours here. That's what it takes to get a real paycheck," says Domenic Bozzotto, president of Boston's hotel and restaurant workers union, whose members are drowning in a sea of work. Two-job families? Those were the good old days, he says. "We've got four-job families." The recent influx of immigrants has also raised hours. I. N. Yazbek, an arrival from Lebanon, works ninety hours a week at three jobs. It's necessary, he says, for economic success.[14]

This decline of leisure has been reported by the Harris Poll, which has received widespread attention. Harris finds that since 1973 free time has fallen nearly 40 percent—from a median figure of 26 hours a week to slightly under 17. Other surveys, such as the 1989 Decision Research Corporation Poll, also reveal a loss of leisure. Although these polls have serious methodological drawbacks, their findings are not far off the mark. A majority of working Americans—professionals, corporate management, "working" mothers, fathers, and lower paid workers—are finding themselves with less and less leisure time.[15]

THEORIES OF THE TIME SQUEEZE

Although the symptoms of time squeeze are relatively uncontroversial—an acceleration in the pace of life, a rise in time-saving innovations, increasing stress, and role overload—analysts differ sharply in how they understand these phenomena. Social critic Jeremy Rifkin believes that what has changed is our perception of time itself. Everything is speeding up, and the culprit is technology. "The computer introduces . . . a time frame in which the nanosecond is the primary temporal measurement. The nanosecond is a billionth of a second, and though it is possible to conceive theoretically of a nanosecond . . . *it is not possible to experience it.* Never before has time been organized at a speed beyond the realm of consciousness." Once people become acclimated to the speed of the computer, normal human intercourse becomes laborious. Programmers get irritable and impatient. Children complain that their teachers talk too slowly, in comparison with Nintendo or Atari. And even the machines can be too slow. Sue Alstedt, a former AT&T manager, became impatient with the computer she bought to save her time at home: "I couldn't stand to wait for it, even though it was coming out at the rate of speech."[16]

Not everyone blames technology. A second theory is that we are merely victims of our own aspirations. We have become more demanding in terms of activities, goals, and achievements. And today's life styles "offer people more options than ever before," according to John P. Robinson, one of the nation's leading chroniclers of how people spend their time. This theme is echoed by another time-use expert: "We have become walking résumés. If you're not doing something, you're not creating and defining who you are." Since the time available to us to do and to define ourselves cannot increase, we are naturally frustrated. While some have suggested that this is merely a "baby-boom" problem, the evidence suggests it is more widespread.[17]

The idea of rising aspirations echoes views put forward more than twenty years ago by economists Gary Becker and Staffan Linder.[18] Becker's work was based on the simple observation that consuming takes time. As people get richer, and own more and more consumer goods, there is less and less time to spend with each item. Unavoidably, use of the Walkman, the VCR, the camcorder, and concert tickets gets crammed into the space once occupied by the lone record player. Linder also believed that leisure time would eventually become hectic as people tried to keep up with the use of an accumulating mountain of possessions. In *The Harried Leisure Class,* he predicted that growing affluence would lead people to switch to those activities that can be done quickly. Long courtships, leisurely walks on the beach, or lingering over the dinner table were destined for extinction. People would do more things at once and do them faster. Even if the amount of leisure time itself did not change, it would become much more harried.

At first blush, events appear to have borne out Linder's ingenious argument. The *New York Times* has already chronicled the quiet death of the dinner party, as he prophesized. ("Most people I know have turned their ovens into planters," notes one professional woman.) Life *has* become more harried—but probably not so much for the reasons Linder and Becker predicted. They anticipated that rising incomes would cause the frenzy. But for many workers, earning power reached a high point just after Linder's book was published, and has been declining since. By this analysis, their lives should have become *less* harried. What Linder did not foresee was that the growing demands of work would lead to a decline in leisure time itself.[19]

There is undoubtedly truth in the ideas that technology and aspirations have led to an accelerated sense of time. But both these explanations have missed a much more obvious force operating in our lives. Time has become more precious because people have less of it to call their own. We have become a harried *working,* rather than leisure, class, as jobs take up an ever larger part of ever more Americans' lives.

DOING MORE FOR THE PAYCHECK

Behind the mushrooming of worktime is a convergence of various trends. These include an increase in the number of people who hold paying jobs; a rise in weekly hours and in weeks worked each year; and reductions in paid time off, sick leave, and absences from work.

More People Working

The mythical American family of the 1950s and 1960s was comprised of five people, only one of whom "worked"—or at least did what society called work. Dad went off to his job every morning, while Mom and the three kids stayed at home. Of course, the

1950s-style family was never as common as popular memory has made it out to be. Even in the 1950s and 1960s, about one-fourth of wives with children held paying jobs. The nostalgia surrounding the family is especially inaccurate for African-American women, whose rates of job holding have historically been higher than whites'. Even so, in recent years, the steady growth of married women's participation in the labor force has made the "working woman" the rule rather than the exception. By 1990, two-thirds of married American women were participating in the paid labor market (see figure 2.1).[20]

Female employment has justifiably received widespread attention: it is certainly the most significant development afoot. But the expansion of work effort in the American family is not occurring just among women. American youth are also working harder in a reversal of a long decline of teenage job holding, the result of increased schooling and economic prosperity. The likelihood that a teenager would hold a job began to rise in the mid-1960s, just as

Figure 2.1   Married Women's Labor Force Participation Rates

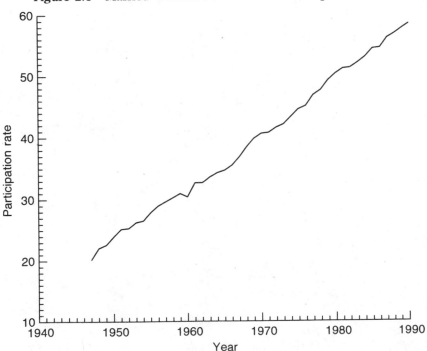

SOURCE: Bureau of Labor Statistics, Special Labor Force Data.

adult hours began their upward climb. By 1990, the labor force
participation rate of teens had reached 53.7 percent, nearly 10
points higher than it had been twenty-five years earlier (see figure 2.2).

Not only are more of the nation's young people working, but
they are working longer hours. A 1989 nationwide sweep by government inspectors uncovered widescale abuses of child labor
laws—violations of allowable hours, permissible activites, and ages
of employment. Low-wage service sector establishments have been
voracious in their appetite for teen labor, especially in regions with
shortages of adult workers. In middle-class homes, much of this
work is motivated by consumerism: teenagers buy clothes, music,
even cars. Some observers are worried that the desire to make
money has become a compulsion, with many young Americans
now working full-time, in addition to full-time school. A New
Hampshire study found that 85 percent of the state's tenth- to
twelfth-graders hold jobs, and 45 percent of them work more than

Figure 2.2   Teenage Labor Force Participation Rates

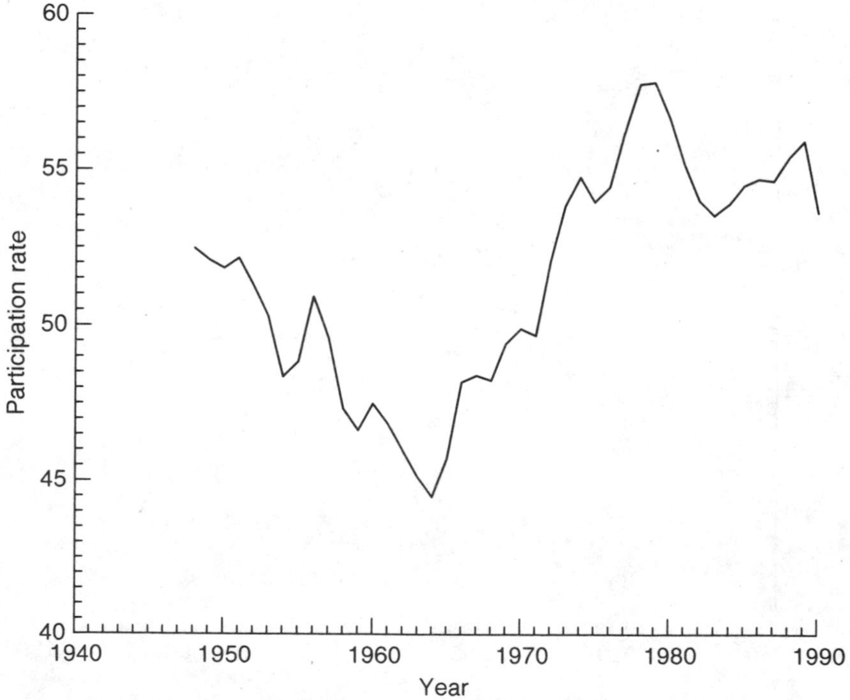

SOURCE: Bureau of Labor Statistics. Sixteen- to nineteen-year-olds.

twenty hours a week. At 10 P.M. on a school night, Carolyn Collignon is just beginning hour eight on her shift at Friendly's restaurant. Teachers report that students are falling asleep in class, getting lower grades, and cannot pursue after-school activities. Robert Pimentel works five days a week at Wendy's to pay off loans on his car and a $5,600 motorcycle, the purchase of which he now describes as a "bad move." Pimentel averages "maybe six hours of sleep a night. If you consider school a job, which it pretty much is, I put in a long day." He wants to go to college, but his grades have suffered.[21]

This is the picture in suburban America. In large urban centers, such as New York and Los Angeles, the problem is more serious. Inspectors have found nineteenth-century-style sweatshops where poor immigrants—young girls of twelve years and above—hold daytime jobs, missing out on school altogether. And a million to a million and a half migrant farmworker children—some as young as three and four years—are at work in the nation's fields. These families cannot survive without the effort of all their members.[22]

There is one ironic exception to the general trend of rising labor force participation: Dad, the mainstay of the 1950s family, is more likely to be out of the labor force than ever before. As women's rates of job holding have risen, men's have fallen. The male decline is somewhat less, from 89 percent in 1948 to 78 percent in 1987, but still substantial (see figure 2.3). This pattern for men should give us pause. Does it contradict our picture of overwork in America? Does it represent a trend toward increasing leisure, albeit among only half the population?

There can be little doubt that many men, especially the elderly, are experiencing newfound leisure. In 1948, almost half of all men aged sixty-five and above were in the labor force; by 1987, the figure had fallen to 16 percent. Social security, private pension plans, and prosperity have made possible a longer period of leisure at the end of life than ever before.[23]

Yet it would be a serious mistake to characterize as "at leisure" all the men who are out of the labor force. Among young males, schooling—which counts as productive activity and cannot be properly measured as leisure time—has been a major cause of labor force withdrawal. The underground economy is also a source of unmeasured work for young men. A closer look than the

Figure 2.3   Male Labor Force Participation Rates

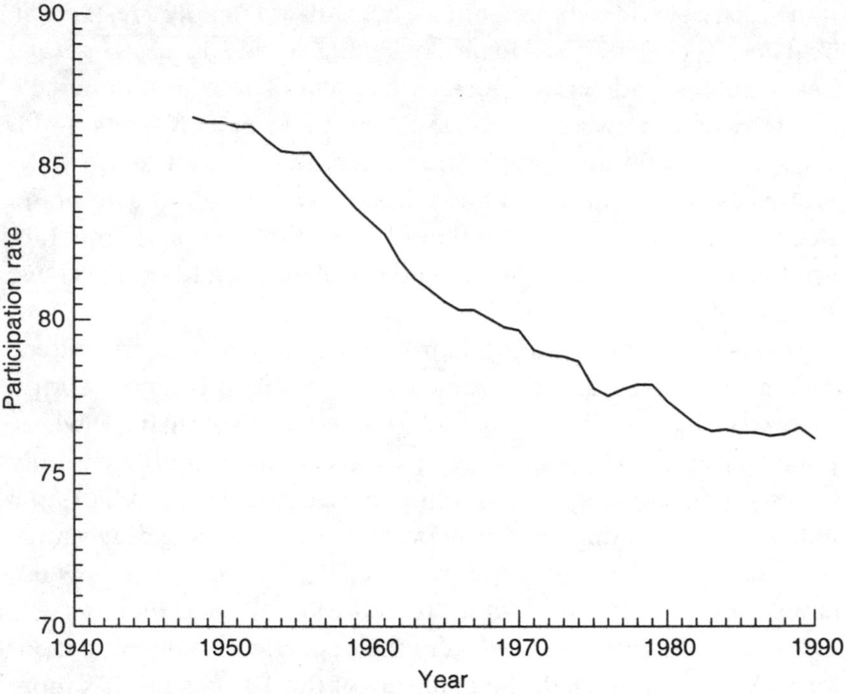

SOURCE: Bureau of Labor Statistics.

standard statistics provide will reveal that much of the "leisure" of older males is involuntary, particularly for the substantial numbers now leaving the labor force before age sixty-five. According to a 1990 survey of men between the ages of fifty-five and sixty-four who are out of the labor force, almost half (45 percent) would prefer to have jobs, a far larger percentage than has previously been recognized. Mandatory retirement and pressures to take early leave have led many unwillingly out of the world of work. Plant closings, corporate restructuring, and ageism have contributed to their difficulties in finding re-employment. Among African-American men, the unemployment situation is about twice as bad as for whites, and participation rates have fallen far more.[24]

More Hours of Work

My estimates—the first comprehensive calculations of worktime spanning the last two decades—confirm not only that more people are working, but that they are working more. (Data are not available for earlier years.) These statistics solve several problems associated with most measures: These are annual, rather than simply weekly, figures. They account for changes in jobs and hours worked which are made within any one year. They are calculated at comparable points in the business cycle to avoid spurious trends. And perhaps most important, they correct for the growth of unemployment and underemployment which artificially reduces the uncorrected figures. (For a description of my data and methods, see the appendix.)

According to my estimates, the average employed person is now on the job an additional 163 hours, or the equivalent of an extra month a year (see table 2.1). Hours have been increasing throughout the twenty-year period for which we have data. The breakdown for men and women shows lengthening hours for both groups, but there is a "gender gap" in the size of the increase. Men are working nearly one hundred (98) more hours per year, or two and a half extra weeks. Women are doing about three hundred (305) additional hours, which translates to seven and a half weeks, or 38 added days of work each year. The research shows that hours have risen across a wide spectrum of Americans and in all income categories—low, middle, and high. The increase is common to a variety of family patterns—people with and without children, those who are married, and those who are not. And it has been general across industries and, most probably, occupations.[25]

The extra month of work is attributable to both longer weekly schedules and more weeks of work, as table 2.2 indicates. As long

TABLE 2.1
Annual Hours of Paid Employment, Labor Force
Participants[a]

	1969	1987	Change 1969–87
All participants	1786	1949	163
Men	2054	2152	98
Women	1406	1711	305

SOURCE: Author's estimates; see appendix for details.
[a]Includes only fully employed labor force participants.

TABLE 2.2
Hours Worked per Week, Labor Force
Participants[a]

	1969	1987
All participants	39.8	40.7
Men	43.0	43.8
Women	35.2	37.0

Weeks Worked per Year, Labor Force
Participants[a]

	1969	1987
All participants	43.9	47.1
Men	47.1	48.5
Women	39.3	45.4

SOURCE: Author's estimates; see appendix for details.
[a]Includes only fully employed labor force participants.

as work is available, people are on the job more steadily through-out the year. This factor accounts for over two-thirds of the total increase in hours. It has been especially important for women, as they are increasingly working full-time and year round. Women now take less time off for the birth of a child and are not as likely to stop working during the summer recess in order to care for children.[26] For better or worse, the pattern of women's employment is getting to look more and more like men's.

Weekly schedules are also getting longer, by about one hour per week (54 minutes, to be exact). This is the first sustained peacetime increase in weekly hours during the twentieth century. What is especially surprising is that it is not just women whose days are getting longer, but men as well. And after twenty years of increase, the proportion of employees on long schedules is substantial. In 1990, one-fourth of all full-time workers spent forty-nine or more hours on the job each week. Of these, almost half were at work sixty hours or more.[27]

Frequently, trends in weekly hours of work are caused by changes in a country's occupational or industrial makeup. Because doctors tend to have longer hours than teachers, an employment shift toward doctors and away from teachers will cause average hours to rise. Surprisingly, recent changes in the relative sizes of industries have on balance had no impact on hours. The growth in "short-hour" service jobs, such as those in retail trade, have been offset by rising numbers in "long-hour" areas, such as those that hire large numbers of professional or managerial workers, all of whom have above-average hours. My analysis shows that the shifts in industries have just about canceled each other out.[28]

So what's pushing up hours? One factor is moonlighting—the practice of holding more than one job at a time. Moonlighting is now more prevalent than at any time during the three decades for which we have statistics. As of May 1989, more than seven million Americans, or slightly over 6 percent of those employed, officially reported having two or more jobs, with extremely high increases occurring among women. The real numbers are higher, perhaps twice as high—as tax evasion, illegal activities, and employer disapproval of second jobs make people reluctant to speak honestly. The main impetus behind this extra work is financial. Close to one-half of those polled say they hold two jobs in order to meet regular household expenses or pay off debts. As one might expect, this factor has become more compelling during the 1980s, with the disappearance of stable positions that pay a living wage and the increase of casual and temporary service sector employment.[29]

A second factor, operating largely on weekly hours, is that Americans are working more overtime. After the recession of the early 1980s, many companies avoided costly rehiring of workers and, instead, scheduled extra overtime. Among manufacturing employees, paid overtime hours rose substantially after the recession and, by the end of 1987, accounted for the equivalent of an additional five weeks of work per year. One automobile worker noted, "You have to work the hours, because a few months later they'll lay you off for a model changeover and you'll need the extra money when you're out of work. It never rains but it pours—either there's more than you can stand, or there isn't enough." While many welcome the chance to earn premium wages, the added effort can be onerous. Older workers are often compelled to stretch themselves, because many companies calculate pension benefits only on recent earnings. A fifty-nine-year-old male worker explains:

Just at the point in my life where I was hoping I could ease up a little bit on the job and with the overtime, I find that I have to work harder than ever. If I'm going to have enough money when I retire, I have to put in five good years now with a lot of overtime because that is what they will base my pension on. With all the overtime I have to work to build my pension, I hope I live long enough to collect it.

[Apparently he didn't—he was diagnosed with incurable cancer not long after this interview.][30]

The Shrinking Vacation

One of the most notable developments of the 1980s is that paid time off is actually shrinking. European workers have been gaining vacation time—minimum allotments are now in the range of four to five weeks in many countries—but Americans are losing it. In the last decade, U.S. workers have gotten *less* paid time off—on the order of three and a half fewer days each year of vacation time, holidays, sick pay, and other paid absences. This decline is even more striking in that it reverses thirty years of progress in terms of paid time off (see figure 2.4).

Part of the shrinkage has been caused by the economic squeeze many companies faced in the 1980s. Cost-cutting measures often included reductions in vacations and holidays. DuPont reduced its top vacation allotment from seven to four weeks and eliminated three holidays a year. Personnel departments also tightened up on benefits such as sick leave and bereavement time. As employees became more fearful about job loss, they spent less time away from the workplace. Days lost to illness fell dramatically. So did unpaid absences—which declined for the first time since 1973.[31]

The other factor reducing vacations has been the restructuring of the labor market. Companies have turned to more "casual" work-forces—firing long-term employees and signing on consultants, part-timers, or temporaries. Early retirements among senior workers also reduced vacation time. Because the length of vacations in this country is based on duration of employment, these changes have all contributed to lowering the amount of time off people

Figure 2.4   Hours Worked as a Fraction of Hours Paid

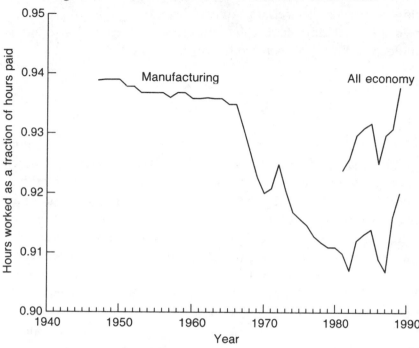

SOURCE: Bureau of Labor Statistics.

actually receive. The growth of service sector occupations, where the duration of employment tends to be shortest, has also been a factor.[32]

Since my data exclude paid time off and commuting, and thus may be biased in one direction or another, I have made a rough calculation of these two factors. The prevailing view is that paid time off has risen substantially. Indeed, business has expressed concern about what one researcher, in 1984, dubbed "the gradual erosion of the annual workyear." Particularly in view of recent reductions in paid time off, this assessment appears to have been premature. By my calculations, the net change in paid time off has been minimal during the period covered by my data (1969–87). The two methods I have used yield estimates of increases in paid time off of between only three and twelve hours a year.[33]

Increases in commuting time have eliminated even this modest gain. Travel time to and from work began rising after 1975, for an overall increase of about three days (23 hours) a year. Together with the change in paid time off, I find an additional rise in work-time of between eleven and twenty hours—or one and a half to two and a half days. If anything, my figures appear to have slightly understated the real increase in working time.[34]

but movement from free to pt-time?

THE TIME SQUEEZE AT HOME

Along with the work people are paid for—time spent at "regular jobs"—almost an equal amount of work is done every year which is not paid for—most of it housework, child care, and other "domestic labor." To get the full story on changes in leisure time, we need estimates of this labor, too. However, as one might expect, calculating hours of household work is not a simple matter. The major difficulty is that the government does not provide any information—despite requests from scholars for official household record keeping which date back more than a hundred years. A second problem is that household labor tends to be less regimented than many forms of paid work. There are no time clocks to punch, and schedules can be erratic. Partly for this reason, researchers have found that the most accurate method for measuring household labor is through minute-by-minute records—or diaries—of people's activities. But this procedure is expensive. Because diary surveys have been carried out exclusively by university-based research institutes, the expense has kept their efforts small and sporadic; and the data are not always representative of the U.S. population.[35]

To ameliorate these drawbacks, I carried out a statistical procedure that combines the time diaries with the large-scale data set on which my earlier calculations are based. In essence, I have constructed estimates of how much household labor each person in my sample is doing, on the basis of information taken from the diaries.[36] This procedure allows one not only to predict trends in household labor but also to identify those factors that determine how much of this work is done at any point in time. The margin of error with these data is, however, greater than with the earlier figures.

Accounting for household labor does not reverse the upward trend in worktime. On average, employed people are doing the same amount of household work they did twenty years ago (I find only a one-hour difference per year!). There have been big changes:

women are doing much less at home and men are doing more. But on balance these changes exactly cancel out. *In terms of total hours—that is, market plus household—the extra month of work remains* (see table 2.3).

While employed people have maintained their hours of domestic labor, the population as a whole is doing less. The social changes of recent decades—women's employment, reduced marriage rates, lower births, and changes in gender roles—have substantially decreased women's ability, need, and willingness to perform household work. Men are doing more, but they haven't fully compensated for the reduction by women.

To explore these developments, I turn to a second set of estimates—hours worked per adult American (rather than per employed person). This measure (table 2.4) allows me to capture worktime changes caused by movements in and out of the workforce, as well as what's happening with those who are out of the labor force altogether. The hours-per-person measure has another advantage: it shows, succinctly, the total quantity of work required for a society to sustain its standard of living. On the other hand, it is an average measure, which does not account for the distribution of either work or income among the population. Because it

TABLE 2.3
Total Annual Hours, Labor Force Participants[a]

	1969	1987	Change 1969–87
Market Hours			
All participants	1786	1949	163
Men	2054	2152	98
Women	1406	1711	305
Household Hours			
All participants	889	888	−1
Men	621	689	68
Women	1268	1123	−145
Total Hours			
All participants	2675	2837	162
Men	2675	2841	166
Women	2674	2834	160

SOURCE: Author's estimates. See appendix for details.
[a]Includes only fully employed labor force participants.

TABLE 2.4
Total Hours Worked per Year, Entire Population

	1969	1987	Change 1969–87
Market Hours			
All Persons	1199	1316	117
Men	1759	1680	−79
Women	723	996	273
Household Hours			
All Persons	1227	1157	−70
Men	683	834	151
Women	1689	1440	−249
Total Hours			
All Persons	2426	2473	47
Men	2442	2514	72
Women	2412	2436	24

SOURCE: Author's estimates. See appendix for details.

includes those who are not employed, it yields far lower figures than those I have been considering so far.[37]

These figures show that Americans as a whole have also experienced a decline in leisure time. If I correct (once again) for the growth in unemployment and underemployment, leisure time has fallen by 47 hours a year.[38] On average, hours of employment are up, and hours of domestic labor are down. But men and women have had very different experiences. Among women, the labor market has been the driving force. In general, the more work women do for pay, the less work they do without it. A major change has been the disappearance of the full-time housewife and the rise of the "working woman." During this period, the fraction of married women who were housewives fell from 30 percent to 15 percent of the adult female population. This exodus from the home has had a large impact on the quantity of household labor currently being done. Each additional hour a woman puts into her paid job reduces her household work by nearly half an hour. She spends less time with her children, cooks fewer meals, and does less cleaning. There is also a one-time, extra reduction of up to four hours per week when a woman initially joins the labor force. According to my calculations, of the 223 hour decline in women's household labor, slightly over half is due to increased hours of employment.

To some extent, women have been able to substitute commercial services for their own labor, using their newly earned paychecks to pay the bill. Expenditures on precooked food—either at restaurants or from the neighborhood deli—professional child care, and dry cleaning have risen rapidly in recent years. Indeed, there is a self-reinforcing nature to this process, as the growing demand for commercially produced products draws more women into service sector employment. But the buying-out of domestic responsibilities has limits. For both two-earner families and single mothers, the reduction in women's time at home has led to a painful cutback in "household services." Children are left in the care of others or even by themselves, there are shortcuts in cooking and cleaning, and the extras provided by 1950s-type "Moms" disappear. Unless husbands are willing and able to pick up the slack, these changes are virtually inevitable: employed women just do not have the time. Their workloads have already climbed above virtually all other groups.[39]

The changing labor market of the 1970s and 1980s has had just the opposite effect on patterns of men's labor. Their market hours have fallen—by 79—and hours of domestic work have increased—by 151. But men's trends have been slightly more complicated. As I showed earlier, employed men are working more, not less. But for the whole population, men's market hours have fallen because there are far fewer of them in the labor force (see table 2.4). Each man who drops out of the labor force reduces his hours so substantially that this effect has outweighed the longer hours of men who are employed. Overall, a smaller proportion are working longer hours, and a larger proportion are without jobs.

The lower market hours of men have been partially replaced by more work at home, thereby making up for some of women's vanishing labor. The average man is doing just under three additional hours a week. A detailed breakdown of activities shows that men are occupying themselves not only with traditional male tasks such as outdoor work and home repairs, but with cooking and cleaning as well. They are also taking on a larger proportion of child care. This combination of more domestic work by men and less by women means that men are now doing almost 60 percent as much as women, up from 40 percent two decades ago.[40]

Despite this rise, it is premature to conclude that we are on the fast track to gender equality with regard to household labor. Most of the increase in men's domestic labor has been caused by the fact that many more men are out of the labor force. Quite naturally, they do more at home (approaching twice as much) than their counterparts with paying jobs. This has been true for decades. Among men who are employed, the increase is far less—amounting to slightly more than one additional hour per week. For the great majority of employed women who also have working husbands, their spouses have provided only partial relief.

The labor market is not the only factor causing a decline in domestic labor. Housewives' hours have finally started to fall. According to my estimates a middle-class, married mother of three is putting in two fewer hours of work a week than she was in 1969. There are also far fewer women who fit this once common demographic profile. Women (and men) are having fewer children and are far less likely to be married. Both these factors have further reduced domestic hours. The influence of children should be obvious: they require tremendous amounts of time, especially when they are young. With marriage, which I define as the presence of a spouse in the household, the effect is more subtle. It turns out that the acquisition of a spouse (especially a husband) leads to more work: homecooked meals, and bigger houses and apartments to care for. Married people also try to save more (to buy those houses or raise their children), which cuts down on the purchasing of services. For women, gaining a husband adds about five hours of domestic work per week. (The case of men is a bit ambiguous; not until the 1980s did they do more when they married.)

During the last twenty years, the married proportion of the adult population fell from about 70 percent to 60 percent. At the same time, the average number of children declined, from one child per person in 1969 to slightly over one-half child today. By 1987, only one-third of the population had children under eighteen years of age, a ten-percent fall. These factors together reduced domestic labor in the neighborhood of one hundred hours a year for women. Of course, declining birth and marriage rates are not independent of the growth of work. Women's employment has also been a cause of fewer births and even later and shorter marriages.[41]

INVOLUNTARY LEISURE:
UNDEREMPLOYMENT AND
UNEMPLOYMENT

There is at least one group of Americans for whom time squeeze is not a problem. These are the millions who cannot get enough work or who cannot get any at all. They have plenty of "leisure" but can hardly enjoy it. One of the great ironies of our present situation is that overwork for the majority has been accompanied by the growth of enforced idleness for the minority. The proportion of the labor force who cannot work as many hours as they would like has more than doubled in the last twenty years. Just as surely as our economic system is "underproducing" leisure for some, it is "over-producing" it for others.

Declining industries provide poignant illustrations of the coexistence of long hours and unemployment. The manufacturing sector lost over a million jobs in the 1980s. At the same time (from 1980 to 1987), overtime hours rose by fifty per year. Many of those on permanent layoff watch their former co-workers put in steady overtime, week after week, year after year. Outside manufacturing, unemployment also rose steadily. At the height of each business expansion (1969, 1973, 1979, and 1987), the proportion of the labor force without a job was higher—rising from only 3.4 percent in 1969 to almost twice that—6.1 percent—in 1987.

Enforced idleness is not just confined to those who have been laid off. Underemployment is also growing. The fraction of the labor force working part-time but desiring full-time work increased more than seven times. The fraction employed only part of the year, but wanting a job year-round, nearly doubled. Those who had neither full-time nor full-year work, but wanted both, rose four times. All told, in the first year of my study, 7 percent of the labor force were unable to obtain the work they wanted or needed. Twenty years later, this category had more than doubled—and stood at almost 17 percent (see table 2.5).

The trend toward underemployment and unemployment signals a disturbing failure of the labor market: the U.S. economy is increasingly unable to provide work for its population. It is all the more noticeable that growing idleness is occurring at a time when those who are fully employed are at their workplaces for ever longer

TABLE 2.5

Fraction of Labor Force Experiencing Unemployment and
Underemployment

	1969	1973	1979	1987
Total unemployed and underemployed	7.2	9.8	16.2	16.8
No Work All Year	0.4	0.7	0.8	1.6
Part Year/Part-Time	1.0	1.8	4.0	4.4
Full Year/Part-Time	0.2	0.3	0.9	1.5
Part Year/Full-Time	5.6	7.0	10.5	9.3

SOURCE: Author's estimates from *Current Population Survey*.

hours. Like long hours, the growth of unemployment stems from the basic structure of the economy. Capitalist systems such as our own do not operate in order to provide employment. Their guiding principle is the pursuit of profitability. If profitability results in high employment, that is a happy coincidence for those who want jobs. If it does not, bottom-line oriented companies will not take it upon themselves to hire those their plans have left behind (see chapter 3 for the relationship between the pursuit of profits, unemployment, and long working hours). Full employment typically occurs only when government commits itself to the task.

In the last twenty years, full employment has become ever more elusive as a result of high interest rates, declining investment, sluggish productivity, takeovers and mergers, increased market uncertainty, and stiffer foreign competition. At the same time, Washington has abdicated its responsibility for maintaining jobs. The "golden age" of Western capitalism is over, and with it went the promise of high employment. The rise and fall of the golden age is a long story in itself, which I, along with others, have told elsewhere.[42] What is important here is that the pressures on businesses have spurred a search for cost-cutting measures. Rather than hire new people, and pay the extra benefits they would entail, many firms have just demanded more from their existing workforces. They have sped up the pace of work and lengthened time on the job. In an atmosphere of high unemployment and weak unions, workers have found it difficult to refuse. The result has been a labor market characterized by a glaring inequity.

As unemployment rose in the 1970s, some labor economists and educators began to advocate shorter hours. Harking back to the labor movement's longstanding traditions, they argued that reductions in weekly hours would put millions of people back to work. But despite their obvious appeal, these proposals received little serious attention. Even as the unemployment problem worsened during the 1980s, work sharing continued to be virtually ignored. Yet if "spreading-the-work" is a sensible and humane solution to a clear irrationality of our economic system, why has it failed? As I shall argue in the next chapter, the ostensible rationality of work-week reductions fails to come to terms with a "larger" capitalist logic. Employers have strong incentives to keep hours long. And these incentives have been instrumental in raising hours and keeping them high. In retrospect, the reformers underestimated the obstacles within capitalism itself to solving both the nation's shortage of jobs and its shortage of time.[43]

CHAPTER 3

"A Life at Hard Labor": Capitalism and Working Hours

The labouring man will take his rest long in the morning; a good piece of the day is spent afore he come at his work; then he must have his breakfast, though he have not earned it, at his accustomed hour, or else there is grudging and murmuring: when the clock smiteth, he will cast down his burden in the midway, and whatsoever he is in hand with, he will leave it as it is, though many times it is marred afore he come again; he may not lose his meat, what danger soever the work is in. At noon he must have his sleeping time, then his bever in the afternoon, which spendeth a great part of the day; and when his hour cometh at night, at the first stroke of the clock he casteth down his tools, leaveth his work, in what need or case soever the work standeth.

—the Bishop Pilkington

One of capitalism's most durable myths is that it has reduced human toil. This myth is typically defended by a comparison of the modern forty-hour week with its seventy- or eighty-hour counterpart in the nineteenth century. The implicit—but rarely articulated—assumption is that the eighty-hour standard has prevailed for centuries. The comparison conjures up the dreary life of medieval peasants, toiling steadily from dawn to dusk. We are asked to imagine the journeyman artisan in a cold, damp garret, rising even before the sun, laboring by candlelight late into the night.[1]

These images are backward projections of modern work patterns. And they are false. Before capitalism, most people did not work very long hours at all. The tempo of life was slow, even leisurely; the pace of work relaxed. Our ancestors may not have been rich, but they had an abundance of leisure. When capitalism raised their incomes, it also took away their time.[2] Indeed, there is good reason to believe that working hours in the mid-nineteenth century constitute the most prodigious work effort in the entire history of humankind.

Therefore, we must take a longer view and look back not just one hundred years, but three or four, even six or seven hundred. Admittedly, there is a certain awkwardness in this exercise. Such calculations are by necessity rough. Since there are no comprehensive, average figures for any time but the recent past, we must use individual estimates for various types of workers, as well as data representing the typical, rather than average, working day and working year. Also, in medieval times the information that does exist is mainly for men. Descriptions of women's household labors are available, but, to my knowledge, there are no estimates of the amount of time women spent doing them. (As I argue in chapter 4, the demands of domestic work have been variable over time.) The greater regularity of women's tasks (cooking, animal husbandry, care of children) suggests their workyear was more continuous, and therefore longer in total, than the male workyear; but we have no direct evidence on this. The other caveat is that because no medieval estimates are possible for America, I have oriented this part of my discussion to Western Europe and mainly England. (For a discussion of "why England?" see the notes.) Despite these shortcomings, the available evidence indicates that working hours under capitalism, at their peak, increased by more than 50 percent over what they had been in medieval times (see figure 3.1).[3]

Consider a typical working day in the medieval period. It stretched from dawn to dusk (sixteen hours in summer and eight in winter), but, as the Bishop Pilkington has noted, work was

Figure 3.1 Eight Centuries of Annual Hours

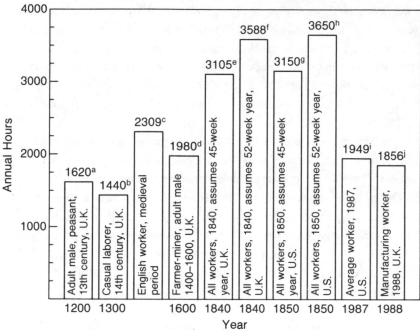

[a]Calculated from Gregory Clark's estimate of 150 days per family, assumes 12 hours per day, 135 days per year for adult male ("Impatience, Poverty, and Open Field Agriculture," mimeo, 1986).

[b]Calculated from Nora Ritchie's estimate of 120 days per year. Assumes 12-hour day. ("Labour Conditions in Essex in the Reign of Richard II," in E. M. Carus-Wilson, ed., *Essays in Economic History,* vol. II [London: Edward Arnold], 1962.)

[c]Calculated from Ian Blanchard's estimate of 180 days per year. Assumes 11-hour day. ("Labour Productivity and Work Psychology in the English Mining Industry, 1400–1600," *Economic History Review,* 31 [1 (1978)]: 23.)

[d]Author's estimate of average medieval laborer working two-thirds of the year at 9.5 hours per day.

[e]Average worker in the United Kingdom, assumes 45-week year, 69 hours per week (weekly hours from W. S. Woytinsky, "Hours of Labor," in *Encyclopedia of the Social Sciences,* vol. III [New York: Macmillan], 1935).

[f]Average worker in the United Kingdom, assumes 52-week year, 69 hours per week (weekly hours from ibid.).

[g]Average worker in the United States, assumes 45-week year, 70 hours per week (weekly hours from Joseph Zeisel, "The Workweek in American Industry, 1850–1956," *Monthly Labor Review,* 81 [January 1958]: 23–29).

[h]Average worker in the United States, assumes 52-week year, 70 hours per week (weekly hours from ibid.).

[i]From table 2.4.

[j]Manufacturing worker in the United Kingdom, calculated from Bureau of Labor Statistics data, Office of Productivity and Technology.

intermittent—called to a halt for breakfast, lunch, the customary afternoon nap, and dinner. Depending on time and place, there were also midmorning and midafternoon refreshment breaks. These rest periods were the traditional rights of laborers, which they enjoyed even during peak harvest times. During slack periods, which accounted for a large part of the year, adherence to regular working hours was not usual. According to Oxford Professor James E. Thorold Rogers, the medieval workday was not more than eight hours. The worker participating in the eight-hour movements of the late nineteenth century was "simply striving to recover what his ancestor worked by four or five centuries ago."[4]

The pace of work was also far below modern standards—in part, because the general pace of life in medieval society was leisurely. The French historian Jacques LeGoff has described precapitalist labor time "as still the time of an economy dominated by agrarian rhythms, free of haste, careless of exactitude, unconcerned by pro-ductivity—and of a society created in the image of that economy, *sober and modest,* without enormous appetites, undemanding, and incapable of quantitative efforts." Consciousness of time was radi-cally different. Temporal units we take for granted today—such as the hour, or the minute—did not exist. There was little idea of time saving, punctuality, or even a clear perception of past and future. Consciousness of time was much looser—and time had much less economic value.[5]

But the pace of work was slow not only for cultural reasons. On the basis of our knowledge of caloric intake, we can infer that work had to have been a low-energy affair. The food consumption of all but the rich was inadequate to sustain either a rapid pace or contin-uous toil. (This may be why lords provided substantial meals to laborers during harvests.) A long, hard day of agricultural labor requires well over three thousand calories per day, an amount out of the range of common people. As more food became available over the nineteenth and twentieth centuries, a significant fraction of those additional calories have been burned up by an accelerated pace of work.[6]

The contrast between capitalist and precapitalist work patterns is most striking in respect to the working year. The medieval calendar was filled with holidays. Official—that is, church—holidays included not only long "vacations" at Christmas, Easter, and midsummer but also numerous saints' and rest days. These were spent both in sober churchgoing and in feasting, drinking, and merrymaking. In addition to official celebrations, there were often weeks' worth of ales—to mark important life events (bride ales or wake ales) as well as less momentous occasions (scot ale, lamb ale, and hock ale). All told, holiday leisure time in medieval England took up probably about one-third of the year. And the English were apparently working harder than their neighbors. The *ancien régime* in France is reported to have guaranteed fifty-two Sundays, ninety rest days, and thirty-eight holidays. In Spain, travelers noted that holidays totaled five months per year.[7]

The peasant's free time extended beyond officially sanctioned holidays. There is considerable evidence of what economists call the backward-bending supply curve of labor—the idea that when wages rise, workers supply less labor. During one period of unusually high wages (the late fourteenth century), many laborers refused to work " 'by the year or the half year or by any of the usual terms but only by the day.' " And they worked only as many days as were necessary to earn their customary income—which in this case amounted to about 120 a year, for a probable total of only 1,440 hours annually (this estimate assumes a 12-hour day because the days worked were probably during spring, summer, and fall). A thirteenth-century estimate finds that whole peasant families did not put in more than 150 days per year on their land. Manorial records from fourteenth-century England indicate an extremely short working year—175 days—for servile laborers. Later evidence for farmer-miners, a group with control over their worktime, indicates they worked only 180 days a year.[8]

The short workyear reveals an important feature of precapitalist society: the absence of a culture of consumption and accumulation. There was far less interest in and opportunity for earning or saving money. Material success was not yet invested with the overriding significance it would assume. And consumerism was limited—both by the unavailability of goods and by the absence of a middle class with discretionary income. Under these circumstances, the lack of compulsion to work is understandable.[9] Of course, those who object to this characterization argue that free time in the middle ages was not really leisure but underemployment. If work effort was low, they claim it is because the economy provided few opportunities for earning money.

What are we to make of these claims? It is certainly true that holidays were interspersed throughout the agrarian calendar, falling after the peak periods of planting, sowing, and harvesting. And in both agriculture and industry, the possibilities for earning additional income were limited. Yet cause and effect are hard to untangle. If more work had been available, it is not obvious that many people would have taken it. The English case provides considerable evidence that higher incomes led to less not more labor—for example, the casual laborers of the thirteenth century, the farmer-miners of the sixteenth, and even the early industrial workers who resisted work whenever their incomes allowed it. Just after wages were paid, as employers learned, absenteeism, failure to work, and much-decried "laziness" resulted. But wherever one stands on the causes of medieval leisure, one fact remains: steady employment, for fifty-two weeks a year is a modern invention. Before the nineteenth—and, in many cases, the twentieth—century, labor patterns were seasonal, intermittent, and irregular.[10]

The argument I will be making is that capitalism created strong incentives for employers to keep hours long. In the early stages, these incentives took the form of a fixed wage that did not vary with hours. In the twentieth century, this incentive would reappear in the guise of the fixed annual salary, which proved to be a major reason for the white-collar worker's long hours. Other incentives also came into play by the end of the nineteenth century, such as employers' desires to keep machinery operating continuously, and the beneficial effects of long hours on workplace discipline. Later, peculiarities in the payment of fringe benefits would have an impact. Each of these factors has been important in keeping hours long. Of course, there have been countervailing pressures, the most important of which was the trade union movement, which waged a successful hundred-year struggle for shorter hours. But once this quest ended after the Second World War, reductions in hours virtually ceased. Not long after unions gave up the fight, the American worker's hours began to rise.

CAPITALISM AND THE EROSION
OF LEISURE

Moments are the elements of profit.
—Leonard Horner, English factory inspector

Capitalism steadily eroded the leisure that pervaded medieval society. Telltale signs—in the form of modern conflicts over time—appeared in at least one "capitalist" enclave as early as the fourteenth century, when the textile industry was faced with an economic crisis. The first response of the cloth makers to this crisis was predictable: they announced reductions in wages. But they also tried something new: the imposition of a longer, "harsher" working day. To enforce this new regime, employers introduced what historians believe are the first public clocks, which appeared in textile centers across Europe. These work clocks—or *Werkglocken,* as they came to be called—signaled to workers when they should arrive at work, the timing of meals, and the close of the day. The idea was that the clock would replace the sun as the regulator of working hours. But unlike the sun, the clocks would be under the control of the employer.

As soon as the *Werkglocken* were introduced, they became objects of bitter antagonism. As they were actually not mechanical clocks but bells which were rung manually, workers, employers, and city officials vied for control of them. Workers staged uprisings to silence the clocks, fighting what the historian Jacques LeGoff has termed "the time of the cloth makers." City officials responded by protecting employers' interests. Fines were levied against workers who disobeyed the injunctions of the bells, by coming late to work or leaving early. Harsher penalties—including death—awaited those who used the bell to signal a revolt.[11] Faced with the alliance of employers and state, the workers' resistance failed; and they resigned themselves to the longer hours, the higher pace of work, and the regimentation of the clocks.

The crisis of labor time in the textile industry illustrates two important points about capitalism and work. First, employers used *time* itself to regulate labor. In medieval Europe, consciousness of time was vague. The unit of labor time was the "day." It was tied to the sun and, as I have noted, tended to be approximate. Modern time consciousness, which includes habituation to clocks, economy of time, and the ownership of time, became an important weapon which employers used against their employees. In the words of the English historian E. P. Thompson, time became "currency: it is not passed but spent." As employers consolidated control over their workforces, the day was increasingly split into two kinds of time: "owners' time, the time of *work*"; and "their own time, a time (in theory) for *leisure*." Eventually, workers came to perceive time, not as the milieu in which they lived their life, but "as an objective force within which [they] were imprisoned."[12]

The second point is that working time became a crucial economic variable, profoundly affecting the ability of businesses to survive and prosper. In the textile case, the impetus of the employers to raise hours emanated from an immediate crisis in their geographically widening and fiercely competitive market. In order to earn sufficient profits to survive, employers took advantage of an intensification of labor. They learned that the market system has a structural imperative to exploit labor: those who do not succeed in raising hours of work or accelerating the pace of production may very well be driven out of business by their competitors. The rigors of the market are particularly demanding during the inevitable depressions in trade which lower prices and choke off demand for products.

As capitalism grew, it steadily lengthened worktime. The change was felt in earnest by the eighteenth century. The workday rose in the cottage industries which sprang up throughout the English countryside. Rural people, especially women, took on spinning, weaving, lacemaking, and other handicrafts, in their own cottages, in order to earn a little cash to survive. The time commitment ranged from a few hours a day for the better-off, to eight, ten, or twelve hours a day for those who were poor. And this was in addition to regular domestic responsibilities. Outside the cottage, workdays rose as employers encroached on customary periods for eating and resting. Farm laborers, hired by the day, week, or season, were subjected to tighter discipline and stricter schedules. The invention of factories, in the late eighteenth century, allowed employers to squeeze out the vestiges of precapitalist work habits. Eventually, when artificial lighting came into use, the working "day" stretched far into the night, and scheduled hours climbed.

Some workers—such as the most highly skilled, well-organized male craft workers in England—were able to withstand increases beyond the ten-hour mark. But even in some skilled trades, such as baking and potteries, the men could not hold out. In any case, skilled male workers were a minority of the workforce. The majority of laboring people, in both England and America, would eventually work longer days. Men, women, and children in home-based and factory labor, farm laborers, slaves, domestic servants, and even a large fraction of male craftsmen experienced a progressive lengthening of work hours. Twelve-, fourteen-, even sixteen-hour days were not uncommon.[13]

A second change was the loss of nearly all the regular holidays medieval people had enjoyed. The Puritans launched a holy crusade against holidays, demanding that only one day a week be set aside for rest. Their cause was aided by the changing economic incentives of the market economy, particularly the growing commercialization of agriculture which resulted in more year-round activity. In the sixteenth century, the long rise in holidays was arrested; and during the seventeenth, reversed. The eighteenth saw the demise of the laborer's long-honored Saturday half-holiday. By the nineteenth century, the English agricultural laborer was working six days per week, with only Good Friday and Christmas as official time off. A similar process occurred in the United States, during the nineteenth century, as steady employment grew more common.[14]

Taken together, the longer workday and the expanding work-year increased hours dramatically. Whereas I estimate a range of 1,440 to 2,300 hours per year for English peasants before the seventeenth century, a mid-nineteenth-century worker in either England or the United States might put in an annual level of between 3,150 and 3,650 hours.

Workers' progressive loss of leisure stemmed from structural imperatives within capitalism which had no counterpart in the medieval economy. The European manor survived on its own efforts, mainly consuming what it produced itself. Neither peasants nor their lords were dependent on markets for basic subsistence. They were not exposed to economic competition, nor driven by a profit motive. Their time was their own. Medieval industry was also protected from market pressures. Guilds had strictly defined hours of work, and apparently "few conflicts arose over the time of work."[15] Custom, rather than competition, dictated economic activity. And custom dictated strictly limited work effort.

The growth of markets, both national and international, thrust workers out of their world of custom and into a competitive dynamic. Capitalist businesses, in contrast to medieval manors, strove for maximum profits. They lived or died by the bottom line. Time off was costly, hence bitterly resisted. Whenever one employer managed to squeeze a bit more work out of his workers, others were compelled to follow. As long as a critical mass of employers was able to demand longer hours, they could set the standard. Workers became victims in a larger-than-life struggle for financial dominance. When textile workers in Manchester lost an hour a day, the repercussions would be felt in Lancashire or maybe far across the seas in Lowell. As local outposts were knitted together into a world market, an economic relay system was created—and it operates to this day. American textile workers, who enjoy paid vacations and official five-day weeks, are rapidly losing out to their counterparts in China, where daily, weekly, and hourly schedules are far more arduous.

Given the high value medieval people placed on a leisurely way of life, why did they accede to grueling hours and the loss of their free time? The answer is straightforward. Capitalists were successful because workers lacked alternatives. In the medieval economy, peasants—whether serfs or freepersons—had secure, time-honored access to land. And land was what nearly everyone depended on for survival. Crop failures might lead to hunger or starvation, but most ordinary people retained *social* rights to some part of their manor's holdings, and hence to food. They were not dependent on the market for their "subsistence." Indeed, a "market" in land did not even exist. Custom dictated its use and disposition.

The growth of a world market led to the uprooting of the peasantry from the land that had sustained them for centuries.[16] Lords enclosed open fields, in order to claim ownership to carry out commercial schemes. Peasants lost control over what had once been a "common treasury" from which they had derived a measure of independence. Now their survival depended on participation in the market in labor. They had become proletarians, reduced to selling time and toil. An analogous fate befell artisans, with the elimination of the more or less assured upward mobility of journeymen into masters promised by the guild system. Increasingly, masters turned themselves into small capitalists and permanently hired apprentices and journeymen. The labor practices enforced by guild traditions were jettisoned in favor of reliance on "what the market would bear."

These changes degraded the status of many common people: "To lose control over one's own (and one's family's) labour was to surrender one's independence, security, liberty, one's birthright." In England, this "commodification" of labor had occurred by the seventeenth century. In the United States, the process took place much later and followed a different path; but by the mid-nineteenth century, similar pressures were operating. In the words of E. P. Thompson, "enclosure and the growing labour-surplus at the end of the eighteenth century tightened the screw for those who were in regular employment; they were faced with the alternatives of partial employment and the Poor Law, or submission to a more exacting labour discipline." As a result, living standards were depressed, and widespread poverty developed. Observers in seventeenth-century England suggest that between a quarter and a half of the rural population lived in poverty. Many commentators maintained that poverty was necessary: "It is only hunger which can spur and goad [the poor] on to labour." The struggle for subsistence had become the paramount fact of life for many people—and in the process, leisure time became an unaffordable luxury.[17]

The Daily Wage and the Expansion of Worktime

The growth of a world market and the creation of a proletariat were major social developments which formed the backdrop for the rise of working hours. Specific features of the emerging labor markets also exacerbated pressures toward long hours. For example, capitalists followed the centuries-old custom of fixing wages by the day, the week, or even the month—in contrast to the modern practice of payment by the hour, which had not been introduced. The daily wage was largely invariant to hours or intensity of labor, a worker earning neither more nor less as the working day expanded or contracted. This flexibility of working hours was a departure from past practice. On medieval manors, serfs' labor obligations to their lords were spelled out in detail, and a certain amount of effort was expected. But with the decline of serfdom, these labor obligations faded away.

The fact that daily wages were fixed gave employers a simple incentive to raise worktime: *each additional hour worked was free.* And because workers were unable to resist the upward pressure on hours, worktime rose dramatically—especially in factories in England and the United States. Marx's famous description of early factories was a harsh reality to the laborers in them: "The 'House of Terror' for paupers, only dreamed of by the capitalist mind in 1770, was brought into being a few years later in the shape of a gigantic 'workhouse' for the industrial worker himself. It was called the factory. And this time the ideal was a pale shadow compared with the reality."[18]

In these "Satanic mills," the custom of a fixed daily wage led the owners to extend hours of toil by whatever means they could manage. They tried "petty pilferings of minutes." They "nibbl[ed] and cribbl[ed] at mealtimes." These methods produced pure profit.[19] One factory operative explained:

> In reality there were no regular hours: masters and managers did with us as they liked. The clocks at the factories were often put forward in the morning and back at night, and instead of being instruments for the measurement of time, they were used as cloaks for cheatery and oppression. Though this was known amongst the hands, all were afraid to speak, and a workman then was afraid to carry a watch, as it was no uncommon event to dismiss any one who presumed to know too much about the science of horology.[20]

Testimony of this sort was not uncommon:

> We worked as long as we could see in summer time, and I could not say at what hour it was that we stopped. There was nobody but the master and the master's son who had a watch, and we did not know the time. There was one man who had a watch. . . . It was taken from him and given into the master's custody because he had told the men the time of day.[21]

Similar strategies were in use in the United States, where factory hours might range from seventy-five to ninety hours a week by the second quarter of the nineteenth century.[22]

Of course, workers did not passively accept the theft of their time. Resistance was widespread and took a variety of forms as workers acquired their own timepieces, failed to show up at work on time, or went on strike to recoup lost leisure. In a New Jersey factory, the young hands went on strike to protest the shifting of the dinner hour. One observer noted: "the children would not stand for it, for fear if they assented to this, the next thing would be to deprive them of eating at all."[23] However, until the second half of the nineteenth century, factory hours in both Britain and the United States rose rather than fell. Workers' position in the market where they sold their labor was not favorable enough to win back their leisure time.

Although the state stepped in, in both countries, government legislation to limit hours was often ineffective. Factory inspectors found themselves unable to enforce the laws: " 'The profit to be gained by it' (over-working in violation of the [Factory] Act) 'appears to be, to many, a greater temptation than they can resist. . . . In cases where the additional time is gained by a multiplication of small thefts in the course of the day, there are insuperable difficulties to the inspectors making out a case.' "[24]

The incentives to increase hours operated in other parts of the economy as well. Servants were also paid fixed wages. Taken together, farm servants and domestics in middle-class homes made up a significant proportion of workers in both England and the United States in the second half of the nineteenth century. Servants were given room and board, plus some payment, either weekly or perhaps by the season. If their hours of work went up, they received no extra pay. It should come as no surprise, then, that their hours of work were particularly arduous. They would rise in the early hours of the morning and work until evening. The hours of domestic servants frequently expanded to fourteen or fifteen hours a day and were typically above those of factory workers. "I used to get up at four o'clock every morning, and work until ten P.M. every day of the week," recounted one Minneapolis housemaid. "Mondays and Tuesdays, when the washing and ironing was to be done," she began at 2 A.M. Time off was often minimal, as families were reluctant to do without their "help." In the United States, free time was one evening or half-day every week or every other week until the 1880s, after which Sundays were added. But even on a "day off," servants were required to do an average of seven and a half hours.[25]

Similar dynamics operated where labor was formally enslaved. Slaves in the American South received a subsistence living—meager food, clothing, and shelter, which did not vary with their hours of work. Field hands worked "every day from 'fore daylight to almost plumb dark"; and during picking season, lighting kept them going at night, often sixteen hours a day. One slave noted: "Work, work, work. . . . I been so exhausted working, I was like an inchworm crawling along a roof. I worked till I thought another lick would kill me." If the owners were able to squeeze out an extra hour here or there, it was purely to their benefit. Slaves' "wages" did not rise.[26]

Employers (and slaveowners) managed to push working hours to the brink of human endurance because they were far more powerful than the common people they hired (or owned). They had the law on their side, to punish those who went on strike or fled the plantation. They had superior resources, to outlast a work stoppage or buy off opposition. They could also invoke the discipline of the market. When businesses are squeezed from above, workers below may find it impossible to resist. In the end, labor lost the battle over working time because it was just too dependent on capital for its very survival.

Piece Rates: "Under-Pay Makes Over-Work"

Not all workers were paid by daily rates. Where it is possible to measure an individual's output, as in the sewing of garments or the cutting of machine tools, there can be payment by the "piece"— that is, on the basis of actual work accomplished. This form of labor contract would seem to vitiate the pressure toward long hours. In theory, the worker can choose a level of effort, and the employer can pay for only what is done. There is no obvious incentive to long hours.

Piece rates were common in the first phase of industrialization in both England and the United States. As I have noted, this phase did not take place in factories but was a small scale, low-tech affair, operating out of cottages in the countryside. Similar arrangements also developed in cities. Because the work took place in a worker's own dwelling, this arrangement has come to be called the "putting out," "domestic," or "outwork" system. Workers received raw materials from a capitalist entrepreneur and returned finished goods. In both countries, the bulk of putting out was in textiles, but it was also used for other handicrafts.

Unlike the factory, where the boss or his representatives kept watch over the worker, in the putting-out system the laborer would appear to retain control over the pace and conditions of work. This is certainly the classic interpretation: after turning in finished goods and receiving their pay on Friday or Saturday, workers might spend the next few days drinking, relaxing, and working at a leisurely pace, if at all. Only on Wednesday or Thursday, as the deadline for handing in finished goods approached, did the pace of work pick up. "Whatever else the domestic system was, however intermittent and sweated its labour, it did allow a man a degree of personal liberty to indulge himself, a command over his time, which he was not to enjoy again."[27] In fact, this "degree of personal liberty" was enjoyed mainly by adult men and mainly in the early days of the system. The system's freedom was illusory. Eventually piece rates would spawn a rise in work effort even more prodigious than that engendered by the factory.

Piece rates led to long hours partly because the rates were set so low. These low rates had a variety of causes. For one thing, the system was dominated by women, whose pay has always been low. A second factor was that there were virtually no barriers to participating in putting out: there was little capital, and materials were advanced by the capitalist "putters-out." With so many people involved, the putters-out could easily reduce rates. Finally, the structure of these industries has typically been highly competitive, often leaving the capitalist with a small profit margin. Margins were frequently squeezed during downturns in trade, and rates cut to compensate.

For the many piece-rate workers who were perched perilously close to the line between survival and starvation, work was a veritable imperative. The historian J. D. Chambers has provided an apt description of an English village swept up in the system: "They knitted as they walked the village streets, they knitted in the dark because they were too poor to have a light; they knitted for dear life, because life was so cheap." In New York City tenements, women all but sewed themselves to death. They often toiled fifteen or sixteen hours a day in cold, badly ventilated tenements. The introduction of the sewing machine further drove down rates, by increasing productivity and consequently the supply of garments. The system also extended working lives. Both the very old and the very young were led to participate, to raise family income. Three- and four-year-olds were put to work, helping their parents in the cottages or slum dwellings. In England, "schools" were started, where, by age five or six, girls would be taught the discipline of twelve- to fifteen-hour days of lacemaking, knitting, or sewing.[28]

The piece-rate workers were caught in a vicious downward spiral of poverty and overwork, a veritable catch-22. When rates were low, they found themselves compelled to make up in extra output what they were losing on each piece. But the extra output produced glutted the market and drove rates down farther. The system kept them poor. A pair of aphorisms summarized their dilemma: "Over-work makes under-pay" and "Under-pay makes over-work."[29]

Eventually the putting-out system declined in importance in both England and the United States. Piece rates did not disappear but were introduced in factories, spurred on in the early twentieth century by reformer Frederick Winslow Taylor's philosophy of "scientific management." Taylor aimed to eliminate the conflict between capital and labor, by paying strictly on the basis of actual work done—that is, by the piece. In order to make the setting of rates "scientific," and thereby insulate them from conflict, scientific management pioneered the use of time-and-motion studies to determine the pacing of individual tasks within factories, or what were termed "standard times." Piece rates were then calculated on the basis of these standards.

But scientific management was unable to eliminate workplace conflict. The process of discovering standard times became a game of cunning between the operative and the man with the stopwatch. An operative in a machine tool shop explains: "If you expect to get any kind of a price, you got to outwit that son-of-a-bitch! . . . You got to add in movements you ain't going to make when you're running the job! . . . They figure you're going to try to fool them, so they make allowances for that. . . . It's up to you to figure out how to fool them more than they allow for." Once a rate is set, the conflict does not end. Management can always change it. When workers show that they can do more than they have been allocated for, the company frequently reduces its rate: thus, "a couple of operators (first and second shift on the same drill) got to competing with each other to see how much they could turn in. They got up to $1.65 an hour, and the price [rate] was cut in half." With lower rates, they had to work more. The tendency for underpay to create overwork thus reappeared in another guise.[30]

WAGE WORKERS' RISING HOURS

The resistance of workers to long hours did not lead back to the earlier, more relaxed patterns of work but to cementing the link between hours of work and pay. As employers demanded more work, workers demanded more money. Eventually, the principle of paying by the hour (or even smaller units) became the dominant form of labor contracting. Although tying wages to workhours would seem to eliminate the employer's preference for long hours, with extra hours no longer being free, other factors perpetuated the employer's interest in long hours. These were increased mechanization in the second half of the nineteenth century, the use of long hours and the concept of employment rent, to promote workplace discipline, by the twentieth century, and the bias created by the structure of fringe benefits since the Second World War.

The Demands of Mechanization

For about a hundred and fifty years, manufacturing industries have been on a path of increasing mechanization. The machinery started out simple but over time grew more complex and costly. By the twentieth century, corporations were spending fantastic sums on expensive equipment. Once capital is invested, its owner has strong financial incentives to see that it is used as intensively as possible. If employees opt to work short hours, the machinery may well sit idle—an expensive proposition for the firm, which may have borrowed money to buy it or need high production to fill its orders. This drive to use machinery intensively has been an important cause of long hours, whether workers are paid by the hour or the piece or a fixed rate. Employers typically prefer to hire fewer people and keep them on long schedules because they cannot count on finding additional workers of comparable quality and experience.[31]

This helps explain why some of the most heavily capitalized industries, such as steel and railways, have had especially long hours. The U.S. steel industry did not relinquish its "twin relics of barbarism"—the twelve-hour day and the seven-day week—until 1923.[32] For a company operating around the clock, two twelve-hour shifts require far fewer workers than three eight-hour ones. This is one reason companies in the manufacturing sector (where investment is high) remain opposed to reforms such as the six-hour day. Low capitalization is also one reason hours are shorter in the service sector.

Workplace Discipline and the Employment Rent

For some employees, the job is defined by the "task." The piece-rate worker gets paid by the piece. Many professionals are paid to "get the job done," rather than by the hour. The person who pays (be it employer or customer) may have little or no financial incentive in the amount of time it takes. The wage worker, by contrast, sells not a finished product, but time itself. It falls to the employer to make sure that the time purchased is used productively. But what ensures that workers actually work during all the hours for which they are being paid? Who sets the pace of work? How is the quality of the product maintained? In order to solve these problems, capitalists took on the role of "boss."[33]

Employers found the first generation of industrial workers almost impossible to discipline. Attendance was irregular, and turnover high. Tolerance for the mindlessness and monotony of factory work was low. "The highlander, it was said, 'never sits at ease at a loom; it is like putting a deer in the plough.' " Employers devised various schemes to instill obedience. They posted supervisors, levied fines, and fired their workers. Beatings were common, especially among slaves and child laborers. One early factory owner explained: "I prefer fining to beating, if it answers . . . [but] fining does not answer. It does not keep the boys at their work."[34]

Many employers and social reformers became convinced that the adult population was irredeemably unfit for factory work. They looked to children, hoping that "the elementary school could be used to break the labouring classes into those habits of work discipline now necessary for factory production. . . . Putting little children to work at school for very long hours at very dull subjects was seen as a positive virtue, for it made them 'habituated, not to say naturalized, to labour and fatigue.' "[35] Schooling ameliorated, but did not solve, the discipline problem. As late as the beginning of the twentieth century, capitalists still had not consolidated their control within the workplace, in either the United States or Britain. Then, in 1914, Henry Ford devised a sophisticated approach to labor discipline which would change the face of worker resistance for decades to come.

Ford's first step was a technical innovation. In order to speed the flow of work through the massive Highland Park (Michigan) plant, he installed a moving conveyor belt. This technology ceded to management far more say over the pace of work than the system it replaced, in which teams of workers rotated among stationary placements of unfinished automobiles. But using machinery to set the pace of work was only a partial solution. Not all production steps or products are amenable to moving-process technology. The more serious problem was that workers did not respond well to the new system: they found the rapid pace and the loss of autonomy unpleasant. Ford was still faced with absenteeism, lateness, and constant turnover of workers.[36] Therefore, as a complement to the conveyor belt, he instituted a new financial strategy—the five-dollar day. This dramatic reform would ultimately prove to be a powerful weapon in the employer's arsenal. The five-dollar day created a "carrot"—a sophisticated economic incentive, which we call the "employment rent."

In its simplest terms, the employment rent is the value of a job to the worker. The term *rent* follows economists' usage. Owners are able to command rents when the "property" they own is fixed in supply. Owners of land, oil sheiks, star basketball players, and Noble Prize laureates can all garner rents. When Henry Ford announced the five-dollar day, he made jobs at Ford far more valuable than at any other auto plant. The going rate was then about $2 a day. By paying his men (only men were eligible)[37] $5 a day, Ford gave them an employment rent of $3—the difference between working for him or for Studebaker or Packard.

Eventually employment rents spread throughout the economy, albeit with less fanfare and smaller wage increases. Unions played a major role in the creation of rents, as the organizing drives and sitdown strikes of the 1930s transformed high-turnover, low-paid "mass production" jobs into valued positions. In the process, capitalists consolidated their control over production. At Ford, observers described the men as "absolutely docile" after the five-dollar day came in. Common sense suggests the connection: when a job pays a rent, a worker is less willing to lose it. There is more willingness to work hard, show up regularly, and follow company rules. My research has borne out this common sense. In a study of British factory operatives, the higher the rent, the faster factory operatives work. The willingness of workers to go on strike or quit a job is also directly correlated with the size of their employment rent. Overall, the greater the employment rent, the more disciplined and profitable a workforce will be (see figure 3.2).[38]

Long hours raise the employment rent, thereby giving employers an incentive to schedule them. If the employment rent is the difference between income on the job and expected income if a worker is terminated, the effect of long hours is clear. By the same reasoning, employers are also reluctant to reduce hours. Consider Bert Johnson, who works in a Houston oil refinery where the Oil, Chemical and Atomic Workers Union has successfully bargained for an hourly wage of $17. Johnson's regularly scheduled workweek is 40 hours, and weekly pay is $680, excluding benefits. Even at regular hours the job yields a substantial rent, because union jobs are not easy to get. If Johnson loses this one, he anticipates he wouldn't be able to get another in the industry, and might be unemployed for a while. He thinks he'd have to return to machining, with its hourly wage of $11 to $12 and substantial loss in benefits.[39]

When his hours go up, the job becomes even more economically valuable. Johnson works overtime, on average one eight-hour shift a week. At time and a half (or $25.50 an hour), this extra work brings in an additional $200 a week. As with most of his co-workers, the pay has made it possible for Johnson to leave the polluted inner-city neighborhood that surrounds the refinery, and buy a house in a cleaner, safer middle-class suburb. For many of the workers, the acquisition of a house has also made the job at ARCO more valuable: losing the high pay and the long hours might well mean losing the house as well.

While ARCO does not relish paying time and a half, it does prefer it to hiring additional employees. The structure of fringe benefits, as I shall discuss, is part of the reason. The rest is that the company makes back part of the additional outlay because a forty-eight-hour week ordinarily yields a higher employment rent.[40] At the higher rent, workers are willing to put in more effort on the job. Every hour is therefore more "productive" (see figure 3.2). With a higher rent, they are also less likely to be absent or to quit altogether. Because their jobs are hard to replace, they're more productive and hence more profitable employees.

Figure 3.2   Productivity and the Employment Rent

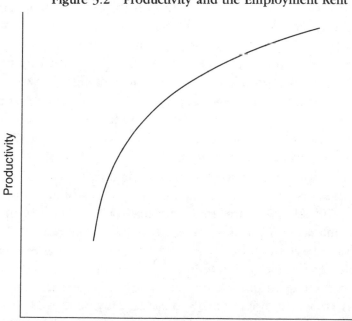

Value of the employment rent

The other way to think of it is that the longer hours make the
worker more dependent on the company, at least in income terms.
Dependency translates into control and, ultimately, profitability.
This is why employers have traditionally liked company towns
(there's no alternative employment) or prefer married men to single
ones (family responsibilities make them more reluctant to challenge management's authority). Today two factors exacerbate this
dependence. The first is the scarcity of high-paying jobs. The disappearance of unionized blue-collar work means that many men like
Bert Johnson are unable to find comparable positions if they lose
their current jobs. White-collar, managerial types face a similar
dilemma, owing to recent retrenchments in corporate America.
Second, the extra income earned in long hour jobs locks workers
into costly expenditures. Debt is an important part of dependence:
paying off a mortgage, a car loan, and a credit card balance can
make long hours absolutely necessary. So, too, is the enthusiasm of
children for the market's latest fad—the skateboard, "Air-Jordans,"
or an acid-washed jean jacket. (See chapter 5, where I explore how
consumption habits have perpetuated long hours.)

Concern about employment rents is one source of employers'
opposition to reductions in hours. Unless a shorter workweek is
accompanied by higher wages, it will lower the employment rent.
And employers are usually reluctant to grant higher wages, because
they fear costs will rise. As I show in chapter 6, there are cases in
which this fear is unfounded: hours can be lowered profitably.
Nevertheless, employers have been skeptical of this possibility,
preferring to remain with the long-hours status quo. And the conservatism of some affects the rest. Once long hours proliferate, as
they did, it becomes difficult for individual firms to break out of the
mold. Custom and inertia take hold.[41]

The connection between long hours and high employment rents
can be seen across the occupational and industrial structure of the
economy. The jobs with the highest rents—white-collar professional and managerial positions or the best-paying manufacturing
jobs—tend to have the longest hours. Men's jobs pay higher rents
than women's jobs—and tend to have longer hours. In the parts of
the economy where employment rents are low or nonexistent, such
as the service sector, hours are shortest. Employment at McDonald's can be had at almost any time, at a rate of pay which will be

instantaneously matched by Burger King. McDonald's pays no employment rent. And the McDonald's and Burger Kings have short workweeks and hire lots of part-time workers.[42]

The high-rent jobs are more demanding. When Henry Ford raised wages, he also expected more effort. According to one production foreman, "[They] called us in and said that since the workers were getting twice the wages, [the management] wanted twice as much work. On the assembly lines, we just simply turned up the speed of the lines." Thus, the logic of capitalist labor relations points in the direction of jobs becoming all-consuming. According to the economist Chris Nyland, the conclusion that "average intensity levels in industry have risen significantly over the last century has been generally accepted by scholars familiar with the work of fatigue researchers."[43]

As a result, our employers ask for more and more from us—and get it on account of the lure of the carrot (the employment rent) and the fear of the stick (dismissal for failure to meet the demands). One autoworker notes:

> Where I work at the auto plant, the workers are just dropping like flies. When there's a lot of work because of a new model coming out, they make people work 10 and 12 hours every day, 6 days a week. Lots of people, even the younger ones, are developing high blood pressure, having accidents on the job, or car accidents on the way to and from work, or other serious health problems. But they have to do it. If you don't like it, you can just quit.[44]

The situation in the auto plant suggests that there are physical limits to this process. If the demands of work are too great, productivity suffers, because people are just not capable of maintaining the pace. In the early twentieth century, opponents of long hours marshaled a great deal of evidence to show that worker fatigue was impairing efficiency. The pace of work and the availability of leisure time also influence employees' valuations of jobs. If employers push the pace too far or demand too many hours, they may face resistance or find their workers quitting. There is a point beyond which it is no longer profitable for employers to raise hours. On the other hand, the employee's valuation of leisure time does not always rise as free time falls. Long hours can reduce the value of time

The loss of desire for leisure

off the job, as the workaholic syndrome erodes people's ability to function outside the work environment. Many people who have especially long hours find themselves unable to cope with leisure time.[45]

The Role of Fringe Benefits

For both salaried and hourly workers, in the second half of the twentieth century, pensions, health and life insurance, paid vacations, and other fringe benefits have become a powerful incentive for the perpetuation of long hours. Since most of these additions to basic earnings are paid on a per-person basis, rather than by the hour,[46] they create a strong discontinuity in cost structures. It becomes far more profitable for a company to hire a smaller number of people for long hours than to extend those hours over more workers (who would also be paid benefits). The long hours of the postwar period owe a lot to the "bias of fringe benefits."

This bias has grown in recent years, as the value of fringes relative to wages and salaries has mushroomed. The standard figure of 15 percent (fringes as a percentage of pay) which prevailed in the 1950s has risen sharply. By 1987, total benefit payments as a percent of wages and salaries stood at 36.2 percent; at some firms, the figure reaches as high as 60 percent (see table 3.1).[47]

Tax structures for government-administered programs have added to this effect, even when paid on an earnings rather than a per-capita basis. Employers' contributions to social security, unemployment insurance, and other programs are capped, so that no taxes are levied after a certain level of earnings. This creates a further bias toward requiring extra hours for existing workers, because no additional tax liability is incurred. If a new employee is added instead, the tax bill rises.

These institutional arrangements have led firms toward the use of overtime and against incremental hiring. The overtime premium required by the Fair Labor Standards Act of 1938 was included in the bill precisely to discourage employers from this reaction. But it has turned out to be a weak sanction. Economists Ronald Ehrenberg and Paul Schumann have found that firms use more overtime

TABLE 3.1
The Growth of Fringe Benefits
(Expressed as a Percentage of Wages
and Salaries)

1955	17.0
1965	21.5
1975	30.0
1986	35.5
1987	36.2

SOURCE: Research Center, Economic Policy Division, U.S. Chamber of Commerce, *Employee Benefits 1988 Edition: Survey Data from Benefit Year 1987* (Washington, D.C., 1988), 33, table 17. Estimated from U.S. Department of Commerce data.

when the ratio of fringe benefits to wages rises. While the magnitude of the effect differed with various statistical techniques, in all cases it was substantial.[48]

Additional factors have created similar incentives. As the economist H. G. Lewis noticed, in a paper written almost twenty years ago, firms that provide on-the-job training—as many companies surely do—will not be indifferent to the hours their employees choose, because there are fixed costs associated with each worker.[49] Recruiting and hiring new employees lead to other fixed costs which encourage firms to prefer long hours for existing employees. As these costs rise, their pull becomes more powerful.

In the aftermath of the early 1980s recession, this set of incentives was a strong brake on employment growth. In the steel industry, which was particularly hard hit by unemployment, it was estimated that the price of the overtime hours worked by employed workers was ten thousand fewer jobs. In 1983, USX issued a directive to plant managers (which was subsequently leaked) ordering them to use overtime, specifically so that they could avoid calling back laid-off workers. This decision was based on the desire of the company to avoid re-entitling workers to benefits. The situation in the mining industry at the time was similar; the coal companies demanded overtime in the midst of severe unemployment. And in the auto industry, the United Autoworkers' Union has calculated that in 1988 overtime resulted in the loss of eighty-eight thousand jobs. Once again, we see the paradox of long hours in the midst of unemployment.[50]

THE SALARIED LABORER'S FREE HOURS

The 80-hour man has far more sizzle. Nine out of ten companies will take the guy who's always there, whose example is one of brute force of effort. His example filters down to those beneath him.

—a corporate recruiter[51]

Pressures toward long hours may be strongest for the third major form of labor contract—payment by salary. Like those early industrial workers who received a fixed daily or weekly wage, the earnings of the salaried worker do not vary with hours. Extra hours are therefore gratis to their employers.

Salaried employment increased substantially in the twentieth century, as firms added white-collar workers—managers, engineers, and a variety of professionals, from lawyers to social workers. Today almost 40 percent of all U.S. employees are paid by salary, rather than hourly wages.[52] As my analysis predicts, salaried workers have longer hours of work than workers paid by the hour. Half the nation's salaried workers belong to the "managerial and professional specialty" group, the occupational category with the longest hours.

Some salaried groups are still toiling at nineteenth-century schedules. Medical residents, investment bankers, corporate lawyers, and many other professionals can be expected to work 70 or 80 hours routinely, with extra effort during particularly hectic times. A 1970s study found that most managers at *Fortune* 500 corporations put in from 60 to 70 hours a week, excluding business travel: "They'd leave home at 7:30 A.M. and return at about the same time that evening. They'd also bring home a few hours of work each day."[53] Not only the top echelons, but employees down the hierarchy, are expected to put in the hours.

Rosabeth Moss Kanter's classic study, *Men and Women of the Corporation* (1977), describes the prodigious effort large corporations traditionally expect of managers:

[They] tended to put in many more hours than workers, and they spent more of their so-called leisure time in work-related activities. . . . Question: How does the organization know managers are doing their jobs and that they are making the best possible decisions? Answer: Because they are spending every moment at it and thus working to the limits of human possibility. Question: When has a manager finished the job? Answer: Never. Or at least, hardly ever. There is always something more that could be done.

When hard times led a California corporation to cut back worktime by 10 percent, managers spent a quarter of this "leisure" time at the office, working without pay.[54]

Many of these workers find that they cannot escape such long hours and remain successful on the job. Their employers require total commitment, expecting more than nine to five; they want Saturdays and nights. Even those near the bottom of the hierarchy feel the pressure:

Upper management expected you to come in on Sundays too—not to work, but just to be seen on the premises—supposed to show how much you loved the damn place. . . . Well, I have a family. What are you supposed to do, live at the plant? Lots of the foremen came down to the lounge on Sunday and drank coffee for a couple of hours. I did a few times, and then said to hell with it—it's not worth it. . . . I started to get passed over on promotions, and I finally asked why. My boss said they weren't sure about my attitude.[55]

More recently, a forty-one-year-old public relations worker in a major corporation expressed these sentiments: "I can't imagine having a baby, which I want to do, and still keeping this job. All corporate jobs are like this—you're valued according to the long hours you are willing to put in, and the schedule is so rigid that anyone who wants to do it differently has to leave."[56]

Similar pressures exist outside large corporations, in smaller professional "shops." Architecture and law firms, universities, publishers, and consulting agencies demand long hours from their salaried workers. Not even government workers are immune these days. One state official warned a job candidate: "We feel that anybody serious has got to be willing to work at least 60 hours a week. If you're not, we know we can get someone who will." Competitive forces operate on the self-employed as well. This group, which clocks in some of the country's longest hours, faces an exceptionally harsh economic climate, as small makes for costly.[57] Ominously low survival rates for the self-employed make self-exploitation virtually inevitable.

The pressures on professionals to work long hours have grown more intense in recent years. In the 1980s, reported weekly hours rose almost an hour a week for both men and women. The impetus has come largely from companies, in response to market conditions. Kanter's qualitative research at the nation's innovative firms bears out the quantitative evidence: " 'enough' is defined not by some pre-existing standard like the length of the workday but by the limits of human endurance."[58]

Some observers feel that it is not employers who enforce long hours of work, but a pervasive workaholism. Indeed, there is historical precedent for the idea that Americans are obsessed with work; as early as 1648, Massachusetts legislated idleness a punishable crime. There is no denying what the historian Daniel Rodgers described as the nation's tendency to "the elevation of work over leisure . . . an ethos that permeated life and manners." Yet it is important not to overstate the case. The work ethic was the doctrine of the northeastern middle class and "never penetrated very far" into the urban working classes or into the South. But however strong this cultural predisposition to hard work, "workaholism" is to some extent a creation of the system, rather than its cause. As long as there are even a few workaholics, competition will force others to keep up. Employers will prefer the hard workers, and these will win out over their colleagues who, either out of personal preference or because they have family responsibilities, do not put in the hours. One engineer noted, "I don't like to put in 80 hour weeks, but a lot of people do. And those are the people who get the projects and promotions." This suggests that the workaholic can set the standard to which others are compelled to adhere. Co-workers may not like the grind. They may not be psychologically invested in it like a classic workaholic. But the eventual outcome—in terms of hours—will be just the same.[59]

Other observers say that since, after all, workers *can* leave their jobs, it is a mistake to place the onus of long hours on employers. If employees are unhappy enough, companies will be unable to retain personnel and will encounter difficulty hiring and promoting into these long-hour jobs. While there is some truth in this logic, it ignores two realities of the economic system. First, companies themselves are subject to harsh competition which drives the market standard: those who cannot induce long hours from their workforces are at a disadvantage in comparison with those who can. The companies that get the hours set the pace.

The second reason is that employers have a structural advantage in the labor market, because there are typically more candidates ready and willing to endure this work marathon than jobs for them to fill. These surpluses of candidates exist because the jobs in question are either on the high rungs of the occupational ladder or are necessary lower rungs. They are the most desirable prizes the market has to offer, carrying high incomes, excellent benefits, and many perquisites. And these employment rents are not just financial but associated with superior status and job satisfaction. For example, managers have higher job satisfaction than other major occupational groups. As one moves down the occupational ladder, satisfaction declines. Managers and professionals are in a better position to escape many of the petty tyrannies that make the worklives of many Americans frustrating, stressful, and unrewarding.[60]

I have used the term *occupational ladder*. While the world of work often does involve a climb from bottom to top, the structure of jobs resembles a pyramid more than a ladder. There are far more people at the bottom than at the top. A manager has many underlings who are managed. A supervisor watches over whole groups of workers. The pyramidal shape virtually guarantees that the best jobs are in short supply. The employer will have the pick of many actual or potential applicants. For every aspiring manager determined to limit his or her hours, there are usually many more willing to give the company whatever time it demands.

In some occupations, the process that created surpluses of labor has been deliberate. Professional organizations (the American Medical Association, the American Bar Association, and their counterparts in other occupations) have intentionally limited entry into their respective fields. They "control," in vital ways, the professional schools, licensing processes, and social networks. As a result, incomes are kept high and unemployment low. But favorable job prospects within the professions are mirrored by surpluses of potential members outside the charmed circle, as would-be doctors, lawyers, and engineers occupy positions as nurses, paralegals, or draftspersons.

Some professionals and managers are starting to refuse the long hours. The rising numbers of professional women with children and a new ethos of fathering are leading many in long hour jobs to desire more time away from work. It is likely that these demands will grow, rather than recede. Yet at the moment, few who feel this way have been able to reconcile the conflicting demands of employer and family. The vast majority of salaried workers are still subject to elastic hours. Unless larger numbers of people both make their voices heard and start voting with their feet, the overworking of salaried men and women is likely to continue.

THE FIGHT FOR SHORTER HOURS

The fact that the market typically favors employers does not mean that they will always be able to raise working hours, or that a transition to a "short hours" economy is impossible. As I noted at the beginning of the chapter, there was one long period during which hours fell, rather than rose. After 1850, the U.S. workweek began to decline and was eventually almost halved.[61] This decline occurred because of pressure from the other side of the market. Workers, through their unions, waged a protracted, bitter, and ultimately successful struggle to reduce working time.

The first documented activity in support of shorter hours in the United States occurred in the 1780s. The participants were unionized male artisans and craftsmen. These were the workers who had already been most able to resist the expansion of working time which capitalism brought for their wives, children, and less well-positioned male counterparts. Their quest was for a ten-hour day, an unthinkable goal for most workers. The struggle was confined to skilled artisans until the 1840s, when women operatives in the textile industry joined the fray. An 1845 petition summarized their grievances: we are "toiling from thirteen to fourteen hours per day, confined in unhealthy apartments, exposed to poisonous contagion of air [and] debarred from proper exercise." Unlike their artisan counterparts, these factory workers did not readily win their cause and would not see ten hours until after the Civil War.[62]

There is little dispute about what motivated these groups of workers: "The most frequent cause of complaint among working people [during the Age of Jackson] was the lack of leisure." Pure exhaustion was an important part of what was driving workers into the streets. Throughout the nineteenth century and into the twentieth, the call for leisure continued to propel the struggle. Workers articulated the need for more family time, time for cultural activities, and eventually just "eight hours for what we will." As the nation became more prosperous, even leisure for leisure's sake started to become culturally acceptable.[63]

The second stage of struggle began after the Civil War, with the birth of the eight-hour-day movement. This time, labor explicitly tied shorter hours to higher pay. As the wife of Ira Steward, a leading eight-hours agitator, quipped, "Whether you work by the piece or work by the day, decreasing the work increases the pay." But despite its appeal for many workers, the eight-hour goal took fifty years to reach. Even the massive protests of 1886 were insufficient to move employers. What finally proved crucial were the intervention of President Woodrow Wilson and the willingness of Henry Ford to grant eight hours. Favorable labor market conditions also played a role.[64]

Business Opposition

Although there were some exceptions such as Ford, the vast majority of employers opposed workers' demands for shorter hours. They used a wide range of tactics and arguments but did not waver in their message. Shorter hours were un-American, indecent, unprofitable, and a threat to prosperity. In 1831, when Pittsburgh carpenters went on strike, their masters had them indicted and tried on grounds of conspiracy. In the 1840s, factory women were "lazy Devils," and business blocked their petitions for state legislation. In the 1880s, after the Haymarket explosion, those held responsible were executed, vilified as "vipers," "serpents," and foreign traitors. A few decades later, the National Association of Manufacturers argued for the American workman's right to work more than 480 minutes of a calendar day. As Saturday work was contested, business "equated increased leisure . . . with crime, vice, the waste of man's natural capacity, corruption, radicalism, debt, decay, degeneration, and decline." Businessmen warned that idleness breeds mischief and—even worse—radicalism. The common people had to be kept at their desks and machines, lest they rise up against their betters.[65]

Business also countered the shorter-hour demands by appealing to the bottom line. Time after time, they put forward grim predictions: shorter hours would lead to financial ruin; their workers were driving them out of business. Employers coupled their threats with displays of brute power. They locked out employees and hired strikebreakers. They called in the police, national guards, and their private army—the Pinkertons. They blackmailed and fired workers. They used their influence with the newspapers, the courts, and the politicians. The tactics of business are far more moderate today, as well they might be. Union opposition has been considerably tamed, and the great struggle between capital and labor blunted. Still, employers as a whole retain their dislike of short hours. M. A. Bienefeld, author of a prominent work on hours reductions, identifies a crucial asymmetry between labor and capital: "the employer usually values the maintenance [of hours of work] more highly than the employee values their reduction."[66]

The Last Major Battle: The Thirty-Hour Week

The 1930s mark a turning point in a struggle that had been going on for a hundred and fifty years. This was to be labor's last major battle for shorter hours. In the midst of depression, the urgency of mass unemployment dominated the agenda, and calls for higher wages and more leisure time were put aside. Ironically, mass unemployment became the route to leisure. The thirty-hour week was first and foremost a plan to spread employment and put people back to work. The crux of thirty-hour logic was that employers would hire back those workers they had already laid off. A one-quarter reduction in hours (from forty to thirty) would reabsorb the 25 percent of the workforce who had become unemployed. It appeared that full employment, labor's elusive but persistent goal, could finally be achieved. But this was not to be. As soon as thirty-hour legislation passed the Senate and the real possibility of enactment appeared, business threw up fierce opposition, barraging the Roosevelt administration with pressure and threats. Quickly changing course, the President abandoned his support for thirty hours. Sixty years later, we are still far from full employment and even farther from a thirty-hour week.

The opposition of business to the thirty-hour week points up an additional structural incentive operating against short hours. When working hours are reduced for many workers simultaneously, the pool of unemployed workers shrinks. This makes employers uncomfortable, for at least two reasons. The first is the effect on the employment rent and, hence, on labor discipline. The great Polish economist Michal Kalecki argued, in a now-classic article:

> [U]nder a regime of permanent full employment, 'the sack' would cease to play its role as a disciplinary measure. The social position of the boss would be undermined and the self assurance and class consciousness of the working class would grow. . . . [Business leaders'] class instinct tells them that lasting full employment is unsound from their point of view and that unemployment is an integral part of the normal capitalist system.[67]

Rephrased in our terms, Kalecki's point is that full employment reduces the employment rent, because workers know the market is full of companies eager to hire them. Under these conditions, employers are in danger of losing the upper hand.

The second problem is that hiring new workers suddenly becomes much more difficult. They are harder to find, cost more, and are less experienced. Such shortages of labor are extremely costly for a firm. At my own place of work, Boston's low unemployment rate during the late 1980s induced the Harvard Corporation to turn its own personnel into bounty hunters: employees who brought in new recruits were given cash rewards.

These considerations help to explain why full employment has been rare. With the exception of wartime, this country has never experienced a sustained period of full employment. The closest we have gotten is the late 1960s, when the overall unemployment rate was under 4 percent for four years. But that experience does more to prove the point than any other example. The trauma caused to business by those years of a tight labor market was considerable. Since then, there has been a powerful consensus among business, government, and the economics profession that the nation cannot withstand such a low rate of unemployment. Economists have defined and redefined upward their "full employment rate of unemployment" to justify the considerably higher rates of the 1970s and 1980s. Meanwhile, the government has assiduously avoided counting all the unemployed and underemployed, sticking instead to a narrow statistic that missed, during the last decade, over half the relevant persons. Business opposition also accounts for the paradox of long hours and unemployment. The forced idleness of some helps perpetuate the forced overwork of others. It is possible that everyone would be better off with a more equitable distribution of work, but capital has maintained a veto on such a solution.[68]

In recent years, the attitudes of business have been far less visible on the hours question. In the absence of a union challenge, there has been little need for employers to show their hand. Once the issue disappeared from the social agenda, hard evidence of employers' opposition has become difficult to find. Nevertheless, there are signs that their longstanding opposition has not disappeared. Corporate lobbying in the late 1970s against the Humphrey-Hawkins bill—in part, a spread-the-work measure—was a rare display of employer sentiment. And in recent years there have been a few surveys of corporate executives. In one, not a single executive would lend support to hours reductions; in fact, the sentiment was for increases. A *Fortune* poll of CEOs indicates similar views: three-quarters say that global competition will require them to push their managers "harder"; and only 9 percent think they are already demanding too much. My own interviews with labor union officials confirm this view: employers are still typically far more willing to grant wage increases than cede control over scheduling hours of work.[69]

Labor Gives Up the Fight

After the Second World War, labor made far less progress on the worktime issue. While a shorter workweek was achieved in a few industries, such as printing, rubber, and ladies' garments, on average there was no further decline in full-time weekly hours. Unions did bargain for longer vacations and other paid time off, and some contracts contain generous provisions. But the gains for workers as a whole were modest. Especially in comparison to prewar objectives such as the thirty-hour week, the postwar efforts appear negligible. The shorter-hours movement, which once mobilized millions, had become a peripheral concern. What happened? Why did the AFL, and then the AFL-CIO, stray so far from the cause that had virtually constituted its identity? Why has the shorter-hours movement laid "dormant for nearly half a century?"[70] Although it is difficult to provide a full accounting, as no in-depth studies of the shift have been done, the outlines of an answer can be identified.

To a certain extent, labor abandoned the cause because it was losing. The inability to win thirty hours had left the unions in a weak position. A key problem was ideological: the unemployment issue had crowded out all others in the discourse over hours. Earlier, labor had based its struggle on positive values, such as the need for family or civic time, the need for leisure, or, in the 1920s, an anticonsumerist message. In the 1930s, these had given way to the purely defensive spread-the-unemployment rationale. Under the circumstances, defensiveness was probably inevitable, but in the long run it proved damaging. As employment revived, labor was left without a compelling rationale for its cause.

Once the Second World War began, the pressure for longer hours was unstoppable. The manufacturing workweek rose more than seven hours between 1940 and 1944. Capital used the war to attack labor at home, laying military defeats at the feet of the forty-hour week. War heroes were paraded across the country speaking against worktime reductions. At war's end, the anticommunist hysteria which swept the nation proved a further obstacle. Virulent anti-union legislation was enacted, and a major drive to organize the South failed. In alliance with conservative forces outside the labor movement, centrists and right-wingers within the CIO expelled eleven unions for allegedly being communists. Labor's own move to the right had a profound impact on the hours question. Although shorter hours had traditionally been a demand for all of labor, it came to be increasingly associated with the left wing. Now the cause itself was questioned. In 1957, the machinists' newspaper queried: "Will Soviets Cut THEIR Overtime?" Unions were adopting the longstanding rhetoric of management.[71]

The conservatism of the postwar years also led labor to be far more accepting of capitalism as an economic system. Labor's earlier opposition to unbridled growth and consumerism disappeared. At the AFL–CIO's first joint conference in 1956—ironically, on the topic of the shorter workweek—one official summed up the new position: "[W]e should emphasize that we do not welcome shorter hours if they reflect the fact that the nation's total level of production is not keeping up the pace." Labor should counter "the impression that the nation is threatened by too much output and excessive possibilities for leisure." Along with almost everyone else, unions had jumped on the growth bandwagon.[72]

The flip side of growth was the emerging climate of consumerism. As a middle-class standard of living came within the reach of more and more working-class people, their desires for shorter hours could no longer be taken for granted. At the 1956 conference, one official claimed confidently that workers had become "eager to increase their income, not to work fewer hours." For males, who were now earning the overtime premium of one and a half or two times their hourly pay, this claim may have been correct. However, as a second official noted, *her* 300,000 mainly female telephone operators wanted shorter hours more than anything else. Given the waning influence of women within the labor movement during the 1950s, it is not surprising that these voices were ignored.[73]

Gender politics aside, it is certainly possible that "the end of shorter hours"[74] was due partly to workers' preferences for money over free time. The immediate postwar years witnessed a surge of pent-up consumer demand. The baby boom and the spread of home ownership encouraged the acquisition of consumer goods. Workers wanted and were getting the American dream. To say, however, that long working hours merely reflect workers' desire for income is simplistic and misleading. As I argue in chapter 5, the consumer boom itself was partly driven by employers' ability to get long hours. The nation became locked into a pattern of work and spend. Leisure was left out of the loop.

THE RISING HOURS OF THE
POSTWAR ERA

During the early postwar era, employers' natural inclination to push up hours was kept in check by prosperity. Labor's inattention to the hours question was not decisive. This was the "golden age" of U.S. capitalism, the "fat years."[75] American corporations had virtually no international competitors, and the domestic market was booming. For their part, unions still retained considerable economic clout. They were able to capture a substantial share of the large profits business was accumulating. Had firms attempted to raise working hours, it is unlikely they would have been successful. In any case they did not. Firms were flush with money and could afford to give rather than to take.

These circumstances produced what was essentially a period of stable hours. Although the data needed to calculate our annual hours measure are not available for the early postwar decades, alternative measures indicate stability in hours. Between 1948 and 1969, the most comprehensive measure—hours worked per adult—rose modestly—from 1,069 to 1,124 per year. Hours per labor force participant fell only slightly, from 1,968 to 1,944. (The difference between the two is accounted for mainly by women's increased participation in the labor force. Because women work fewer hours than men, their inclusion lowers the labor force trend.) Surprisingly, weekly hours for nonstudent men were virtually constant over the period (39.9. to 39.5), even when increases in vacation and holidays are included. The claims of some researchers that paid time off greatly reduced annual hours appear to have been exaggerated: paid time off increased by fewer than four days a year for the average worker.[76]

After 1969, hours began to rise. The workweek crept up, especially for women, as did the percentage of the year people found themselves on the job. As I showed in chapter 2, labor force participants would eventually register an annual increment equivalent to an extra month of work. At the most general level, this rising work effort can be traced to the economic problems that ended the era of high prosperity. The golden age of the 1950s and 1960s was followed by oil price increases, a slowdown in productivity growth, heightened international competition, and sluggish demand.

Corporate profits, which had been at record highs, fell substantially. Recessions became deeper and more damaging. Businesses were under increasing pressure to cut costs and improve profit margins. Predictably, a large portion of the burden was "downloaded" onto employees—particularly during the 1980s, when the squeeze on many U.S. corporations hit hardest. Their strategy has been to require workers to do more for less.

This economic distress has raised hours in two ways. The first method was direct: employers simply demanded longer hours and more work effort. The 1980s were a period of increased overtime and reductions in vacations, rest periods, and other paid time off. Among better-paid white-collar employees, large-scale layoffs and the cutthroat environment made greater commitment of time and energy necessary to retain one's job. At the low-wage end of the labor market, sweatshops reappeared, with nineteenth-century style conditions. The government contributed by eroding legal protections for employees, as well as failing to enforce existing regulations.

The second cause of longer hours has been a steady reduction in hourly rates of pay. Workers paid by the hour—a majority of U.S. employees—saw their average wage peak in 1973. Since then, it has declined substantially and now stands at its mid-1960s level. This erosion has had a profound effect on hours: in order to maintain their current standard of living, these employees must now put in longer hours. Like the piece-rate workers who were forced to produce more as the rates fell, a large number of American families are now in a similar bind. Many men—the group that bore the lion's share of the decline—have expanded their worktime through overtime and second jobs. Unmarried men especially have had a tremendous rise in hours (334 per year). Many of these men are young—the group that suffered the biggest earnings decline. Unmarried women have also increased hours substantially. Among married couples, wives, rather than husbands, have had the largest growth in worktime. By adding a second income or increasing the wife's hours, many families have averted a real decline in their material standard of living. The trends in income have led to a public consensus that it is no longer possible for families to "make it" on a single income—a view that eight out of ten Americans now hold. While our understanding of what we "need" turns out to be

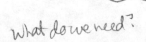

what do we need?

quite complicated (see chapter 5), there is no denying that the perception of financial necessity is widespread.[77]

In one sense, workers are choosing these extra hours. No one forces Valerie Connor to work two eight-hour shifts or Bert Johnson to put in the overtime. But the pressure to work the hours *has* come from companies. In return for a 1970s standard of living, employers are now demanding far more hours. For the production and nonsupervisory employees who make up 80 percent of the labor force, these demands have been substantial. According to our calculations, *just to reach their 1973 standard of living, they must work 245 more hours, or 6-plus extra weeks a year.*[78]

Among salaried workers as a whole, earnings have not declined.[79] These employees also tend to have higher incomes to begin with, so they have been less affected by the financial hardship that has plagued many less well-off families. However, their hours have also risen. Some of the increase has come from employers, who have cut back on paid time off and subtly (or not so subtly) required longer weekly hours. But financial incentives have also affected salaried workers. Although their incomes have not fallen, they have not grown by much either. Therefore, to keep up with the ever-more-expensive middle- or upper-middle-class life style, more work has been necessary. Finally, among women, the desire to pursue a career, independent of the monetary rewards, has also led to increases in total working time.

Only now are the consequences of labor's blindness to the hours question fully visible. Workers, both as individuals and through their unions, have been virtually powerless to stop the onslaught of work. Amidst the high unemployment and economic insecurity of recent years, there have been few solid impediments to long hours. And the problem is not only economic. The nation no longer possesses a culture of resistance to long hours or a political movement to press for government reforms. There have been few ideological vantage points from which to stake a claim to leisure.

The importance of labor's inaction can be seen by a comparison with Europe. In Europe, labor did retain interest in shorter hours, keeping this issue at the top of its agenda throughout the postwar period. When economic crisis hit, unions were determined to resist the inevitable pressures for longer hours. Despite the severity of the economic downturn in Europe, weekly hours have continued to

TABLE 3.2
Paid Vacation in European Countries

Country	By Law	By Agreement
Austria	5 weeks	cf. law
Belgium	4 weeks	5 weeks
Denmark	—	5 weeks
Spain	30 civil days	4½ to 5 weeks
Finland	5 weeks	5 to 6 weeks
France	5 weeks	5 to 6 weeks
Great Britain	—	4 to 6 weeks
Greece	4 weeks	cf. law
Ireland	3 weeks	+/− 4 weeks
Iceland	4 weeks, 4 days	cf. law
Italy	—	4 to 6 weeks
Luxembourg	5 weeks	25 to 30 days
Malta	4 weeks	cf. law
Norway	4 weeks, 1 day	cf. law
Netherlands	4 weeks	4 to 5 weeks
Portugal	30 civil days	4½ to 5 weeks
FRG	3 weeks	5½ to 6 weeks
Sweden	5 weeks	5 to 8 weeks
Switzerland	4 weeks	4 to 5 weeks

SOURCE: European Trade Union Institute, *Collective Bargaining in Western Europe in 1988 and Prospects for 1989* (EuroInt; 1988/89), 62, table XI.

fall. After bitter strikes through the 1980s, the large German union IG Metall has now won a 35-hour week for its members, a gain that is expected to spread throughout the labor force. And vacation hours have risen substantially. Collective agreements have set annual leave at 5 to 6 weeks in France, 5.5 to 6 in West Germany, and 4 to 6 in Great Britain (see table 3.2). Partly as a cure for unemployment and partly in search of a higher quality of life, European workers have successfully articulated a vision of a more leisured society. That vision is still missing in America, not only in the workplace but in the home as well.

US – no vision of a more leisured society –

========== CHAPTER 4 ==========

Overwork in the Household

As a society we have been loathe to acknowledge the chronic overwork that plagues the American household, preferring to romanticize the role of housewife and mother. Yet the shortage of time is not merely a problem of our paying jobs—we spend just as much time working in the home as we do outside of it. Houses, yards, and children devour our time, seemingly without limit. For many with two jobs—so-called working mothers—the burden is enormous. In addition to the forty-plus hours of work a week a full-time woman employee puts in on the job, different studies estimate that she does anywhere from twenty-five to forty-five hours in the home.[1]

All this household work often seems unavoidable, like death and taxes. Children have to be cared for, and food needs to be cooked. When attention is directed to the time squeeze, it is rarely suggested that we should curtail household work. The message is that we need time so we can do *more* at home. And perhaps we do—at least with existing methods for taking care of home and family. But we need to consider the possibility that we have gotten locked into a household technology and a culture of domestic work that are more inefficient, time consuming, and onerous than they need to be.

The long hours of the housewife have a variety of causes. One is the continual upgrading of standards of performance. A second is that commercial alternatives to private provision were stymied at an early stage of development. A third is that since housework was never professionalized, it has not benefited from specialization. Underlying each of these was a common economic factor: the low cost of the housewife's labor. Because married women were largely excluded from the labor force, the incentives to conserve their labor were blunted. Instead, a powerful bias toward using up their time developed. This led, quite naturally, to higher expectations regarding household services and to an artificial inflation of the costs of commercial alternatives and professionalization, in comparison with the do-it-at-home solution. Although in recent years household hours have begun to fall, progress has been hampered by a culture and a technology of domestic labor that is far more difficult, labor-intensive, and inefficient than it needs to be.

By looking at domestic labor in economic terms—such as the "cost" of a housewife and the "efficiency" of home technologies—we can better see the economic structures that have determined how we feed ourselves, clean our houses, and even raise our children. Yet the household has traditionally been out of the purview of economics, being rather the domain of sociology and anthropology. We have preferred to think of our private lives as exempt from those factors that rule the market.[2] We have also avoided putting into the same category what we do in our jobs and what we do at home. Domestic activity has been excluded from the realm of labor. As any woman can attest, the query, "Do you work?" is meant to distinguish between those who are employed in the market economy, and those whose labors are confined to the home. The expected answer of the housewife to this question would typically be "No"—at least until recently, when the feminist movement has attempted to overcome her economic invisibility.

This was not always so. In the colonial period, women's household activities were not devalued by being denied the status of work. Economist Nancy Folbre notes: "In 1800, women whose work consisted largely in caring for their families without pay were widely considered productive workers. By 1900, however, they had been formally relegated to the census category of 'dependents' that included infants, young children, the sick, and elderly." The dominant discourse characterized women as "supported" by their husbands.[3]

The official statistics measuring the yearly flow of production and income embody this sexist bias as well. As virtually every introductory economics textbook points out in its opening chapter, if a man marries his housekeeper, the gross national product will fall. The paid labor of the housekeeper is replaced by the unmarketed services of the wife, and the country looks to be poorer as a result. The reality is that the actual work being performed may well be identical, and the reduction in GNP is a statistical artifact. At this point, the textbook writer moves on and never looks back. So, too, have most economists, who have chosen the trivial method of identifying work with income-generating activity and shunned the household as "uneconomic."[4]

If we care to look, we can see that the American household really is an economic institution. Food preparation, child rearing, laundry services, house cleaning, the transportation of people, care of the sick and elderly, the acquisition of goods and services (shopping), gardening and lawn care, home and car maintenance and repair, and financial accounting are all services typically produced in American homes. Perhaps the most convincing argument that these are economic activities—real and valuable work—is the fact that as the paid employment of women grows, and with it family income, more and more of these services are purchased in the market. Children are placed in day-care centers. Meals are eaten in restaurants. Shirts are sent to the laundry. Those who can afford it hire cleaning help, accountants, car mechanics, gardeners, and people to paint their houses.

Of course, there are big differences between household labor and the experience of being "on the job." The two do not share the same structures of pay, accountability, control, or technology. Many people will (and have) protested that taking care of children is not work, but a meaningful and pleasurable part of life. So it is. But the fact that we can enjoy our labor or find it satisfying does not mean that it is not work. If we consider the differences between a corporate executive or an orchestra conductor (highly satisfied occupational groups) and the lowly counterperson in a fast-food establishment, it is obvious that the world of "real work" is characterized by differences equally profound as those separating home and market.

THE CONSTANCY OF HOUSEWIVES' HOURS

The twentieth century radically transformed America. We went from the horse and buggy to the Concorde, from farm to city and then to suburb, from silent movies to VCRs. Throughout all these changes, one thing stayed constant: the amount of work done by the American housewife. In the 1910s, she was doing about fifty-two hours a week. Fifty or sixty years later, the figure wasn't much different.

This conclusion comes from a set of studies recording the daily activities of full-time housewives. The first was carried out in 1912–14 by a Ph.D. candidate at Columbia University named John Leeds. Leeds surveyed a group of sixty middle-class families, with employed husbands, full-time homemakers, and an average of 2.75 children. After watching the routine of the housewives in his group, Leeds found that they spent an average of fifty-six hours each week at their work. This number is actually slightly higher than most subsequent findings, but the difference appears not to be meaningful and is attributable to some peculiarities of Leeds's families.[5]

Over the next few decades, many more housewives were surveyed under the auspices of the U.S. Bureau of Home Economics. Another Ph.D. candidate, Joann Vanek from the University of Michigan, compiled the results of these surveys, all of which followed a common set of guidelines. Vanek found that in 1926–27, and again in 1929, housewives were putting in about fifty-two hours. The strange thing is that in 1936, 1943, and 1953, years of additional studies, the findings were unchanged. The housewife was still logging in fifty-two hours. In the 1960s and 1970s, more surveys were undertaken. A large one in Syracuse, New York, in 1967 and 1968 found that housewives averaged fifty-six hours per week. And according to my own estimates, from 1973, a married, middle-class housewife with three children did an average of fifty-three hours of domestic work each week (see figure 4.1).[6]

Figure 4.1   The Constancy of Housewives' Weekly Hours[a]

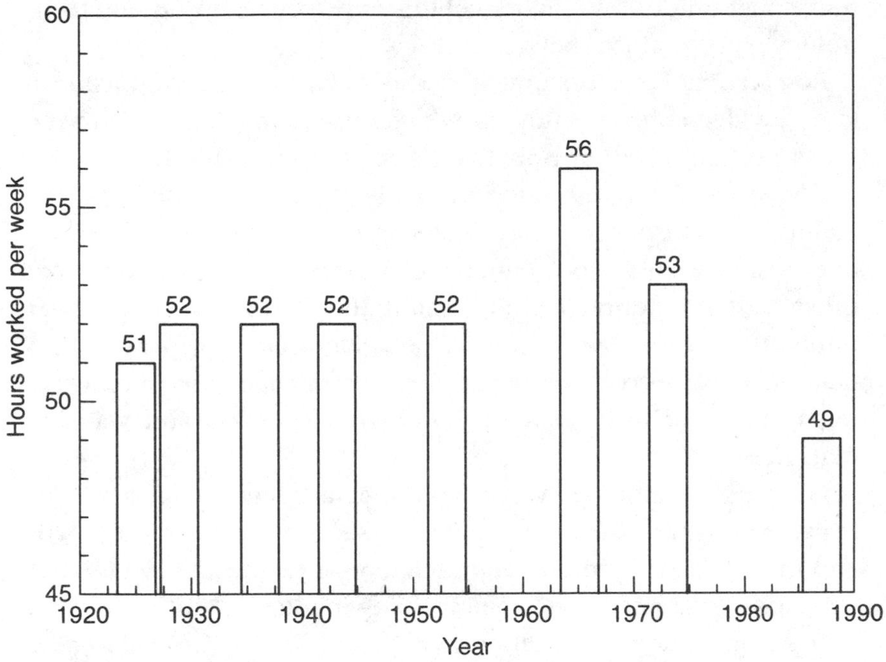

SOURCE: Estimates from 1926–27 through 1965–66 are from Joann Vanek, "Time Spent in Housework," *Scientific American,* 231 (5 November 1974): 116–20. 1973 and 1987 are author's calculations.
[a]All data are for full-time housewives.

The odd thing about the constancy of hours is that it coincided with a technological revolution in the household. When the early studies were done, American homes had little sophisticated equipment. Many were not yet wired for gas and electricity. They did not have automatic washers and dryers or refrigerators. Some homes even lacked indoor plumbing, so that every drop of water that entered the house had to be carried in by hand and then carried out again.[7]

By 1950, the amount of capital equipment in the home had risen dramatically.[8] Major technological systems, such as indoor plumbing, electricity, and gas, had been installed virtually everywhere. At the same time, many labor-saving appliances also came into vogue—automatic washing machines and dryers, electric irons, vacuum cleaners, refrigerators and freezers, garbage disposals. By the 1990s, we had added dishwashers, microwaves, and trash compacters. Each of these innovations had the potential to save countless hours of labor. Yet none of them did. In terms of reducing time spent on domestic work, all this expensive labor-saving technology was an abject failure.

Researchers have documented this failure. After conducting a large, twelve-country study, in which conditions ranged from the most modern to rather primitive (lack of indoor plumbing, appliances, and so forth), the authors tentatively suggested the opposite: technical sophistication may *increase* the amount of time given over to household work. Studies of U.S. women also found that those with more durable equipment in their homes work no fewer hours than those with less. Only one major appliance has been shown to save significant amounts of time (the microwave oven). Some actually increase housework (freezers and washing machines).[9]

Of course, technology was not without its effects. Some activities became less time consuming and others more. Between the 1920s and the 1960s, food preparation fell almost ten hours a week, but was offset by a rise in shopping, managerial tasks, and child care. Certain innovations were labor saving on their own, but led to new tasks. The refrigerator eliminated the need for daily shopping and storing ice at home, but helped drive the door-to-door vendor out of business, thereby contributing to the rise of the supermarket, with its self-service and greater travel time.[10]

THE UPGRADING OF STANDARDS AND THE EXPANSION OF SERVICES

Laundry provides the best example of how technology failed to reduce labor time. During the period from 1925 to 1965, automatic washers and dryers were introduced. The new machines did cut the time needed to wash and dry a load of clothes. Yet laundry time rose. The reason was that housewives were doing more loads—in part, because investment in household-level capital undermined commercial establishments. Laundry that had previously been sent out began to stay home. At the same time, standards of cleanliness went up.[11]

The escalation of standards for laundering has been a long

process, stretching back to colonial times. In those days, washing would be done once a month at most and, in many families, much less—perhaps four times per year. Nearly everyone wore dirty clothes nearly all the time. Slowly the frequency of washing rose. When the electric washer was introduced (1925), many Americans enjoyed a clean set of clothes (or at least a fresh shirt or blouse) every Saturday night. By the 1950s and 1960s, we washed after one wearing.[12]

Standards have crept up for nearly everything housewives do—laundry, cooking, care of children, shopping, care of the sick, cleaning. Estimates from a mid-1970s survey show that the housewife spent an average of 10.3 hours a week getting the floors "spic and span," cleaning toilets, dusting, and waxing.[13] In recent decades, homes have received "deep cleaning," with concerted attacks on "germs" and an "eat-off-the-floor" standard. Americans have taken seriously the dictum that "cleanliness is next to godliness." One 1920s housewife realized:

> Because we housewives of today have the tools to reach it, we dig every day after dust that grandmother left to a spring cataclysm. If few of us have nine children for a weekly bath, we have two or three for a daily immersion. If our consciences don't prick over vacant pie shelves or empty cookie jars, they do over meals in which a vitamin may be omitted or a calorie lacking.[14]

But we were not always like this. Contemporary standards of housecleaning are a modern invention, like the vacuum cleaners and furniture polishes that make them possible. Europeans (and Americans) joined the cleanliness bandwagon quite recently. It was not until the late eighteenth century that people in England even began to wash themselves systematically. And it was only the rich who did so. Body odors and excretions offended no one. For example, menstrual blood just dripped onto the floor. In terms of personal hygiene, a crust of dirt was thought to foster a good complexion underneath. Noses would be blown onto clothing; feces were often left lying around the house, even among the genteel classes.

In other parts of the world, higher standards of hygiene prevailed. Medieval and early modern European travelers to Asia, for example, were considered to be extremely uncouth. In matters of housekeeping, filth and neglect were the order of the day. Anything more was considered "a waste of time." These habits were transported to America with the first European settlers, whose bodies and homes reproduced European-style filth. The culture of cleanliness was at least a century away.[15]

It was delayed because it was expensive. The labor of colonial women was far too valuable to be spent creating spic-and-span. For most colonists, survival entailed the labor of both adults (and their children and perhaps someone else's children as well). Women were busy making yarn, cloth, candles, and soap. They were butchering animals, baking bread, churning butter, and brewing beer. They tended gardens and animals, concocted medicines, and cared for the sick. They sewed and mended garments, and typically had time to clean their houses only once a year. According to historian Mary Beth Norton, "it seems clear either that cleanliness was not highly valued or that farm wives, fully occupied with other tasks, simply had no time to worry about sweeping floors, airing bedding, or putting things away." Undoubtedly, some colonial women did take great pains with their homes, but sanitation could be infeasible. Rural dwellings were rudimentary, with dirt floors and few pieces of furniture or other possessions. Open-hearth fires spewed out soot. Hauling and heating water was arduous and expensive; it was used sparingly for luxuries such as washing dishes.[16]

The less well-off segments of U.S. society, who were by no means a minority, faced similar living conditions throughout the nineteenth century. Slaves, and then sharecroppers, lived in primitive cabins, which were "extremely difficult to keep clean and tidy."[17] In urban tenements, housekeeping was hard even to recognize:

> There was no furniture to speak of, few clothes to wash, little food to prepare. . . . Washing and cleaning were difficult since all water had to be carried up the stairs. People tracked in dirt from the muddy streets; plaster crumbled; chimneys clogged and stoves smoked. . . . Cleaning was only a small part of complicated and arduous family economies. The major effort went into acquiring necessities—food, fuel and water.[18]

As the nation grew richer, it got cleaner. Prosperity freed many married women from the burdens of earning money and producing necessities and gave them time to devote to housekeeping. As they did, higher standards emerged. The shift began among the middle classes and eventually filtered down to the less well-to-do. By the last quarter of the nineteenth century, America was well into its longstanding affair with the immaculate. Victorian-era homes were subjected to strenuous cleaning exercises, which were further complicated by the clutter and bric-a-brac that was the fashion of the day. In households with servants, requirements would be even more exacting. By the turn of the century, the once-yearly cleaning had given way to a daily routine. Each and every morning, women would be sweeping, dusting, cleaning, washing, and straightening up.[19] And those were just the daily tasks. Bigger jobs (washing clothes, ironing clothes, baking, canning, washing walls, and so on) were done on a weekly, monthly, and seasonal basis. The rituals had become endless.

The trend to more and better was not confined to housecleaning and laundry but included activities such as cooking and baking. To some extent, what occurred was a shift from the production of the food itself (gardening, raising animals, making butter or beer) to more elaborate preparation. In earlier days, "the simplest and least exerting forms of cooking had to be utilized most frequently; hence the ubiquity and centrality of those classic 'one-pot' dishes, soup and stew." Now women learned the art and craft of cooking, as soup and stew gave way to fried chicken and angel food cake. Nutrition and esthetics became preoccupations. All these changes in the standards of housekeeping helped keep the housewife's hours long even as progress made it possible to save her labor. But the area where the upgrading was most dramatic was in the care of children.[20]

Being a mother—and increasingly, being a father as well—is a highly labor-intensive and demanding job. It is an article of faith that infants and small children need constant attention, supervision, and love. As they grow older, they also require education and moral training. All these needs translate into countless hours. One might have thought that mothering was always like this. Newborn babies in the fifteenth century were just as helpless as those in the twentieth. But three hundred years ago, parents acted very differently. Children were hardly "raised" in today's sense of the term. Historians of the family and "private life" have discovered that we cannot project contemporary child-rearing practices backward in time. Like housecleaning, laundering, cooking, and many other domestic labors, the standards and norms of mothering have been dramatically upgraded.

Part of the transformation has been psychological. In the past (before about the sixteenth century in England and later in other parts of Europe), parent-child relationships appear to have been much less emotional. What is seen today as a deep biological bond between parent and child, particularly mother and child, is very much a social construction. For the most part, children were not "cared for" by their parents. The rich had little to do with their offspring until they were grown. Infants were given to wet-nurses, despite widespread evidence of neglect and markedly lower chances of survival. Older children were sent off to school. Those in less economically fortunate families fared no better. They would be sent as servants or into apprenticeships, often in the homes of strangers. In all social classes, infants and children were routinely left unattended for long periods of time. To make them less of a nuisance, babies were wrapped in swaddling clothes, their limbs completely immobilized, for the first months of their lives. Another custom was the violent rocking of infants "which puts the babe into a dazed condition, in order that he may not trouble those that have the care of him." However harmful these practices may have been for children, they were convenient for their elders.[21]

Among the poor and laboring classes, economic stress made proper care virtually impossible. In the worst cases, there was not sufficient income to feed children, and infanticide and abandonment were not unusual.[22] When families did keep (and feed) their offspring, they could rarely spare even the ill-paid labor of women. Time for mothering was an unaffordable luxury. Women had to work for pay, and the children were frequently left alone:

> The children are then in many cases left without any person in charge of them, a sufficient quantity [of opium] being given by the parents to keep them in a state of stupor until they return home. . . . When under the influence of this mixture, the children lie in a perfectly torpid state for hours together. "The young 'uns all lay about on the floor," said one woman to me who was in the habit of

dosing her children with it, "like dead 'uns, and there's no bother with 'em. When they cry we gives 'em a little of it—p'raps half a spoonful, and that quiets 'em."[23]

The relative lack of parental love and attention can partly be explained by the high probability that children might not survive. The ephemerality of life until at least the mid-eighteenth century is revealed by the practice of giving two children the same name, in the expectation that only one would live. Under these circumstances, the absence of deep emotional ties to children is understandable. But the picture is actually more complicated. Parental indifference was not merely a result of infant mortality. It was also a cause. Historians now realize that one reason many children died is that their parents did not, or could not, take sufficient pains to keep them alive. Neglect and abuse were dangerous, in both rich and poor families.[24]

More caring attitudes began to emerge in the eighteenth century, in both Europe and the United States. Eventually some of the more odious child-rearing practices started to fade away, such as swaddling; and by the end of the century, wetnursing was in decline. Parental affection became more common, and the individuality of the child was recognized. Middle-class families, often religious reformers, began to devote considerable attention to the education of their children. The biggest changes came in the nineteenth century. The idealization of mother love, vigilant attention to the needs of children, and recognition of the unique potential of each individual came to dominate child-rearing ideology. These beliefs may appear natural; but, as a leading historian of the family has noted, "motherhood as we know it today is a surprisingly new institution."[25]

By the last quarter of the nineteenth century, what historians have called "conscious motherhood" and a bona-fide mothers' movement emerged. As the "century of the child" opened, mothers were providing their children with all manner of new services. They breast-fed. They began to toilet-train, schedule, and educate. They learned to worry about germs, nutrition, and the quality of the air. They practiced "scientific nursing" on sick children. The long legacy of child neglect gave way, particularly in America, to the most labor-intensive mothering process in human history.

Children benefited from all this attention. "But the burden that it placed upon the new American housewife was immense. Children had to be kept in bed for weeks at a time; bedpans had to be provided and warmed . . . utensils had to be boiled, alcohol baths administered, hands scrupulously washed, mouths carefully masked."[26] And all these practical duties were embedded in a new cultural icon: the selfless mother. She was a romantic ideal, but eventually became a reality. Mothers actually did become altruistic—and unsparing with their time.

In all these ways, then, was the American household and the labor of its mistress transformed. The old tasks of animal husbandry, sewing, and candlemaking disappeared, and women took on new ones. They made their family's beds and breast-fed their own babies. The motto was more and better. Looking back on this history, some observers have noted the operation of a Parkinson's Law of housework, in which "work expands to fill the time available for its completion." And there is a certain amount of truth in this characterization: the housewife's work *did* expand to fill her customary schedule. As the market economy produced low-cost versions of what women had made at home, they transferred their labor to other tasks. Housewifery remained a full-time job irrespective of the appliances or the technological systems at the housewife's disposal. The 1950s and 1960s were particularly labor-intensive. Middle-class women were trapped in a stultifying domesticity, following "Hints from Heloise" on how to prepare homemade dog food or turn Clorox bottles into birdfeeders.[27]

THE PARKINSON'S LAW OF HOUSEWORK: LOW-COST LABOR

In my view, the most important explanation for the operation of Parkinson's Law in housework was the increasing isolation of the housewife from the market economy and the resulting devaluation of her time in comparison with what she could be earning in market work. In economic jargon, the opportunity cost of an hour of labor was reduced, because the market wage—an "opportunity"—was eliminated as an alternative (and lucrative) use of a housewife's time. The loss of this option artificially deflated the value of a housewife's time. Once deflated, the tendency to fill that time with household work was powerful. From the institution of the full-time housewife, it was but a short step to cleaning the floor a second time or spending more time with the children.

Why were housewives effectively excluded from the market? Among middle-class women, outright prohibitions on suitable jobs played a crucial role. In teaching and clerical work, women faced "marriage bars"—restrictions against the hiring of married women, or the firing of single women once they did marry. According to economic historian Claudia Goldin, at their peak, these bars were used by 87 percent of local school districts and covered 50 percent of office workers.[28] Teaching and office work were two of the most important occupations for middle-class women whose class position would prevent them from going into factories or other work from which they were not barred. By eliminating major potential occupations for reasonably well-off women, this overt discrimination undermined the opportunity cost of their time.

In the working class, married women were also excluded from the labor market. The (male) trade-union movement had long argued against women's employment in manufacturing industries. The men were concerned to limit competition from women, who were inevitably lower paid. Part of their justification was that the frailer sex should not have to endure the horrors of the capitalist workplace but should be "free" to stay at home. Men fought to be paid a "family wage"—remuneration generous enough to "support" a wife at home.[29] But it was not only outright discrimination that kept women out of the labor market. There was also the sense that a family with a full-time housewife had achieved a privileged position in society.

At least until late in the nineteenth century, most families could not afford to devote the labor of an adult solely to housecleaning, cooking, and mothering. Although social mores confined them to the home, married women, especially among the working classes and the poor, remained enmeshed in the cash economy. They earned income by taking in laundry, accepting boarders, or doing piecework. In rural areas, they worked on family farms. A large fraction of the population relied on this money for survival.[30]

With prosperity, more and more families could afford a housewife. It became a status symbol, almost a definition of being in the middle class, to have a wife who "didn't work." This was an ideal which was aspired to (and realized for a time) by most American families. Robert S. and Helen Merrell Lynds' classic study of a middle American town reveals that of forty business-class families, only one wife worked for money between 1920 and 1924, and she was "semi-artistic." Even in the working class, fewer than half the wives were employed. "One of the most strongly rooted of Middletown's values is that concerning the goodness of a wife's being a homemaker rather than a toiler in the rough outside world of men." Of course, even prosperous wives did work, they just didn't get paid. The lady of leisure may have been a powerful ideological symbol, but it was a reality for only the tiniest fraction of the populace. Middle-class women "faced a paradoxical set of expectations. They were to work but . . . not seem to work. . . . They were to run a household, yet return themselves in the census as unemployed."[31]

The combination of marriage bans, trade-union pressure, the lure of the "wife who didn't work," and, of course, family responsibilities were sufficiently strong to keep women out of the market. Between 1890 and 1940, the official labor-force participation rate of married women ranged from only 5 percent to 15 percent. And while the official rate leaves out many actual participants, by the 1920s it was nevertheless the case that, for the middle class especially, a paying job was a severely circumscribed—if not nonexistent—option. Meanwhile, the possibilities for earning income inside the home were being eliminated, as families bought their own washing machines, and rising incomes reduced the supply of potential boarders. As the century wore on, it became increasingly true that by working at domestic tasks women were not forgoing income.[32]

Had the labor market (or even cash-earning activities within the home) exerted a pull on the housewife, it would have limited her work at home as she weighed off each additional hour spent on spic-and-span or gourmet desserts with the cash she could have earned in a paying job. If the "price" of each hour of domestic labor had been higher, families would have "bought" less of it, and standards and services would not have escalated nearly as much. But discrimination and social mores prevented the true opportunity cost of women's labor at home from being taken into account. *As it was, women's time became an artificially undervalued resource.*

In exactly the same way that we use up too much clean air and water because it has no price, the housewife's time was squandered.[33] On the other hand, in recent decades, as married women have entered the labor force in large numbers, few families continue to give no thought to a woman's income-earning potential. The opportunity cost of a housewife's time is now increasing; and, predictably, the time she spends on domestic labor has finally begun to shrink.

I have attributed the escalation of standards and the constancy of housework to a distortion in the value of women's time. But most historians of domestic labor have pointed to the growth of a class of experts in homemaking and child rearing who imposed ever-more exacting practices on American women. Early examples were Catherine Beecher and her sister, Harriet Beecher Stowe, who aimed to upgrade, make scientific, and professionalize housework. Eventually these reformers created a new "domestic science" and a home economics movement which spread their gospel into homes, schools, and the media. Home economists, child psychologists, and social workers were purveyors of the war on germs, scientific cooking, and the century of the child.[34]

A second strand of argument indicts corporate America. Businesses subjected women to a barrage of advertising and social pressure, in order to sell more products. Housework was functional for capitalism. Lysol warned that even "the doorknobs threaten [children] . . . with disease." Grapenuts told mothers that breakfast cereal would determine the course of their child's life. The moral demands on the housewife extended down as far as her floor. According to one polish manufacturer: "By Their Floors Shall Ye Judge Them. . . . It is written that floors are like unto a mirror, reflecting the character of the housewife." Corporate marketing and the home economics movement converged as experts such as Christine Frederick became spokespersons for individual companies, endorsing products as scientific. They helped spread the message that a woman who did not purchase the growing array of consumer goods was jeopardizing her family and missing out on the best life had to offer. Valuable as they are, what is missing from these accounts is the economic context in which the experts and the admen operated. In my view, long domestic hours cannot be attributed solely to their efforts. Their message found receptive ears precisely because of the structure of incentives operating on the use of women's time.[35]

Of course, my interpretation has left at least one nagging question. Even without the possibility of earning income, household work does have an opportunity cost—the housewife's leisure time. If it had been highly valued, the promise of leisure would have inhibited the proliferation of services and standards. Why didn't it count for more?

One answer is the power of the work ethic. Especially in the middle classes, idle hands were often thought to do the devil's work. Cultural exaltation of work and denigration of leisure were ever present. Considerations of equity within the family also played a role. A substantial discrepancy in free time in wives' favor might well have made their husbands feel resentful and insecure, especially because women earned no money. Large increases in women's leisure would have had to be matched by equivalent gains for husbands. Women, for their part, were sensitive to this issue of worktime parity. Many felt (and feel) that the "luxury" of staying home entails a moral obligation to hard work. Of course, this is a difficult point to prove. But it is suggestive that until just recently, as "housewifery" is dying out, the twentieth-century housewife's workweek has not been exceeded by her husband. In the early part of the century, adult men were working a few hours less, and their hours fell until about 1950.[36]

Another factor that kept hours long is that husbands desired the services their wives' labor provided. Domestic labor was not merely busywork, as some scholars have suggested, but resulted in real benefits. Women were acting, in some sense, as domestic servants for their families.[37] Men liked the fancy cooking, clean homes, and healthier children their wives produced. They encouraged, or even demanded, the services. These benefits meant that, for men, women's leisure time had a tangible cost.

Ironically, what did not have a cost—at least directly—were these extra services. Men got them free. And herein lies another source of bias. A housewife is not paid directly for her domestic labors. She receives a share of her husband's income, but as with the salaried worker, this does not vary with the workload: in both cases, each additional hour worked imposes no cost on the "employer." So when husbands—or children—demand work from their wives (or mothers), *they* incur no cost. Although this absence of a wage for domestic labor is taken as almost axiomatic, maybe we should regard it as a curious development. After all, capitalism turned so much else into "commodities"—that is, activities or products whose production and exchange is governed by prices. In a world in which almost every form of labor came to be bought and sold (from brainpower to sex), why should the housewife's labor be exempted?[38]

Finally, the very gender division of labor itself has kept housewives' hours long. Society has rarely been self-reflective about relegating to women responsibility for the labors of hearth and home. Although the feminist movement, in its many incarnations (late nineteenth century, early twentieth, and the contemporary period), did question men's exclusion and women's seclusion, historically it made little headway. If feminism had been successful, the hours of household labor probably would not have remained constant. Men's labor time was valued far more highly than women's. Men were paid a higher wage. And they were not confined to the home by cultural taboos that inhibited comparisons among various types of labor. Had men been cooking, cleaning, and taking care of children, there almost certainly would have been a lot less of it.

THE PERPETUATION OF
DOMESTIC INEFFICIENCY

There is little doubt that the upgrading of standards and the expansion of services contained an element of overkill. Floors can be too clean, and shirts too well ironed. It is even possible to read too many baby manuals or overpower children with what the child psychologists called "smother-love." On the other hand, much of what women were producing was useful and appreciated. Even the most ardent opponent of housework would probably not advocate a return to the child neglect or filth of earlier eras. But approving of these clean kitchens or well-attended children does not settle the question. The method of provision is still at issue.

The history of the twentieth-century household is replete with technologies and methods of provision that were ignored, discarded, or undeveloped. Many of these possessed superior efficiency. They failed because the undervaluation of household time created a strong bias against them. They saved labor in a world in which labor cost very little.

An obvious alternative to the path we followed was the commercialization and professionalization of household services. Major phases of commercialization had already occurred. Spinning and weaving had been replaced by store-bought cloth and then by ready-mades. Food, and eventually processed food, was being purchased. The market was providing lower-cost alternatives, because it could take advantage of the savings from high-volume production and specialization. But to date, the commercialization of services has been sporadic. In the period from 1870 to 1930, a wide variety of commercialization schemes were tried. Companies prepared high-quality, nutritious meals and delivered them, piping hot, to individual homes. Commercial vacuum-cleaning services existed. Laundries flourished for a time. Boarding houses and apartment hotels, which kept chores to a minimum, were briefly popular. These experiments were, however, basically defunct by the depression of the 1930s. Instead, housewives continued to do for themselves.

There were also major reversals in the market. At one time, nearly all middle-class families employed servants or paid help for cleaning or, at the very least, for laundry. But eventually a servant shortage developed, and widespread hiring of in-home help declined substantially for all but the rich. The shortage was caused mainly by the lack of respect given to domestics. They had virtually no time to call their own, were at the beck and call of often-tyrannical employers, and were subjected to petty rituals of class distancing. Had domestic servants been able to standardize conditions, thereby professionalizing their jobs, and ensuring a shred of dignity, housework might have become a wholly marketed service. As it was, the unavailability of paid help led middle-class women back to washing their own floors. Another reversal occurred in laundry services. Hired laundresses and commercial laundries made great headway, especially in the 1920s. But automatic washing machines and dryers eventually put them out of business. Housewives did their own.

Commercialization and professionalization did not fail for lack of recognition. Beginning in the last quarter of the nineteenth century, prominent advocates argued that the privatization of domestic labor in individual homes was inefficient, anachronistic, and a central factor in the oppression of women. Between 1870 and 1930, a movement that historian Dolores Hayden has named "material feminism" attempted to socialize domestic work, through the establishment of day-care centers, public kitchens, and community dining clubs. Caught up in the swing, the *Ladies' Home Journal* prophesized in 1919 that "the private kitchen must go the way of the spinning wheel, of which it is the contemporary." Material feminists argued that socialized housework was far less costly due to economies of scale and specialization, and that professionalization could raise the quality of services. They decried the backwardness of privatized domestic labor. "By what art, what charm, what miracle, has the twentieth century preserved *alive* the prehistoric squaw!" asked an exasperated Charlotte Perkins Gilman, the noted feminist and economist. She and her associates called for kitchenless houses organized like hotels, with individual living spaces and common eating areas. They supported commercial laundry services and professional childrearing. Communitarians and socialist-feminists built model villages in which women shared housework. But most, such as Gilman, advocated "making a legitimate human business of housework; having it done by experts instead of by amateurs; making it a particular social industry instead of a general feminine function. . . . [This] is one of the greatest business opportunities the world has ever known."[39]

So what happened? Why have so many women continued to do their own laundry, cooking, cleaning, and child care more than half a century after the material feminists articulated a viable escape? What *was* the "art" or "charm" by which this "great business opportunity" came to so little?

Some scholars have argued that business preferred the existing system, because it allowed companies to sell more vacuum cleaners and washing machines. Others point to men, suggesting that they preferred individual attention from their wives. A third view has been offered by historian Ruth Schwartz Cowan, who believes that Americans consciously chose "to preserve family life and family autonomy." They wanted privacy (the single-family residence,

home-cooked meals eaten together by families, and privately owned household tools), even at the expense of "technical efficiency and community interest."[40]

It is true that Americans have traditionally revealed a taste for the privatized and individualized. But I believe that Cowan lays too much stress on this cultural imperative, and that the more important culprit has been the devaluation of the housewife's labor. Commercial services were too expensive in a situation where the housewife was restrained from earning cash to pay for them. By contrast, her labor had no monetary cost; to purchase what she could produce was a waste of a cheap resource. Marketed services couldn't compete, because the structure of prices was stacked against them.

This distortion also helps to explain why we haven't made more progress in streamlining home and appliance design. Had housewives' time been at a premium, our homes would look very different. For starters, they'd probably be much smaller. And they'd be easier to clean. We would have done away with the maddening burners and knobs on our stoves. Ditto for toilet bowls, with their hard-to-reach places. Other species marked for extinction would be odd-shaped rooms (hard to vacuum), intricate woodwork and cabinets, and knickknacks (dust collectors). Home appliances, which break far more frequently than commercial varieties, would be more reliable if housewives weren't there to wait for repairmen. The household versions also have more crevices and moving parts, which raise cleaning time. A look at the history of home and appliance design reveals that in many areas we are mired in outdated styles and habits. The kitchen, a major site of household labor, has not been redesigned since the 1930s. It's hard to believe that clever inventors and architects couldn't have saved us substantial amounts of time—if the economic incentives to do so had been there.[41]

The failure to socialize domestic labor ultimately contributed to the long hours of the housewife. The feminists were right that public provision, through either the market or nonprofit outfits, was more efficient. The total social labor devoted to cleaning, feeding, and caring for people could certainly have been reduced. But technical efficiency does not necessarily translate into economic cost. The devaluation of household labor made a less efficient technology cheaper. The labor-saving potential of socialized housework will be chosen only when women's time is highly valued.

HOUSEWORK TODAY AND TOMORROW

Things have started to change. As my estimates of working hours indicate, American women are finally finding some relief from long domestic schedules. They are having fewer children. They are marrying later and unmarrying earlier. Both these factors reduce the demands and commitments of the home. Women's paid employment has also made a major difference. Employed women do about two-thirds as much housework and child care as their non-employed sisters. In families where mothers work for pay, the insidious effects of undervalued labor are attenuated: there is just no time for the domestic routines of a full-time housewife.

Much of the decline in women's household labor is due to the disappearance of the group that devotes the most time to the home: married housewives with children. These are the women who have experienced the long-term constancy in hours—the ones who have put in fifty-plus hours a week for seventy years. In the last decade, we have finally seen a crack in this stability. My own estimates show a decline of two hours a week in three-children households. John Robinson's findings from the 1985 time-use study suggest the decline may be larger.[42] The processes that raised hours are now operating in reverse: standards are falling, and the range of household services is contracting. The culture of cleanliness is in abeyance.

And there are signs that men are doing more. This is a sharp break from earlier studies which consistently showed that men did not increase their help at home when their wives went into the labor force. Until recently, the attitude of this man, whose wife held a full-time job, was all too common: "My dad never did it. Why the hell do I have to?" Or this fellow: "I'd want her home when the kids come home from school or at least when I get home from work. I'm sure as hell not cooking my own supper. I didn't get married for that." Women are still doing about twice as much household work as men. But that's far less than before. Studies show that where couples live together, husbands are helping much more with child care. Robinson found greater male involvement in all household tasks, including things men were never before willing to do, such as house cleaning. My estimates yield similar results.[43]

Values are changing, too. Solid majorities of both women *and* men now believe that when a woman works for pay, household responsibilities should be shared. The idea that a woman's hours of employment are irrelevant for the distribution of household work no longer holds the power it once did. Of course, old habits die hard and many men who "believe" in sharing housework are not actually willing to take on much of this often-unrewarding work. Twenty-four percent of employed wives are still saddled with *all* the household work, and an additional 42 percent do "the bulk" of it.[44] However, things are improving, especially among young people. It is likely that the future holds more, not less, household equality.

The commercialization of household services remains a question mark. There has, of course, been a tremendous rise in the purchasing of services formerly produced at home. Americans are buying more restaurant meals and precooked food, day care, dry cleaning, and nursing home stays for their parents. Curiously, the rising demand for these things is not directly due to women's increased labor force participation. Demand is up because income is up. Most studies show that patterns of consumer spending on these services do not differ much by whether wives have paid employment. But how far will commercialization go? Will it wipe out household work altogether, so that women no longer face the double day? The quality and variety of many market substitutes remains limited. For top dollar, almost anything is available; but in the middle- to low-price range which most Americans can afford, the alternatives are frequently unappetizing. Perhaps the legacy of bias against commercialization has inhibited traditions of fine taste and quality at reasonable cost. There is also a cultural problem: the market for domestic services is often hollow and soulless. McDonald's and Kentucky Fried Chicken are not acceptable substitutes for people with a choice. We have yet to find a method of provision that is both quick and efficient and can reproduce the warmth and pleasures of home and family. And then, too, there is the prior question of how much domestic labor we want to keep within the home, because we prefer to raise our own children or cook our own meals. These can be deeply satisfying kinds of work, the stuff of which families are made. Ultimately, our choices about domestic labor will be made in conjunction with those concerning consumption as a whole, the subject to which I now turn.

CHAPTER 5

The Insidious Cycle of Work-and-Spend

SHOP 'TIL YOU DROP *because it's work, not because it's consumerism*

We live in what may be the most consumer-oriented society in history. Americans spend three to four times as many hours a year shopping as their counterparts in Western European countries.[1] Once a purely utilitarian chore, shopping has been elevated to the status of a national passion. *?*

Shopping has become a leisure activity in its own right. Going to the mall is a common Friday or Saturday night's entertainment, not only for the teens who seem to live in them, but also for adults. Shopping is also the most popular weekday evening "out-of-home-entertainment." And malls are everywhere. Four billion square feet of our total land area has been converted into shopping centers, or about 16 square feet for every American man, woman, and child. Actually, shopping is no longer confined to stores or malls but is permeating the entire geography. Any phone line is a conduit to thousands of products. Most homes are virtual retail outlets, with cable shopping channels, mail-order catalogues, toll-free numbers, and computer hookups. We can shop during lunch hour, from the office. We can shop while traveling, from the car. We can even shop in the airport, where video monitors have been installed for immediate on-screen purchasing.[2]

we don't know how to rest?

Some of the country's most popular leisure activities have been turned into extended shopping expeditions. National parks, music concerts, and art museums are now acquisition opportunities. When the South Street Seaport Museum in New York City opened in the early 1980s as a combination museum-shopping center, its director explained the commercialization as a bow to reality: "The fact is that shopping is the chief cultural activity in the United States." Americans used to visit Europe to see the sights or meet the people. Now "Born to Shop" guides are replacing Fodor and Baedeker, complete with walking tours from Ferragamo to Fendi. Even island paradises, where we go "to get away from it all," are not immune: witness titles such as *Shopping in Exciting Australia and Papua New Guinea*.[3]

Debt has been an important part of the shopping frenzy. Buying is easier when there's no requirement to pay immediately, and credit cards have seduced many people beyond their means: "I wanted to be able to pick up the tab for ten people, or take a cab when I wanted. I thought that part of being an adult was being able to go to a restaurant, look at the menu, and go in if you like the food, not because you're looking at the prices." This young man quickly found himself with $18,000 of credit card debt, and realized that he and his wife "could have gone to Europe last year on [the] interest alone." For some people, shopping has become an addiction, like alcohol or drugs. "Enabled" by plastic, compulsive shoppers spend money they don't have on items they absolutely "can't" do without and never use. The lucky ones find their way to self-help groups like Debtors Anonymous and Shopaholics Limited. And for every serious compulsive shopper, there are many more with mild habits. Linda Weltner was lucky enough to keep her addiction within manageable financial bounds, but still her "mindless shopping" grew into a "troubling preoccupation . . . which was impoverishing [her] life."[4]

The "shop 'til you drop" syndrome seemed particularly active during the 1980s, a decade popularly represented as one long buying spree. In the five years between 1983 and 1987, Americans purchased 51 million microwaves, 44 million washers and dryers, 85 million color televisions, 36 million refrigerators and freezers, 48 million VCRs, and 23 million cordless telephones—all for an adult population of only 180 million.[5]

Much has, with some justification, been made of the distinctiveness of the decade. The rich made an important social comeback. Not since the 1920s had the country been so tolerant of unrestrained materialism and greed. But in other ways the 1980s were not unique. The growth of personal consumption—the hallmark of 1980s culture—is nothing new. Modern consumerism harkens back to at least the 1920s. The growth of expenditures was temporarily derailed by the Depression and the war but was on track again by the 1950s. Since then, the nation has been feeding on a steady diet of single-family houses, cars, household appliances, and leisure spending. The average American is consuming, in toto, more than twice as much as he or she did forty years ago. And this holds not only for the Gucci set but all the way down the income scale. Nearly everyone participated in the postwar consumption boom. Compared with forty years ago, Americans in every income class—rich, middle class, and poor—have about twice as much in the way of income and material goods (see figure 5.1).[6]

Of course, the consumer boom of the 1980s *has* been different from the earlier decades in one important way—consumerism has been far more an affair of the affluent—the top 20 or 40 percent of the population. Income became far less equally distributed during this decade, and many people, especially those in the bottom quarter of the population, have experienced substantial declines in their standard of living. Others have maintained their incomes only by working longer hours. Had hours not risen, the average American worker's annual earnings would have been lower at the close of the decade than when it began. Still, declining wages have been mainly a phenomenon of the last ten years. From the longer vantage point of the "golden age" of the 1950s, 1960s, and 1970s, the depth and breadth of American affluence comes clearly into view.

Housing expenditures—the largest item in most family budgets—clearly reflect the country's growing wealth. In the 1950s, when developer William Levitt created Levittowns for ordinary American families, his standard house was 750 square feet. In 1963, the new houses were about twice as large; and by 1989, the average finished area had grown to almost three times the Levittown standard—2,000 feet. At the same time, fewer people were living in

Figure 5.1   Consumption per Person (Constant 1982 Dollars)[a]

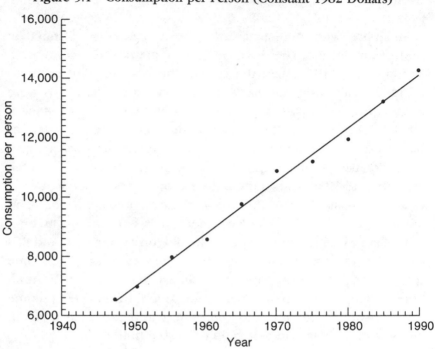

SOURCE: Calculated from *Economic Report of the President*, 1991 edition, tables B–15 and B–32.

[a]Data are in constant 1982 dollars, divided by the population sixteen years of age and over.

these dwellings. The typical 1950s family of four has shrunk to an average of 2.6 persons, so that each individual now has as much space as an entire family of four occupied in 1950. Fifty years ago, only 20 percent of all houses had more rooms than people living in them; by 1970, over 90 percent of our homes were spacious enough to allow more than one room per person.[7] The size and quality of the American housing stock has not been replicated anywhere else on earth.

Houses are not only bigger, they are also more luxuriously equipped. As late as 1940, 30 percent still had no running water, and 40 percent were without flush toilets. Today virtually all houses have both, and three-quarters of single-family dwellings have two or more bathrooms. In 1940, less than 45 percent of homes had electric refrigerators. Now all do. Americans also acquired vacuum cleaners, toasters, irons, radios, and washing machines. Forty years ago, fewer than 5 percent of U.S. homes had air-conditioners, dishwashers, and clothes dryers. Now two-thirds have air-conditioning (a majority

with centralized systems), microwaves, and dryers, and almost half
have dishwashers. Only a quarter of homes had kitchen ranges in
1953; now all do (see table 5.1).[8]

More of us also own our own homes. The difficulties young
people have had buying houses in the 1980s notwithstanding,
overall rates of home ownership have risen impressively—from 44
percent in 1940, to 55 percent in 1950, to 64 percent in 1989.
Homeownership rates for two-person households are even
higher—just over 70 percent. Ownership of motor vehicles has also
grown: in 1935, 55 percent of families had a car: today, 88 percent
of households have a motor vehicle, and the average number of
vehicles per household is two. Over 90 percent of all households
also have color televisions and 80 percent have VCRs. In addition

TABLE 5.1
Improvements in Material Standards of Living

Housing Characteristics	1940	1950	1970	1989
Size of typical home[a] (in square feet)		750		2000
Houses with running water[b]	70%		98%	
Houses with flush toilets[b]	60%		96%	
Home ownership rate[c]	44%	55%		64%

Households with Selected Appliances[d]	1940	1953		1987
Electric refrigerators	44%	89%		100%
Washing machines		76%		75%
Kitchen ranges		24%		97%
Air-conditioners		1.3%		64%
Dishwashers		3%		43%
Microwaves	0%	0%		61%
Color televisions	0%			93%

[a]Witold Rybczynski, "Living Smaller," *Atlantic Monthly*, February 1991, 67–68.
[b]Lebergott, *The American Economy: Income, Wealth and Want* (Princeton, N.J.: Princeton University Press, 1976), 98–99.
[c]Home ownership statistics for 1940 and 1950 from U.S. Department of Commerce, *Statistical Abstract of the United States*, (Washington, D.C.: Government Printing Office, 1971), 673, table 1110. Data for 1989 from Lawrence Mishel and David M. Frankel, *The State of Working America*, (Armonk, N.Y.: M. E. Sharpe), 224, table 8.1.
[d]1940 figure for refrigerators from Lebergott, *American Economy*, 101. All figures for 1953 and 1987 are from *Statistical Abstract*. 1953 figures are from 1971 edition, table 667, 1117. 1987 figures are from 1990 edition, table 723, 1280.

to VCRs and microwaves, Americans are buying many more services—like foreign travel, restaurant meals, medical attention, hair and skin care, and products of leisure industries such as health clubs or tennis lessons. Overall, per-capita service expenditures have risen 2.6 times since 1950—even more than consumer expenditures as a whole.[9]

The consumerism of the postwar era has not been without its effects on the way we use our time. As people became accustomed to the material rewards of prosperity, desires for leisure time were eroded. They increasingly looked to consumption to give satisfaction, even meaning, to their lives. In both the workplace and the home, progress has repeatedly translated into more goods and services, rather than more free time. Employers channel productivity increases into additional income; housewives are led to use their labor-saving appliances to produce more goods and services. Consumerism traps us as we become habituated to the good life, emulate our neighbors, or just get caught up in the social pressures created by everyone else's choices. Work-and-spend has become a mutually reinforcing and powerful syndrome—a seamless web we somehow keep choosing, without even meaning to.

WORK-AND-SPEND IS A MIDDLE-CLASS AFFLICTION

Work-and-spend is not everyone's disease. It is an affliction of affluent, mostly white, Americans. While many middle-class or even upper-middle-class people do not consider themselves affluent or even "well off," in relative terms their economic circumstances are actually quite favorable. A sizable proportion of the U.S. population can reasonably be classified as members of the middle, upper middle, and upper classes. Furthermore, in the last ten years, the better-off segments of society have done especially well economically. And their ranks have swelled—with the growth in two-earner families and the expansion of professional and managerial jobs. The much-heralded decline of the middle class has occurred not only because blue-collar workers have fallen on hard times, but also because large numbers of people have ascended into the income categories "above" the middle.

How large is the group prone to "work-and-spend"? The answer depends in part on how one chooses to define the middle class and what's above it. A simple procedure is to begin from the top of the income scale and move down to the middle. The top 20 percent, whose average income in 1990 was $105,000, over three times the nation's median, will certainly be included in the ranks of the affluent. The next 20 percent, who receive on average $45,000 a year, should also be counted. Adding 10 percent more, or exactly half the population, would bring us, in income terms, all the way down to about $31,000.

Although $31,000 is in the middle of the distribution, it is no longer a sufficient income to put a family into the middle class. Especially for young families, with heavy child-care or housing expenses, it is inadequate. Among the black middle class, responsibility for poorer relatives has put a tremendous strain on earnings, so that even a decent income often can't provide a decent life style. On the other hand, for a single person who owns a house that is paid for, $30,000 or even less may be enough to finance a perfectly comfortable middle-class life. Income is an imperfect measure because individual circumstances—such as family size, age, the price of housing, and where one lives—matter very much. Therefore, to identify the middle class, we may also want to take into account life-style factors—such as the ability to own one's home or finance college educations for the children. On these grounds, we get a range—from about two-thirds for home ownership, to 37 percent for college education.[10]

Though it is clearly difficult to come up with precise estimates from existing statistics, exact numbers are probably not essential for my purposes. Rough notions will suffice. My own preference is to take 40 percent as a lower bound estimate for "eligibility" in the ranks of the well-off and consider the next 20 percent as questionable. At the other end, we will certainly exclude the poorest quarter of the population—the percentage of Americans who in recent years report that they worry "all or most of the time" that they will not be able to meet family expenses and pay the bills.[11]

The worries of the bottom quarter of the population are a reflection of the recent surge in inequality. In earlier decades, the benefits of prosperity were far more evenly distributed, extending even to the least well-off segments of society. In the mid-1970s, a larger proportion of the population could have been identified as "middle class" or above, perhaps as much as two-thirds. At that time, many working-class families, often by dint of considerable overtime hours, were managing a middle-class life style. They financed their own homes and bought nice cars, sometimes modest vacation places. Many survived on one income. This has now changed, as lucrative manufacturing jobs for men have disappeared. The 1980s have also brought a substantial growth in the fraction of the population living on the margins, struggling to get by. According to a 1989 Gallup Poll, 13 percent of those surveyed reported that there were times during the last year when they did not have enough money to buy food. Higher proportions (17 percent and 21 percent) did not have enough income for clothes and medical care. Among people of color, the proportions are far higher, exceeding a third among African-Americans. And because the poll reaches only those with homes (and telephones), these numbers are understated.[12]

Many of these people cannot work long hours even if they want to because their jobs are part-time or intermittent. They may not even have employment, either because they cannot find it or because they cannot afford child care. Among those who do have jobs, hourly pay is very low; long hours or multiple jobs are necessary just to make a subsistence income. They are clearly not working in order to sustain a middle-class life style. Even those with low incomes, however, are not free from pressures to consume. Television, advertising, peer competition, and the ubiquitous example of the economically more fortunate provide continual testaments to the value of high living. The poor are not so much adherents to an alternate (antimaterialist) set of values, as they are unsuccessful at the same game everyone else is playing. Far more than in the past, middle-class culture has insinuated itself throughout the society. If they're not trapped in work-and-spend, it's more because they can't than that they won't.

THE CREATION OF DISCONTENT

I never knew how poor I was until I had a little money.
                                                                —a banker

There is no doubt that the growth of consumption has yielded major improvements in the quality of life. Running water, washing machines, and electrical appliances eliminated arduous, often backbreaking labor. Especially for the poor women who not only did their own housework, but often someone else's as well, the transformation of the home has been profoundly liberating. Other products have also enhanced the quality of life. The compact disc raises the enjoyment of the music lover; the high-performance engine makes the car buff happy; and the fashion plate loves to wear a designer suit.

But when we add up all the items we consume, and consider the overall impact, rather than each in isolation, the picture gets murkier. The farther we get from the onerous physical conditions of the past, the more ambiguous are the effects of additional commodities. The less "necessary" and more "luxurious" the item, the more difficult it is automatically to assume that consumer purchases yield intrinsic value.

In an era when the connections between perpetual growth and environmental deterioration are becoming more apparent, with the quality of public life declining in many areas (public safety, decline of community, failing education system), shouldn't we at least step back and re-examine our commitment to ever-greater quantities of consumer goods? Do Americans need high-definition television, increasingly exotic vacations, and climate control in their autos? How about hundred-dollar inflatable sneakers, fifty-dollar wrinkle cream, or the ever-present (but rarely used) stationary bicycle? A growing fraction of homes are now equipped with jacuzzis (or steam showers) and satellite receivers. Once we take the broader view, can we still be so sure that all these things are really making us better off?

We do know that the increasing consumption of the last forty years has not made us happier. The percentage of the population who reported being "very happy" peaked in 1957, according to two national polls. By the last years these polls were taken (1970 and 1978), the level of "very happy" had not recovered, in spite of the rapid growth in consumption during the 1960s and 1970s. Similar polls taken since then indicate no revival of happiness.[13]

Despite the fact that possessions are not creating happiness, we are still riding the consumer merry-go-round. In fact, for some

Americans the quest for material goods became more intense in the last decade: according to the pollster Louis Harris, "by the mid-1980s, the American people were far more oriented toward economic growth and materialism than before. Most significant, young people were leading the charge back to material values."[14]

Materialism has not only failed to make us happy. It has also bred its own form of discontent—even among the affluent. Newspaper and magazine articles chronicle the dissatisfaction. One couple earning $115,000 tallied up their necessary expenses of $100,000 a year and complained that "something's gone terribly wrong with being 'rich.' " An unmarried Hollywood executive earning $72,000 worried about bouncing checks: "I have so much paid for by the studio—my car, my insurance, and virtually all food and entertainment—and I'm *still* broke." Urbanites have it especially hard. As one New York City inhabitant explained, "It's incredible, but you just can't live in this city on a hundred thousand dollars a year." According to the *New York Times,* the fast lane is not all it's cracked up to be, and Wall Streeters are "Feeling Poor on $600,000 a Year." "When the Joneses they are keeping up with are the Basses . . . $10 million in liquid capital is not rich."[15]

Whatever we think of these malcontents—whether we find them funny, pathetic, or reprehensible—we must acknowledge that these feelings are not confined to those in the income stratosphere. Many who make far less have similar laments. Douglas and Maureen Obey earn $56,000 a year—an income that exceeds that of roughly 70 percent of the population. Yet they complain that they are stretched to the breaking point. Douglas works two jobs "to try to keep it all together. . . . I feel I make a fairly good income that should afford a comfortable lifestyle, but somehow it doesn't. . . . [I'm] in hock up to my eyeballs." The Obeys own their home, two cars, a second rental property, and a backyard pool.[16]

Complaints about life style have been particularly loud among the baby-boom generation. One writer explained a state of mind shared by many in her generation: she was convinced she would not achieve the comfortable middle-class life style enjoyed by her parents (four-bedroom house, two-car garage, private schools for the children, and cashmere blankets at the bottom of the beds): "I thought bitterly of my downward mobility . . . and [had] constant conversations with myself about wanting . . . a new couch, a weekend cottage, a bigger house on a quieter street." Eventually she realized that more money was not the answer. Her needs were satisfied. As she acknowledged: "Discontent was cheating me of the life I *had*."[17]

CAPITALISM'S SQUIRREL CAGE

This materialism (and its attendant discontent) is taken for granted. It is widely believed that our unceasing quest for material goods is part of the basic makeup of human beings. According to the folklore, we may not like it, but there's little we can do about it.

Despite its popularity, this view of human nature is wrong. While human beings may have innate desires to strive toward something, there is nothing preordained about material goods. There are numerous examples of societies in which *things* have played a highly circumscribed role. In medieval Europe, there was relatively little acquisitiveness. The common people, whose lives were surely precarious by contemporary standards, showed strong preferences for leisure rather than money. In the nineteenth- and early twentieth-century United States, there is also considerable evidence that many working people exhibited a restricted appetite for material goods. Numerous examples of societies where consumption is relatively unimportant can be found in the anthropological and historical literature.[18]

Consumerism is not an ahistorical trait of human nature, but a specific product of capitalism. With the development of the market system, consumerism "spilled" over," for the first time, beyond the charmed circles of the rich. The growth of the middle class created a large group of potential buyers and the possibility that mass culture could be oriented around material goods. This process can be seen not only in historical experiences but is now going on in places such as Brazil and India, where the growth of large middle classes have contributed to rampant consumerism and the breakdown of longstanding values.[19]

In the United States, the watershed was the 1920s—the point at which the "psychology of scarcity" gave way to the "psychology of abundance." This was a crucial period for the development of modern materialist culture. Thrift and sobriety were out; waste and excess were in. The nation grew giddy with its exploding wealth. Consumerism blossomed—both as a social ideology and in terms of high rates of real spending. In the midst of all this buying, we can discern the origins of modern consumer discontent.

This was the decade during which the American dream, or what was then called "the American standard of living," captured the nation's imagination. But it was always something of a mirage. The historian Winifred Wandersee explains:

> It is doubtful that the average American could have described the precise meaning of the term "American standard of living," but nearly everyone agreed that it was attainable, highly desirable, and far superior to that of any other nation. Its nature varied according to social class and regional differences, but no matter where a family stood socially and financially, it was certain to have aspirations set beyond that stance. This was the great paradox posed by the material prosperity of the twentieth century: prosperity was conspicuously present, but it was always just out of reach, for nearly every family defined its standard of living in terms of an income that it hoped to achieve rather than the reality of the paycheck.[20]

The phenomenon of yearning for more is evident in studies of household consumption. In a 1928 study of Yale University faculty members, the bottom category (childless couples with incomes of $2,000) reported that their situation was "life at the cheapest and barest with nothing left over for the emergencies of sickness and childbirth." Yet an income of $2,000 a year put them above 60 percent of all American families. Those at the $5,000 level (the top 10 percent of the income distribution) reported that they "achieve nothing better than 'hand to mouth living.' " At $6,000, "the family containing young children can barely break even." Yet these were the top few percent of all Americans. Even those making $12,000—a fantastic sum in 1928—complained about items they could not afford. A 1922 Berkeley study revealed similar sentiments of discontent—despite the facts that all the families studied had telephones, virtually all had purchased life insurance, two-thirds owned their own homes and took vacations, over half had motor cars, and nearly every family spent at least a little money on servants or housecleaning help.[21]

The discontent expressed by many Americans was fostered—

and to a certain extent even created—by manufacturers. Business embarked on the path of the "hard sell." The explosion of consumer credit made the task easier, as automobiles, radios, electric refrigerators, washing machines—even jewelry and foreign travel—were bought on the installment plan. By the end of the 1920s, 60 percent of cars, radios, and furniture were being purchased on "time."[22] The ability to buy without actually having money helped foster a climate of instant gratification, expanding expectations, and, ultimately, materialism.

The 1920s was also the decade of advertising. The admen went wild: everything from walnuts to household coal was being individually branded and nationally advertised. Of course, ads had been around for a long time. But something new was afoot, in terms of both scale and strategy. For the first time, business began to use advertising as a psychological weapon against consumers. "Scare copy" was invented. Without Listerine, Postum, or a Buick, the consumer would be left a spinster, fall victim to a crippling disease, or be passed over for a promotion. Ads developed an association between the product and one's very identity. Eventually they came to promise everything and anything—from self-esteem, to status, friendship, and love.[23]

The psychological approach responded to the economic dilemma business faced. Americans in the middle classes and above (to whom virtually all advertising was targeted) were no longer buying to satisfy basic needs—such as food, clothing and shelter. These had been met. Advertisers had to persuade consumers to acquire things they most certainly did not need. In the words of John Kenneth Galbraith, production would have to "create the wants it seeks to satisfy." This is exactly what manufacturers tried to do. The normally staid AT&T attempted to transform the utilitarian telephone into a luxury, urging families to buy "all the telephone facilities that they can conveniently use, rather than the smallest amount they can get along with." One ad campaign targeted fifteen phones as the style for an affluent home. In product after product, companies introduced designer colors, styles, even scents. The maid's uniform had to match the room decor, flatware was color-coordinated, and Kodak cameras came in five bird-inspired tints—Sea Gull, Cockatoo, Redbreast, Bluebird, and Jenny Wren.[24]

Business clearly understood the nature of the problem. It even had a name—"needs saturation." Would-be sellers complained of buyers' strike and organized a "Prosperity Bureau," urging people to "Buy Now." According to historian Frederick Lewis Allen: "Business had learned as never before the importance of the ultimate consumer. Unless he could be persuaded to buy and buy lavishly, the whole stream of six-cylinder cars, super helerodynes, cigarettes, rouge compacts, and electric ice boxes would be dammed up at its outlets."[25]

But would the consumer be equal to her task as "the savior of private enterprise"? The general director of General Motors' Research Labs, Charles Kettering, stated the matter baldly: business needs to create a "dissatisfied consumer"; its mission is "the organized creation of dissatisfaction." Kettering led the way by introducing annual model changes for GM cars—planned obsolescence designed to make the consumer discontented with what he or she already had. Other companies followed GM's lead. In the words of advertising historian Roland Marchand, success now depended on "the nurture of qualities like wastefulness, self-indulgence, and artificial obsolescence." The admen and the businessmen had to instill what Marchand has called the "consumption ethic," or what Benjamin Hunnicutt termed "the new economic gospel of consumption."[26]

The campaign to create new and unlimited wants did not go unchallenged. Trade unionists and social reformers understood the long-term consequences of consumerism for most Americans: it would keep them imprisoned in capitalism's "squirrel cage." The consumption of luxuries necessitated long hours. Materialism would provide no relief from the tedium, the stultification, the alienation, and the health hazards of modern work; its rewards came outside the workplace. There was no mystery about these choices: business was explicit in its hostility to increases in free time, preferring consumption as the *alternative* to taking economic progress in the form of leisure. In effect, business offered up the cycle of work-and-spend. In response, many trade unionists rejected what they regarded as a Faustian bargain of time for money: "Workers have declared that their lives are not to be bartered at any price, that no wage, no matter how high can induce them to sell their birthright. [The worker] is not the slave of fifty years ago.

. . . he [*sic*] reads . . . goes to the theater . . . [*and*] has established his own libraries, his own educational institutions. . . . And he wants time, time, time, for all these things."[27]

Progressive reformers raised ethical and religious objections to the cycle of work-and-spend. Monsignor John A. Ryan, a prominent Catholic spokesman, articulated a common view:

> One of the most baneful assumptions of our materialistic industrial society is that all men should spend at least one-third of the twenty-four hour day in some productive occupation. . . . If men still have leisure [after needs are satisfied], new luxuries must be invented to keep them busy and new wants must be stimulated . . . to take the luxuries off the market and keep the industries going. Of course, the true and rational doctrine is that when men have produced sufficient necessaries and reasonable comforts and conveniences to supply all the population, they should spend what time is left in the cultivation of their intellects and wills, in the pursuit of the higher life.[28]

The debates of the 1920s clearly laid out the options available to the nation. On the one hand, the path advocated by labor and social reformers: take productivity growth in the form of increases in free time, rather than the expansion of output; limit private consumption, discourage luxuries, and emphasize public goods such as education and culture. On the other hand, the plan of business: maintain current working hours and aim for maximal economic growth. This implied the encouragement of "discretionary" consumption, the expansion of new industries, and a culture of unlimited desires. Production would come to "fill a void that it has itself created."[29]

It is not difficult to see which alternative was adopted. Between 1920 and the present, the bulk of productivity advance has been channeled into the growth of consumption. Economist John Owen has found that between 1920 and 1977, the amount of labor supplied over the average American's lifetime fell by only 10 percent; and since 1950, there has even been a slight increase.[30] The attitude of businessmen was crucial to this outcome. As employers, they had strong reasons for preferring long hours, as I argued in chapter 3. As sellers, they craved vigorous consumption to create markets for their products. Labor proved to be no match for the economic and political power of business.

Finally, we should not underestimate the appeal of consumption itself. The working classes and the poor, particularly those migrating from Europe or the rural United States, grew up in conditions of material deprivation. The array of products available in urban America was profoundly alluring, at times mesmerizing. For the middle classes, consumption held its own satisfactions. Designer towels or the latest GM model created a sense of privilege, superiority, and well-being. A Steinway "made life worth living." Once the Depression hit, it reinforced these tendencies. One of its legacies was a longlasting emphasis on finding security in the form of material success.[31]

[handwritten margin note: why need a critique of consumerism]

THE PITFALLS OF CONSUMERISM

The consumerism that took root in the 1920s was premised on the idea of *dis*satisfaction. As much as one has, it is never enough. The implicit mentality is that the next purchase will yield happiness, and then the next. In the words of the baby-boom writer, Katy Butler, *[handwritten margin note: who is this?]* it was the new couch, the quieter street, and the vacation cottage. Yet happiness turned out to be elusive. Today's luxuries became tomorrow's necessities, no longer appreciated. When the Joneses also got a new couch or a second home, these acquisitions were no longer quite as satisfying. Consumerism turned out to be full of pitfalls—a vicious pattern of wanting and spending which failed to deliver on its promises.

The inability of the consumerist life style to create durable satisfaction can be seen in the syndrome of "keeping up with the Joneses." This competition is based on the fact that it is not the absolute level of consumption that matters, but how much one consumes relative to one's peers. The great English economist John Maynard Keynes made this distinction over fifty years ago: "[Needs] fall into two classes—those which are absolute in the sense that we feel them whatever the situation of our fellow human beings may be, and those which are relative only in that their satisfaction lifts us above, makes us feel superior to, our fellows." Since then, economists have invented a variety of terms for "keeping up with the Joneses": "relative income or consumption," "positional goods," or "local status." A brand-new Toyota Corolla may be a luxury and a status symbol in a lower-middle-class town, but it appears paltry next to the BMWs and Mercedes that fill the driveways of the fancy suburb. A 10-percent raise sounds great until you find that your co-workers all got 12 percent. The cellular phone, fur coat, or _____ (fill in the blank) gives a lot of satisfaction only before everyone else has one. In the words of one 1980s investment banker: "You tend to live up to your income level. You see it in relation to the people of your category. They're living in a certain way and you want to live in that way. You keep up with other people of your situation who have also leveraged themselves."[32]

Over time, keeping up with the Joneses becomes a real trap—because the Joneses also keep up with you. If everyone's income goes up by 10 percent, then relative positions don't change at all. No satisfaction is gained. The more of our happiness we derive from comparisons with others, the less additional welfare we get from general increases in income—which is probably why happiness has failed to keep pace with economic growth. This dynamic may be only partly conscious. We may not even be aware that we are competing with the Joneses, or experience it as a competition. It may be as simple as the fact that exposure to their latest "life-style upgrade" plants the seed in our own mind that we must have it, too—whether it be a European vacation, this year's fashion statement, or piano lessons for the children.

In the choice between income and leisure, the quest for relative standing has biased us toward income. That's because status comparisons have been mostly around commodities—cars, clothing, houses, even second houses. If Mrs. Jones works long hours, she will be able to buy the second home, the designer dresses, or the fancier car. If her neighbor Mrs. Smith opts for more free time instead, her two-car garage and walk-in closet will be half empty. As long as the competition is more oriented to visible commodities, the tendency will be for both women to prefer income to time off. But once they both spend the income, they're back to where they started. Neither is *relatively* better off. If free time is less of a "relative" good than other commodities, then true welfare could be gained by having more of it, and worrying less about what the Joneses are buying.

It's not easy to get off the income treadmill and into a new, more leisured life style. Mrs. Smith won't do it on her own, because it'll set her back in comparison to Mrs. Jones. And Mrs. Jones is just like Mrs. Smith. They are trapped in a classic Prisoner's Dilemma: both would be better off with more free time; but without cooperation, they will stick to the long hours, high consumption choice.[33] We also know their employers won't initiate a shift to more leisure, because they prefer employees to work long hours.

A second vicious cycle arises from the fact that the satisfactions gained from consumption are often short-lived. For many, consumption can be habit forming. Like drug addicts who develop a tolerance, consumers need additional hits to maintain any given level of satisfaction.[34] The switch from black and white to color television was a real improvement when it occurred. But soon viewers became habituated to color. Going back to black and white would have reduced well-being, but having color may not have yielded a permanently higher level of satisfaction. Telephones are another example. Rotary dialing was a major improvement. Then came touch-tone, which made us impatient with rotaries. Now numbers are preprogrammed and some people begin to find any dialing a chore.

Our lives are filled with goods to which we have become so habituated that we take them for granted. Indoor plumbing was once a great luxury—and still is in much of the world. Now it is so ingrained in our life style that we don't give it a second thought. The same holds true for all but the newest household appliances—stoves, refrigerators, and vacuum cleaners are just part of the landscape. We may pay great attention to the kind of automobile we drive, but the fact of having a car is something adults grew accustomed to long ago.

The process of habituation can be seen as people pass through life stages—for example, in the transition from student life to a first job. The graduate student makes $15,000 a year. He has hand-me-down furniture, eats at cheap restaurants, and, when traveling long distances, finds a place in someone else's car. After graduation, he gets a job and makes twice as much money. At first, everything seems luxurious. He rents a bigger apartment (with no roommates), buys his own car, and steps up a notch in restaurant quality. His former restaurant haunts now seem unappetizing. Hitching a ride becomes too inconvenient. As he accumulates possessions, the large apartment starts to shrink. In not too many years, he has become habituated to twice as much income and is spending the entire $30,000. It was once a princely sum, which made him feel rich. Now he feels it just covers a basic standard of living, without much left over for luxuries. He may not even feel any better off. Yet to go back to $15,000 would be painful.

Over time, further increases in income set in motion another round of the same. He becomes dissatisfied with renting and "needs" to buy a home. Travel by car takes too long, so he switches to airplanes. His tastes become more discriminating, and the average price of a restaurant meal slowly creeps upward. Something like this process is why Americans making $70,000 a year end up feeling stretched and discontented.[35]

Of course, part of this is a life-cycle process. As our young man grows older, possessions like cars and houses become more important. But there's more to it than aging. Like millions of other American consumers, he is becoming addicted to the accoutrements of affluence. This may well be why the doubling of per-capita income has not made us twice as well off. In the words of psychologist Paul Wachtel, we have become an "asymptote culture . . . in which the contribution of material goods to life satisfaction has reached a point of diminishing returns. . . . Each individual item seems to us to bring an increase in happiness or satisfaction. But the individual increments melt like cotton candy when you try to add them up."[36]

These are not new ideas. Economists such as James Duesenberry, Edward Schumacher, Fred Hirsch, Tibor Scitovsky, Robert Frank, and Richard Easterlin have explored these themes. Psychologists have also addressed them, providing strong support for the kinds of conclusions I have drawn. My purpose is to add a dimension to this analysis of consumption which has heretofore been neglected—its connection to the incentive structures operating in labor markets. The consumption traps I have described are just the flip side of the bias toward long hours embedded in the production system. We are not merely caught in a pattern of spend-and-spend—the problem identified by many critics of consumer culture. The whole story is that we work, and spend, and work and spend some more.

CAUSES OF THE WORK-AND-
SPEND CYCLE

The irony in all the consuming Americans do is that, when asked, they reject materialist values. The Gallup Poll recently asked respondents to choose what was most important to them—family life, betterment of society, physical health, a strict moral code, and so on. Among a list of nine, the materialist option—"having a nice home, car and other belongings"—ranked *last*. In a second survey, respondents ranked "having nice things" twenty-sixth in a list of twenty-eight. (Only opposing abortion and being free of obligations were less popular.) Over two-thirds of the population says it would "welcome less emphasis on money." Yet behavior is often contrary to these stated values. Millions of working parents see their children or spouses far less than they should or would like to. "Working" mothers complain they have no time for themselves. Volunteer work is on the decline, presumably because people have little time for it. Employed Americans spend long hours at jobs that are adversely affecting their health—through injury, occupationally induced diseases, and stress. My explanation for this paradoxical behavior is that people are operating under a powerful set of constraints: they are trapped by the cycle of work-and-spend.[37]

Work-and-spend is driven by productivity growth. Whether the annual increment is 3 percent, as it was for much of the postwar period, or less, as it has been in recent years, growth in productivity provides the chance either to raise income or to reduce working hours. This is where the cycle begins, with the employer's reaction to the choice between "time and money." Usually a company does not offer this choice to its employees but unilaterally decides to maintain existing hours and give a pay increase instead. As we have seen, for forty years, only a negligible portion of productivity increase has been channeled into free time. Using productivity to raise incomes has become the firmly entrenched "default option."

One might imagine that where wages are set by collective-bargaining agreements employees would have more of a say in the choice between income and time. But less than 20 percent of the workforce is unionized. Furthermore, as union negotiators will attest, employers are frequently fiercely resistant to granting concessions on hours and jealously guard the authority to set schedules. But even if a firm is willing, the reduced worktime option it offers will often be worth less (in dollar terms) than a straight pay increase, because of the extra costs incurred, such as additional fringe benefits for new employees. The company will try and force the employees to bear the expenses associated with shorter working hours. So even with collective bargaining, the choice will be skewed against shorter hours.

Once a pay increase is granted, it sets off the consumption cycles I have described. The additional income will be spent. (The personal savings rate is currently only 4.5 percent of disposable income.)[38] The employee will become habituated to this spending and incorporate it into his or her usual standard of living. Gaining free time by *reducing* income becomes undesirable, both because of relative comparisons (Joneses versus Smiths) and habit formation. The next year, when another increase in productivity occurs, the process starts again. The company offers income, which the employee spends and becomes accustomed to. This interpretation is consistent with the history of the last half-century. Annual productivity growth has made possible higher incomes or more free time. Repeatedly, the bulk of the productivity increase has been channeled into the former. Consumption has kept pace.

What drives this cycle of work-and-spend? One view—that of neoclassical economic theory—contends that it is motivated by the choices of workers. Workers have prior (and fixed) attitudes about how valuable income is to them and how much they dislike work. On the basis of these attitudes they select the number of hours they want to work. Firms are passive and willing to hire workers for whatever quantity of hours they choose. By this account, if factory workers in the nineteenth century toiled twelve, fourteen, or sixteen hours a day, it was because they "preferred" this schedule above all others. If U.S. workers have added a month onto their annual worktime, it is because they want the extra income. Attempts to limit hours of labor will make employees worse, not better off. Invariably, *workers get what they want.*[39]

I turn the neoclassical analysis on its head, arguing that *workers want what they get*, rather than get what they want. My starting point is firms rather than individual workers. Firms set the hours they require of their employees. Associated with those hours is a level of income that determines workers' consumption level. As a

result of habit formation and relative status considerations, people develop preferences to accommodate that level of spending. Attitudes toward consumption are not preordained but are actually formed in the process of earning and consuming itself.[40] These two interpretations—workers get what they want or want what they get—are the polar cases. According to neoclassical theory, attitudes toward consumption are independent of the actual experience of spending, and firms are passive. In my interpretation, firms set hours and workers do most of the adjusting.

Assessing the Neoclassical View

The crux of the neoclassical story is that workers determine hours. But do they? Not according to the evidence. Every study I have seen on this topic has found that workers lack free choice of hours. They are limited in both how much and how little they can work. In one survey of male heads of households, 85 percent reported that they did not have free choice of hours. A second study (of married men) again found that 85 percent were faced with the choice of either no job or a job at hours that were not those they would choose. The men wanted shorter hours, but all the jobs were full-time. The other existing studies report consistent results: workers face constraints on their hours of work. Indeed, institutionalist labor economists (oriented to the "real world") have long maintained that firms choose hours, giving employees a take-it-or-leave-it option. Now this institutionalist view is backed up by statistical evidence.[41]

These findings do not imply that workers have *no* freedom in the matter of working hours. Moonlighting and retirement are options. And hours differ across occupations and industries, so that workers can quit their jobs to find alternate schedules. But the research shows that for most workers these adjustments are not sufficient to eliminate *binding* constraints on hours. As the economist Paul Samuelson noted years ago: "In contrast with freedom in the spending of the money we earn, the modern industrial regime denies us a similar freedom in choosing the work routine by which we earn those dollars." The failure of the neoclassical approach is rooted in its assumption that there is always full employment and that workers' choices are sovereign. As I have argued, this charac-

But then how to explain decline in 19BC of hours in early 20k C?

terization is mistaken. Competition in labor markets is typically skewed in favor of employers: it is a buyer's market. And in a buyer's market, it is the sellers who compromise. Competition for labor is not strong enough to ensure that workers' desires are always satisfied. This is part of why firms are able to set working hours, even when they entail binding constraints on workers.[42]

The second major point of difference between my approach and the neoclassical involves the nature of preferences. Neoclassical economists point to worker attitudes as evidence that the market is delivering the hours they want. Results from a 1985 survey are typical: asked whether they would prefer more, fewer, or just the hours they were currently working, accompanied by commensurate changes in income, about two thirds of workers reported satisfaction with their current hours/income choice.[43]

This evidence may sound compelling. But imagine, for a moment, what the responses would be like in the light of my interpretation, and workers want what they get. *The results would look just the same,* in the sense that majorities would express satisfaction with their current hours. The standard survey evidence is perfectly consistent with both views.

A great deal of psychological evidence casts doubt, however, on the neoclassical interpretation. Psychologists find that people tend to "adapt" to their environments: that is, their preferences adjust over time.[44] The fact that large numbers of people say they are contented with their working hours (or job conditions) may reveal that they are tractable, not that their deeper desires have been fulfilled.

One type of evidence that can differentiate between the two interpretations is forward-looking surveys—questions about trading off future income for leisure. Here workers express markedly different views. In a 1978 Department of Labor study, 84 percent of respondents said that they would like to trade off some or all of future income for additional free time. Nearly half (47 percent) said they would trade *all* of a 10-percent pay raise for free time. Only 16 percent opted for the money with no increase in time off (see table 5.2).

These findings support a key feature of the work-and-spend cycle—the difference in attitudes toward current and future income. As with all the previous surveys, this group was unwilling to

TABLE 5.2
Trading Off Future Income for Free Time
Amount of Ten-Percent Raise Workers Are Willing to Forgo for
Additional Leisure[a]
(in percentages)

	Nothing for Free Time	40% of Pay Raise for Free Time	70% of Pay Raise for Free Time	100% of Pay Raise for Free Time
All Correspondents	15.6	25.4	11.6	47.3
Sex				
Men	16.4	22.8	9.8	51.0
Women	14.1	30.2	15.0	40.8
Occupation				
Prof-Tech	15.6	25.0	10.6	48.9
Managerial	20.2	26.9	9.2	43.7
Clerical-Sales	11.1	30.2	13.5	45.2
Skilled Labor	15.8	21.7	11.3	51.3
Operatives-Laborers	15.1	25.9	10.2	48.8
Service	17.3	25.5	18.4	38.8
Farm	7.7	30.8	7.7	53.8
Education				
Some H.S. or less	19.7	18.7	13.3	48.3
High School Degree	14.2	25.2	10.1	50.6
Some College	14.4	25.8	13.5	46.3
College Degree	12.5	37.5	8.3	41.7
Some Graduate School	18.6	27.5	9.8	44.1
Total Family Income				
Under $4,999	19.0	25.4	11.1	44.4
$5,000–$9,999	19.3	24.1	13.8	42.8
$10,000–$14,999	14.4	30.3	11.3	44.1
$15,000–$19,999	13.1	27.7	12.0	47.1
$20,000–$24,999	11.3	20.3	9.8	58.6
$25,000–$34,999	17.8	20.6	14.0	47.7
Over $34,999	15.3	24.7	8.2	51.8
Major Activity of Spouse				
Men				
Not Married	13.9	17.5	14.6	54.0
Working Full-time	17.1	24.1	7.6	51.3
Working Part-time	23.2	21.7	11.6	43.5

TABLE 5.2 *(Continued)*

	Nothing for Free Time	40% of Pay Raise for Free Time	70% of Pay Raise for Free Time	100% of Pay Raise for Free Time
Unemployed & Off-Job	17.6	5.9	14.7	61.8
Keeping House & Other	15.9	27.5	7.2	49.3
Women				
Not Married	16.4	25.0	14.7	44.0
Working Full-time	13.3	33.7	16.0	37.0
Working Part-time	9.1	45.5	9.1	36.4
Unemployed & Off-Job	13.3	20.0	20.0	46.7
Keeping House & Other	7.7	23.1	7.7	61.5
Number of Dependents				
None	16.5	21.4	12.7	49.4
One	15.9	26.5	9.5	48.1
Two	16.2	25.7	12.6	45.5
Three	13.3	33.3	11.4	41.9
Four or more	12.2	32.4	9.5	45.9
Age				
Under 25	10.5	28.1	22.2	34.2
25–34	14.2	31.9	8.5	45.4
25–49	15.1	22.1	11.6	51.2
50–64	20.5	21.0	8.0	50.4
Over 64	38.5	7.7	0	53.8

[a]Maximum potential income-time tradeoff choice determined by computation of a composite variable which reports the highest proportion of a potential 10-percent pay raise that each respondent states a willingness to exchange for any of five forms of potential gains of free time. For example, a respondent who states a desire to exchange 70 percent of a 10-percent pay raise for a shorter workday, 40 percent of the raise for a reduced workweek, 40 percent for added vacation, 40 percent for an extended paid leave of absence (sabbatical), and no portion of the pay raise for earlier retirement would have a maximum potential tradeoff score of 70 percent of pay raise because the shorter workday choice elicited the highest exchange of all the available choices.

SOURCE: Fred Best, *Exchanging Earnings for Leisure: Finding of an Exploratory National Survey on Work Time Preferences,* (Washington, D.C.: United States Employment and Training Administration, 1980), 77, table 6.

give up its current income (only a small percentage chose that option). Presumably they had become materially or psychologically attached to their existing standard of living. But the desire to consume out of future income was far less compelling, a fact consistent with recent psychological research.[45] In the neoclassical interpretation, there is no explanation for this asymmetry.

Because this study was conducted over ten years ago, we can check to see whether the stated preferences were actually validated. Did 84 percent of the population gain the free time they said they wanted? As we know, they did not. In fact, they lost free time. Of course, what has happened since 1978 is complicated. Some workers, particularly younger less-educated men, have lost purchasing power since 1978. Others have had stagnant incomes. But leisure time did not even increase among those with gains in income. In fact, hours increased substantially for those groups who both did well in the labor market and expressed the strongest desires for more time off—women and people in the higher-paid occupational categories. In 1989, when a similar survey was taken, the results indicated that forward-looking preferences for leisure are still strong. Eight out of ten Americans declared that they would sacrifice career advancement in order to spend more time with their families.[46]

This evidence hardly settles the issue. Many more studies and surveys are necessary, particularly to track working hours and preferences over time. However, the findings do cast doubt on the sanguine view of labor/leisure choices which dominates the economic discourse. It is clear that we can no longer rely on the simple assumption that labor and product markets provide optimal outcomes, in response to what people want and need. The interaction between what we want and what we get is far more complicated.

THE SOCIAL NATURE OF WORK-
AND-SPEND

Part of the power of the work-and-spend cycle is its social pervasiveness. Although individuals are the proximate decision makers, their actions are influenced and constrained by social norms and conventions. The social character of the cycle of work-and-spend means that individuals have a hard time breaking out of it on their own. This is part of why, despite evidence of growing desires for less demanding jobs and disillusionment with "work-and-spend," hours are still rising.[47]

To see the difficulties individuals have in deviating from the status quo, consider what would happen to an ordinary couple who have grown tired of the rat race. John and Jane Doe, like nearly half of all Americans, want more time to spend with their children and each other.[48] What will happen if they both decide to reduce their hours by half and are willing to live on half their usual earnings?

The transition will be most abrupt for John. Few men work part-time, with the exception of teens, students, and some seniors. Among males aged twenty-five to forty-four, virtually none (a meager 2.5 percent) voluntarily choose part-time schedules. Most report that they are not able to reduce their hours of work at all.[49] And of those who do have the freedom to work fewer hours, it is likely that only a small percentage can reduce hours by as much as half. Unless John has truly unusual talents, his employer will probably refuse to sanction a change to part-time work. Chances are he'll have to find a new job.

Given the paucity of part-time jobs for men, John's choices will be limited. It will be almost impossible to secure a position in a managerial, professional, or administrative capacity. Most part-time jobs are in the service sector. When he does land a job, his pay will fall far short of what he earned in full-time work. The median hourly wage rate among male workers is about $10.50, with weekly earnings of $450. As a part-time worker paid by the hour, his median wage will be about $4, or $80 a week. He will also lose many of the benefits that went with his full-time job. Only 15 percent of part-time workers are given health insurance.[50] The total income loss John will suffer is likely to exceed 80 percent. Under these conditions, part-time work hardly seems feasible.

The social nature of John's choice is revealed by the drama of his attempt to go against the grain. Since few adult men choose part-time work, there is almost none to be had. The social convention of full-time work gives the individual little choice about it. Those who contemplate a shift to part-time will be deterred by the economic penalty. There may even be many who would prefer shorter hours, but they will exert very little influence on the actual choices available, because their desires are latent. Exit from existing jobs— one channel for influencing the market—is not available, because they cannot find part-time jobs to exit to. Unless people begin to speak up and collectively demand that employers provide alternatives, they will probably remain trapped in full-time work.

Jane's switch to part-time will be less traumatic. She will find more job possibilities, because more women work part-time. Her earnings loss will be less, because women are already discriminated against in full-time work. (The median hourly wage for women working part-time is almost three-quarters of the full-time wage, compared with one-half for men.) If Jane can get health insurance through John's employment, part-time work may be feasible. But a great deal depends on his earnings and benefits. Even under the best of assumptions, Jane will have to forgo a wide variety of occupations, including most of those with the best pay and working conditions. She will most likely be relegated to the bottom part of the female labor market—the service, sales, and clerical jobs where the majority of women part-timers reside. Social convention and the economic incentives it creates will reproduce inequalities of gender. Despite their original intentions, Jane, rather than John, will end up in part-time employment.

These are the obstacles on the labor market side—low wages, few benefits, and severe limitations on choice of occupations. The dominance of full-time jobs also has effects on the consumption side. Imagine that Jane and John still want to cut back their hours, even under the adverse circumstances I have described. Their income will now be very low, and they will be forced to economize greatly on their purchases. This will affect their ability to fit in socially. As half-time workers, they will find many social occasions too expensive (lunches and dinners out, movies). At first, friends will be understanding, but eventually the clash in life styles will create a social gap. Their children will have social difficulties if they don't have access to common after-school activities or the latest toys and clothes. They'll drop off the birthday party circuit because they can't afford to bring gifts. We can even see these pressures with full-time workers, as parents take on extra employment to live up to neighborhood standards. After her divorce Celeste Henderson worked two jobs to give her children the things their schoolmates had. Ms. Henderson's daughter says her mother "saved her the embarrassment of looking poor to the other children."[51] For a family with only part-time workers, the inability to consume in the manner of their peers is likely to lead to some social alienation. Unless they have a community of others in similar circumstances, dropping down will include an element of dropping out. Many Americans, especially those with children, are not willing to risk such a fate.

Even with careful budgeting, a couple like the Does may have trouble procuring the basics (housing, food, and clothing), because the U.S. standard of living is geared to at least one full-time income and, increasingly, to two. Rents will be high relative to the Does' income. In part, this is because of price increases in the last decade. But there is also a more fundamental impediment. As I have argued, contemporary houses and apartments are large and luxurious. They have indoor plumbing, central heating, stoves, and refrigerators. They have expensive features such as closets, garages, and individual bedrooms. In our society, housing must conform to legal and social conventions that define the acceptable standard of housing. The difficulty is that the social norm prevailing in the housing market is matched to a full-time income (or incomes). It is not only that the cost of living is high these days. It is also that bare-bones housing, affordable on only half a salary, is rare. Even if the Does were willing to go without closets, garages, and central heating in order to save money, they would be hard-pressed to find such a dwelling.

This problem is common to many goods and services. In an economy where nearly everyone works full-time, manufacturers cater to the purchasing power of the full-time income. There is a limited market for products that are desired only by those with half an income. A whole range of cheap products are not even available. Only the better-quality goods will be demanded, and hence only they will be produced. We can see this phenomenon in the continual upscaling of products. We've gone from blender to Cuisinart, from polyester to cotton, from one-speed Schwinn to fancy trail bike. Remember the things that were available forty years ago but have disappeared? The semiautomatic washing machine. The hand-driven coffee grinder. The rotary dial telephone. For those who are skeptical about this point, consider the markets of poor countries.

In India, one can find very cheap, low-quality clothing—at a fraction of the price of the least expensive items in the United States. Semiautomatic washers and stripped-down cars are the norm. On a world scale, the American consumer market is very upscale, which means that Americans need an upscale income to participate in it.

The strength of social norms does not mean that the nature of work cannot be changed. Part-time employment *could* become a viable option for larger numbers of people. But the existence of social norms suggests that change will not come about, as the neoclassical economist predicts, merely through individuals exercising their preferences in the market. Where Prisoner's Dilemmas and vicious cycles exist, change requires intervention on a social level—from government, unions, professional associations, and other collective organizations.

THE PERILS OF HOMO ECONOMICUS

The discipline of economics has traditionally represented human beings by the construct of *homo economicus,* or economic man. Homo economicus is a simple fellow. He has a set of preferences.[52] And he aims to maximize his well-being (defined as "utility"). His behavior is cool and rational, unlike "psychoanalytic man" (who is driven by compulsion) or "sociological man" (who is confined by social norms). Homo economicus is an individual, acting alone, who does what he does because he believes it is the course of action that will bring him the most utility. For my purposes, the most important personality trait of homo economicus is that he can never be satiated. He will always prefer more to less. Although he can become tired of any particular good, there is never a point at which having more goods overall will make him worse off. And because more will always make him better off, his desires are infinite.

Some economists have made grand claims for homo economicus, asserting that he is an adequate representation of human beings in all societies, at all times. "Stone age" peoples, slaves, housewives, and medieval peasants are assumed to live by his maxims.

These claims have led to great (and unresolved) debate among anthropologists, psychologists, historians, and economists. (It should be clear by now that I believe modern consumerism is learned behavior, rather than a trait of human nature equally applicable to primitives and peasants.) But one thing that is probably not controversial is the real-world example from which homo economicus has been drawn. If he describes anyone at all, it is the twentieth-century American consumer. Here we find the quintessential materialist—highly focused on the acquisition of goods, shamelessly hedonistic, and slavishly devoted to the proposition of nonsatiation.

The problem with homo economicus is that nonsatiation shades all too easily into nonsatisfaction. Once he sees (as the perspicacious economic man does) that having more will make him "better off," it is hard to keep from wanting it. If more is better, discontent will not be far behind. Discontent is relieved, over and over again, by acquiring more. Where desires are infinite, the process of acquisition will become infinite itself.

Such a process has serious ramifications. We are committed to perpetual growth, yet the world has finite resources. They are already stretched to the danger point, as we pollute our air, land, and water. Can the earth tolerate more cars, more BTUs, and the felling of more trees? Affluent citizens the world around continue to try to raise their own standards of living, while the globe's poor majority scrape by (or fail to) with little or nothing. If we look at satisfaction as a relationship between wanting and having, it becomes clear that there are two ways to be satisfied. In the economic view, satisfaction comes from increasing what one has. But couldn't one just as well gain happiness by reducing desires?

This is the "Zen" path to happiness. It warns that hedonistic pleasures are shallow and addictive. It asks for renunciation, not necessarily of material goods, but of materialism. In the words of anthropologist Marshall Sahlins, this path holds "that a people can enjoy an unparalleled material plenty—with a low standard of living." The key is to keep desires equally low. English economist Edward Schumacher's "Buddhist economics" produces "extraordinarily satisfactory results" from "amazingly small means."[53]

I have already identified many who have exhibited limited material desires: the fourteenth-century English laborers who responded to higher wages by doing less of the unpleasant work that was their lot in life; the early American workers who craved time away from work to educate themselves; the trade unionists and reformers of the 1920s who foresaw and forswore consumerism. More recently, the affluence of the 1960s helped create a youth culture that shunned the materialism of the American way of life. In Western Europe today, popular "green" movements reject growth and consumerism.

The meaning of *consumption* itself has already gone through one major transformation, from its original negative meaning of "eat up, devour, waste, destroy."[54] Today, a second transformation would entail new ways of wanting, buying, owning, using, and discarding. Instead of craving novelty in consumer goods, we could cultivate attachments to possessions that were high-quality and long-lasting, from clothes to automobiles to gadgets. We would use things until they wore out, not until they went out of fashion or we just grew tired of them. Foresight would be necessary, in order to avoid new products that ultimately leave us no better off. Maybe the Joneses and the Smiths could even cooperate rather than compete. If they were less concerned about acquiring, the two families could share expensive household items that are used only intermittently.

While most Americans may find it hard to understand that such changes are in their interest, many who have made them are confident that getting off the consumer treadmill yields a deeper and truer sense of well-being. When Linda Weltner, a former shopping addict, stopped buying, she didn't "suffer pangs of self-denial" but felt "filled to the brim." Her life has become far richer. And not only will we help ourselves. Forswearing a bankrupting consumerist path, the new consumer of the twenty-first century will be in a far better position to address issues of global inequality and move us off our current collision course with nature. But to do these things, we must be open to major changes in how we run our businesses, households, and the connections between them. And we must organize ourselves to make those changes happen—in spite of all-too-certain opposition from those who benefit from the status quo. In the next chapter, I take up these structural transformations.[55]

=========== CHAPTER 6 ===========

Exiting the Squirrel Cage

It is often said that an economist is a person who knows the price of everything and the value of nothing. On the question of time, we may all have become economists. We are keenly aware of the price of time—the extra income earned with a second job, the wage and a half for an hour of overtime. In the process, we may have forgotten the real worth of time.

The origins of modern time consciousness lie in the development of a capitalist economy. Precapitalist Europe was largely "timeless"—or, in historian Jacques Le Goff's words, "free of haste and careless of exactitude." As capitalism raised the "price" of time, people began to think of time as a scarce resource. Indeed, the ideology of the emerging market economy was filled with metaphors of time: saving time, using time wisely, admonitions against "passing" time. The work ethic itself was in some sense a time ethic. When Benjamin Franklin preached that time is money, he meant that time should be used productively. Eventually capitalism did more than make time valuable. Time and money began to substitute for each other. Franklin's aphorism took on new meaning, not only as prescription, but as an actual description. Money buys time, and time buys money. *Time itself had become a commodity.*[1]

Moneylending was the first example of the sale of time, its nature revealed in the colloquial "to buy on time." Then the sale of time developed in the labor market, and became, for most people, the area where the impact has been greatest. Today the principle of sale of labor time is thoroughly accepted. But this is the result of a long and contentious process. As the British historian Edward Thompson has argued, workers struggled at first from a traditional ideology of "timelessness" against the very idea of time. They resented employers' attempts to impose time and time discipline. As decades passed, they struggled over the ownership of time—how much was theirs, how much the boss's. And today, many fight for *overtime*—the right to sell as much time as they can.[2]

The unencumbered sale of time for money is now a reigning value, its legitimacy so entrenched that it is no longer fully voluntary: most employees can be forced to put in overtime. The monetary equivalence to time has expanded far beyond the labor market. Patients have begun to charge doctors when they are kept waiting. The government pays jurors for each day they spend in court. The legal value of a human life is based on the future sale of working time. Every hour has a price.

The virtues of the sale of time and the equation of time and money are well known: putting a price tag on each hour allows a person (or a society) to use time efficiently.[3] But there are also vices, which are less well recognized. Many aspects of the value of time are difficult to incorporate into a purely market exchange— such as the effects of individuals' use of time on the quality of social life, or the concept of a basic human right to free time. Every society has a culture of time. Has ours perhaps gone too far in the direction of collapsing time into money?

The more time substitutes for money, the more difficult it is to establish an *independent* measure of time's value. And our diminishing ability to make this judgment contributes to long hours. If the market recognizes only the measure of money, then arguing that a job requires "too many hours" makes no sense: it is tantamount to saying that it pays "too much money." The inflated working hours of the Wall Street financier or the corporate lawyer are a fair trade for their inflated salaries. If low-wage employees in the nursing home industry have two full-time jobs, it is because they value money over time. In a culture where time is merely money, we risk perverse effects such as occurred after 1938 with legislation to regulate overtime. This policy was designed to install a forty-hour week, but its disincentive to companies (time and a half) turned into a powerful incentive for workers to work as many hours as they could. In the end, the legislation contracted both leisure and employment, the two things it was designed to expand.

Where time is money, it's hard to protect time for those who— such as low-wage workers, children, aged parents, or community organizations—can't pay for it. And it's hard to protect time for ourselves, for relaxation, hobbies, or sleep. The pressures toward long working hours have become too powerful. But common sense tells us that working hours *can* be too long. Excessive hours are unhealthy and antisocial, and ultimately erode the quality of life.

The commensurability of time and money has other detrimental social effects. It transforms a resource that is equally distributed (time) into one that is distinctly unequal (money). Both wealth and income are unequally distributed. But everyone is born with twenty-four hours in a day. And while money does skew the distribution of time to some extent (higher-income people live longer), "ownership" of time is still far more equally allocated. The sale of time undermines its egalitarianism. As time outside work becomes more precious, those with money can economize on it. And this appears to be happening. Fast-track careerists are hiring people to cook their meals, watch their children, even wait in line for them. Small companies have sprouted up, offering services from grocery shopping to changing light bulbs. The people whose time is being sold are those less economically well situated—as happened earlier, of course, in the nineteenth century when the growth of the middle class spawned a huge demand for servants. Today's scarcity of time puts us in jeopardy of producing a new servant class and undermining the egalitarianism of time.

Establishing a right to free time may sound utopian—but the principle of limiting exchange has already been established. It is not legal to sell oneself into slavery. It is not legal to sell one's vote. It is not legal to sell children. Even the principle of limiting the exchange of time is well established. The state has regulated working hours since the colonial period.[4] The right to free time has been legislated in some forms, such as legal holidays. Most important of all is the social security system, which assumes that workers have a right to leisure for a period at the end of their lives. What I am arguing for is the extension of this right—so that everyone can enjoy free time while they are still young and throughout their lives.

BREAKING THE WORK-AND-SPEND CYCLE

To gain this right—to reduce the reliance on long hours—it will be necessary to break the work-and-spend cycle. Changes must be made on a number of fronts: altering employers' incentives; improving wages for the lowest-paid; creating gender equality; preempting the automatic spiraling of consumption; and throughout, establishing time's value independent of its price, so that it can no longer be readily substituted for money.

New Incentives for Employers

The employer's bias toward excessive hours is strongest for salaried workers. Effective change will therefore lay the burden of extra hours on the employer. What a firm now receives courtesy of its salaried workforce, it should have to pay for. Therefore, I propose that every salaried job be formally (and legally) attached to a standard schedule. Along with annual pay, every position would also have an explicit standard of hours—for example, a nine-to-six schedule—and a specified number of holidays, vacation and personal days, and sick time. Thus, if an employee actually works longer than the standard, the hours would be counted as extra, and the firm must pay for them. Ideally, the firm would designate an annual total of hours and allow flexible scheduling within it. Of course, many, and probably most, salaried positions already have official weekly hours even if they're not adhered to. And paid time off is almost always specified in advance. But standard hours would be a departure in many of the longest-hour fields, such as finance, consulting, upper administration and management, and law. (It should be noted that I am advocating not that limits be set on the amount of standard hours but that the government require firms to set some standard.)

This system would not be a cure-all for the excessive hours of some occupations. Employers could still set very high standard hours and thereby considerably negate the benefits of standardizing hours. A replication of Japanese practices is even possible, where employees are subtly (or not so subtly) pressured to ignore any standard. Salaried employees may fail to claim extra hours, or forgo vacations, in order to advance their careers—as happened in a California firm where a quarter of management came to work without pay.[5] In the most competitive environments, it is almost impossible to prevent the long-hour bias without a transformation of the corporate culture. But clearly defined schedules would both place a useful limitation on employers and give employees the right to be paid for their overtime. And competition for personnel may discourage the setting of excessively long days. If a prospective trainee at Salomon Brothers were asked to guarantee eighty hours and Goldman, Sachs sets seventy, the former would be at a disadvantage. For those employees who *want* their time, the standardization of hours could be effective.

As for paying for extra hours, my second proposal is that the company should pay back time with time, rather than with money. The idea is to transform overtime into "comp" time—and make it voluntary. Every job—salaried, hourly, or piece rate—would have a standard workday, workweek, and workyear. Companies could request—although not demand—extra hours, which would be recompensed in time off. An extra hour worked today would yield an extra hour of paid time off in the future. Workers would be able to bank their overtime hours and accumulate them. They could save up for longer vacations, take sabbaticals, or go to part-time at full-time pay. The shift from overtime to comp time would not only reduce the total number of hours worked, it would also make jobs much more flexible. It would become far easier to go to school, be a parent, or do volunteer work and, at the same time, carry on a full-time job. Of course, there may be limitations on the scheduling of time off. Existing practices involving comp time or programs of voluntary work reduction usually have some restrictions such as prior notification and management approval. But in situations where both sides have shown flexibility and goodwill, these limitations have not been onerous.

Expanding the use of comp time represents a big step toward

eroding the substitution of time and money—and would encounter significant opposition. Employers would like some things about the proposal and not others. Payment by comp time means that workers are remunerated for extra hours at their regular wage rate (which is all they are paid for time off), rather than time and a half. Employers will like this. But it also means that they will have to find more employees to fill in for the additional time off. They will not be happy about this, in part because of the fringe benefits. But I suspect employers will be most averse to the idea of associating standard hours with all salaried jobs. Despite the flexibility built into the proposal (they can choose any level of standard hours and adjust it frequently), they will complain that it is an unnecessary intrusion on their prerogatives.

Many hourly workers, especially men, would be bitterly opposed to the elimination of overtime pay, at least at the beginning. Overtime is the only way many can earn high or even "liveable" rates of pay—a circumstance that has turned more than a few into slaves to their jobs. One union steward noted:

> The people I represent in the union want to work *more* hours, not less. Working overtime is the only way to make decent money, so they're always looking for ways to stretch the work out, or find something that needs to be done over the weekend or into the evening. When I talk to them about working shorter hours, they just laugh like it's a joke. Maybe for some yuppie who already makes enough in twenty or thirty hours, or even forty—but not us. But I know how tired and bored they are after fifty or sixty hours on the line. After sixty hours your mind is still doing that job after you're asleep and dreaming, and then it's up at six and back to the job. It's not that they want to work those hours. There's just no other way to break even.[6]

But the idea that jobs pay more where overtime is available is to some extent an illusion. A recent study shows that workers who get overtime receive lower hourly wages, as firms "undo" some of the effect of the overtime premium.[7] If this research is correct, it is likely that hourly wages would rise in response to the elimination of overtime. Even so, there would be significant resistance to this proposal. In some unionized shops, workers with seniority have opposed work sharing as an alternative to layoffs, preferring to have some workers laid off rather than having all workers' hours reduced.

A much-needed change is to make part-time work more feasible. At the moment, the great majority of part-time positions are low-pay, low-mobility, and largely without benefits. Yet growing numbers of people are expressing interest in reducing their hours. The impediments for professionals and managers are especially powerful. In many places, part-time is tantamount to career suicide. A California study of professionals who opted for shorter hours catalogued the difficulties. When one state employee went to her supervisor with a proposal to work fewer hours, his reaction was typical: "My gawd . . . do you realize what this means to your career?" The private sector is even more discriminatory. A manager in a private public relations firm went on part-time with the birth of her child. After more than a decade of excellent performance, the firm still will not put her on the list for promotion—not until she's willing to return to work full-time.[8] And, despite new thinking by some employers, many still won't give the opportunity to cut back:

> When I asked for six months off from my job after I had a new baby, they treated me like I was lazy. They just turned me down flat. Then I tried asking to come back earlier part-time. And they still said no. The thinking was that if I was serious about my career, that just meant working full-time or nothing. And so I did it. I'd rather give up the money than some of the time with my family, but they just wouldn't offer me that choice.[9]

There are some simple reforms that would enhance the feasibility of part-time work. A first, crucial step is to eliminate the "fringe benefits" penalty. Part-time workers would receive a share of health insurance, pension benefits, and other fringes, prorated by their hours of work. They would also get the option to go to full coverage at their own expense. There are already many full-time workers who would prefer part-time work but don't take it because of the loss of benefits. This provision would allow them to scale back. (A superior solution is universal, government-guaranteed health insurance for all, regardless of employment status. I offer my suggestion in the absence of such a program. Furthermore, granting full employer-paid benefits to part-timers, however desirable, would create a powerful incentive for firms to refuse to offer part-time positions.) A second option is to institute job sharing, in which two people split one position's fringe benefits, responsibility, work, and pay. Each of these changes would reduce existing biases toward long-hour jobs.

The major remaining incentive toward long hours is that associated with the sale of labor by the hour. In chapter 3, I argued that additional hours increase the employment rent and thereby raise productivity. Although there is no simple "institutional" trick for eliminating this bias, there are effective productivity-raising substitutes for long hours. Examples include giving workers more participation and decision-making power on the job, narrowing wage differentials, and humanizing the work environment. A large number of studies show that these reforms raise satisfaction and productivity. The more prevalent they become, the less costly it would be for companies to shorten hours.Other measures can also be effective. One straightforward reform, long overdue, is to outlaw the practice of mandatory overtime. Workers should not be forced, as many currently are, to work more than their normal workweek in order to keep their jobs.

Giving Up Future Income for Time Off

To sever the work-consumption link, we must exploit the psychological difference between income that is already being spent and income that is merely expected. People cling tenaciously to their current paycheck, unwilling or unable to trade it for time, but polls indicate strong sentiment for using future income to fund additional time off. Suppose that companies were required by law to give people this choice. What if, as we take the "productivity challenge" in coming decades, there is no bias toward money?

The company would announce the percentage pay increase it plans to give to each group of employees. Then it would calculate equivalent hours of time off. The employee could decide among the alternatives—from the extremes of all pay or all time, to half and half, or three-quarter/one-quarter splits. The company could offer different forms of time off (reductions in daily hours, part-time schedules, or additional vacation or personal days). Free time could be accumulated from year to year. Administratively, this option could be added on to existing personnel routines. Many firms already allow employees to choose their health coverage, whether to participate in the company savings plan, or how much company-sponsored life insurance to carry. The money/time tradeoff is just one more benefit option.

Exactly how would this choice work out if it were available today? There are two key parameters: the amount of income a company is willing to give, and the fraction of it workers designate toward free time. Let's assume the former is 2 percent plus an adjustment for inflation, and the latter is 100 percent. Then, about a decade from now—in the year 2002, say—the average workyear will have fallen by 340 hours—from 1,960 hours to 1,600 hours per year (see table 6.1). That's enough for an additional two months of vacation or a 6½-hour day. At lower rates of real income growth, the leisure gain is lower. Higher rates produce rapid gains. If a person's real income were to rise by 4 percent a year, and all of it was channeled into time off, after ten years the annual workyear would be near 1,300 hours—a total gain in free time of over 600 hours. This person could go to school one semester a year, take a four-month vacation, or follow a five-hour daily schedule year-round.

If it sounds too good to be true, remember that in my example

TABLE 6.1
Potential Gains in Leisure
Annual Hours If 2 Percent Productivity
Growth Is Transformed into Leisure

Year	Hours	Year	Hours
1991	2000	2002	1608
1992	1961	2003	1577
1993	1922	2004	1546
1994	1885	2005	1516
1995	1848	2006	1486
1996	1811	2007	1457
1997	1776	2008	1428
1998	1741	2009	1400
1999	1707	2010	1373
2000	1673	2020	1126
2001	1641		

purchasing power is completely stagnant. The person who goes 100 percent toward free time for ten years will experience no increase whatsoever in his or her material standard of living. Purchasing power will keep up with inflation, but not go beyond it. The appeal of such a scheme is that what you don't know can't hurt you. As shopping addicts tend to discover, dissatisfaction with their possessions vanish once they stop going into stores and exposing themselves to the newest items. If you can be content tomorrow with the amount you consume today, then trading off future income can be a blessing.[10]

How many people would actually choose to forgo future income? A few voluntary worktime reduction plans for government employees already exist, going by the name of V-Time (the *V* stands for "voluntary"). Participation in these plans is small—typically below even 5 percent. But it would be wrong to read too much into these programs. They require individuals to reduce *current* income, as we already know they are very reluctant to do. Only future-oriented V-time is relevant; and to my knowledge, no such plans exist. But survey data give some idea of how people would respond to them. In the 1978 survey, 84 percent of workers said they would choose to trade off *some* future income—with almost half opting for a 100-percent tradeoff. A 1989 poll asked people which of two career paths they would choose: "one enabling you to schedule your own full-time work hours, and give more attention to your family, but with slower career advancement; and the other with rigid work hours and less attention to your family, but faster career advancement." Nearly eight out of ten preferred the path with more free time. Indeed, large majorities of both men and women (74 percent and 82 percent) chose this option. Fifty-five percent also said they would not be "likely to accept a promotion involving greater responsibility if it meant spending less time with family," compared with 34 percent who said they would. Of course, these are hypothetical questions, with no guarantee that people would actually act in this way. But even if the participation were considerably lower—say, at two-thirds or half—the program would have to be deemed very popular and would eventually have a major impact on worktime.[11]

There would be hard-core resisters. This country has plenty of workaholics—people for whom work is an escape, an obsession, or, if they have nothing better to do, the default option, who will not be interested in my proposal. There are others for whom money is everything, who will avail themselves of almost any opportunity to make a few more bucks. Or those who sell their souls to the highest-paying job they can find—regardless of its working hours, stress level, effect on their family life, or social implications. And half the population has a special problem, as a forty-five-year-old machinist explains: "Being a man means being willing to put all your waking hours into working to support your family. If you ask for time off, or if you turn down overtime, it means you're lazy or you're a wimp."[12] Men are ensnared not only in the traditional breadwinner role but also by the tendency of our culture to equate self-worth with job and pay.

Hard-core resistance to giving up money for time would, I hope, give way in the face of the positive experience of many, such as this group of overtime-loving workers in a British shoe factory:

> It was easy to find volunteers for Sundays as well. I'm sure that there were times when you could have asked them to work seven days out of seven for a whole year; they'd have done it, if they'd been pushed. . . . And there were people who worked after hours as well, cash in hand, as well as their split shift, either through alienation, or sometimes from necessity. You see, when you were working forty-eight hours a week, cash really became the thing you were after. . . . A friend said to me, jokingly (but jokes always have a serious side): "Me, when I'm not working, I don't know what to do, I'm bored stiff, I'm better off at work." Your factory is your life. . . . You have a bit more money, you'll buy as much electrical gadgetry as you can. You'll chase after money, but it won't do you much good in the end.

When hard times hit, the plant went into worksharing:

> Then bit by bit, there was an unbelievable phenomenon of physical recuperation. The idea of money really lost its intensity. I don't mean it had disappeared but eventually even the blokes with families to look after said, "It's better now than before." It's true that we lost a good deal of money [25 percent of former income] . . . but, quite soon, only one or two of the blokes minded.
>
> It was about now that . . . friendships began: we were now able to go beyond political conversation, and we managed to talk about love, impotence, jealousy, family life. . . . It was also at this time that

we realized the full horror of working in the factory on Saturday afternoons or evenings. Before, the blokes had put up with it, but now we were once again learning the meaning of the word living. . . . Similarly for Sundays or Bank Holidays, which were paid at triple time, management admitted to us that they had difficulty finding people. . . . There had been a change of attitude, they weren't able to buy workers as easily as before.[13]

Inequalities of Time

Of course the wages of many Americans are so low, or their conditions of employment so precarious, that they cannot afford to give up any income—present or future. And their numbers are rising. Nearly one-third of all U.S. workers currently earn wages which, on a full-time schedule, are insufficient to lift them out of poverty. As I have stressed, millions can make ends meet only through overtime, moonlighting, and multi-earner families. And many are unable to make ends meet at all.

The danger of increasing leisure time voluntarily is that it could replace one inequity with another—as inequality of income creates inequality of time. The poorest third would work just as many hours as ever—or more, as more work became available—while the top two-thirds would gradually become a leisured class. The people who would gain free time would be those who already had the financial resources that make it possible—education, homes, and a bank account. They would be mainly white and mainly upper and middle class.

To redress these imbalances, I also advocate mandatory increases in free time. The United States stands out among rich countries in its failure to ensure basic rights to vacation or parental leaves. What about government-mandated four-week paid vacations for all employees, independent of length of service? Or six-month paid parental leaves, financed through the social security system? These would be a start in the right direction.

Ultimately, inequality of time must be solved by redressing the underlying inequality of income. Only when the poorest make a living wage can their right to free time be realized. And barring an economic miracle, part of it will have to come from the people at the top. In the 1980s, the rich grabbed a fantastic amount from those below them. Now it's time to give it back.

Raising low incomes is not a simple matter, but at least two strategies will help. First, companies should begin to equalize the large differences in wages and salaries which exist among their employees, by paying more to those at the bottom and less to those at the top. The United States has high levels of wage inequality in comparison with other industrialized nations. Second, the federal minimum wage should be raised and indexed to the economy's average wage. While only a limited fraction of workers receive the minimum, when it rises, it creates upward pressure on those wages which are somewhat higher. Therefore, raising the minimum can be an effective strategy for improving the living standards of many low-wage workers.

Finally, as should be clear from my earlier discussion, the problem of worktime cannot be solved without an equalization of the distribution of work itself. This means we must find a durable solution for the crisis of unemployment and underemployment plaguing this economy. Such a solution will require an ongoing commitment from the federal government to ensure a more equal allocation of total work hours.

My proposals also run the risk of reproducing inequalities of gender. The suggestions themselves—such as making part-time work more desirable or allowing people to trade off income for time—are gender-neutral. Without change in underlying gender roles, however, women will be more likely to take advantage of them. If this occurs, it will reproduce women's current responsibility for housework and child care. Therefore, ongoing feminist efforts to equalize the division of labor within the family are crucial to the larger success of my proposed reforms. If men take considerably more responsibility for children and housework—as many now say they want to—then they too will want to opt for working patterns that are compatible with family duties. In that event, the effect of the proposals will be quite different. They will, as I intend, help undermine rigid gender roles, by making shared parenting and two-career families more feasible. These transformations, however, require that the culture of U.S. workplaces must change, in order to be more accommodating to society's needs for child care, care of the sick and elderly, and other domestic labor. And the change must happen for both men and women.

We must also confront the legacy of inefficiency in household technology, in order to reverse the built-in backwardness of the American home. Architects and product designers should be encouraged to invent new, truly labor-saving household technologies, emphasizing low maintenance and ease of cleaning. Progress against wage discrimination on the basis of sex will also help, by eliminating one source of the bias which devalues women's time. Ultimately, we need a serious public debate on household labor, which addresses both who should do it and how it should be done.

Can America Afford Less Work?

The need for more leisure is not accepted by everyone. A 1989 letter to three hundred business leaders advocating a shorter work-week failed to yield a single favorable response. This reply from the CEO of a *Fortune* 500 company was typical: "My view of the world, our country and our country's needs is diametrically opposite of yours. I cannot imagine a shorter work week. I can imagine a longer one both in school and at work if America is to be competitive in the first half of the next century." I have already mentioned a *Fortune* poll in which three-quarters of CEOs took the view that competing with the Japanese will require them to "push their managers harder." Its fierce opposition even to unpaid parental leave suggests that business thinks it can't afford any concessions.[14]

Of course, employers have been sounding the alarm of foreign competition for at least a century and a half. In 1830, New York employers opposed the ten-hour day on grounds that it would allow foreigners to undersell them. Their laborers put forth the other point of view, in a debate that has changed little since that time: "Are we to slave thirteen or fourteen hours a day, because the Manchester spinner or the Birmingham blacksmith, so slaves?"[15]

In fact, the vast majority of America's competitors work far less than we do. When business claims that Americans must work harder, they show selective vision, looking only East, to Japan and South Korea. Most Japanese workers are on a six-day schedule and half fail to take their allotted vacations. Koreans are still in the factory three Sundays out of four. In manufacturing, the sector where most foreign competition takes place, Japanese workers put in six weeks more each year than their counterparts in the United States. But U.S. workers are already doing eight weeks more than West Germans, and eleven more than Swedes. The West Europeans have managed to maintain their standard of living, cutting neither wages nor time off.[16]

Discrepancies in worktime are often cited as if they were proof enough that the United States must replicate Japanese ways. But the economics of competition is not the economics of mimicry. It's more complex. First, we must be clear about what is being asked for. If it's more hours at existing pay, then it is merely a roundabout way for business to reduce workers' wages. While lower wages help competitiveness in the short term, in the long run they can boomerang, as declining wages leading to declining productivity, through diminished incentives to invest, higher turnover, and lower employee morale. The game of lowering wages can get insidious. Once the highest in the world, U.S. manufacturing wages have fallen substantially for a decade and now rank below many West European nations. How far down should they go? Korea, Brazil, and India are growing competitors. If corporations demand a decline to the poverty wages paid in many countries, should American workers simply accede?[17]

What we should learn from the Japanese, and from our own history as well, is not the need to reduce wages, or raise hours, but the importance of productivity. In the international market, what matters in the long run is not how many hours a person works, but how productively he or she works them. If an American can produce an equivalent computer in fewer hours than a Japanese (at a comparable wage rate), then that computer will sell, whether the American worker has a fifty- or a forty- or a thirty-hour week. And efficient production itself will yield rising wages, as the cases of Japan and Korea reveal. Instead of pushing their employees' standard of living even farther down the international hierarchy, American management should be figuring out how to make the hours they buy more productive.

The irony of corporate America's position is that excessive hours are a serious *problem* in Japan. Consider the white-collar "salarymen," as they are called, who adhere to grueling schedules in a pressure-cooker environment. They face arduous commutes, an extended workday, and obligatory "after work" socializing. They are strongly discouraged from taking their vacations. In recent years, Japan's vibrant economy has brought overtime hours near their all-time high. The result: thousands of workers have become victims of *karoshi,* or "death by overwork." Otherwise perfectly healthy, they keel over at their desks, usually after a prolonged stretch of overtime or a particularly high-pressure deal.[18]

Even those who work fewer hours than the salarymen suffer debilitating consequences from their daily grind. Office employees as a whole put in 225 hours—or almost six weeks—more than they do in the United States.[19] A recent government study found that Japanese productivity (despite its high growth) is lower than that of other advanced countries in part because the working hours are too long. And there is now considerable pressure in Japan to reduce worktime. The government has made 1,800 hours a national goal, which, if achieved, would put Japanese hours below those of the United States. And according to a 1985 opinion poll, most young Japanese workers frown on overtime and would probably prefer a reduction of worktime rather than wage increases. To emulate current Japanese hours would be sheer folly. Those who call for America to replicate the Japanese work culture have forgotten that the point of economic success is to make possible a good life. To impair the quality of life *in the name* of economic success is foolhardy. One young American summed up a common and sensible point of view: "I don't want to be Japanese. . . . I work hard enough as it is."[20]

The fact is that some shorter-hour schedules can actually raise productivity. For example, many people are more productive on Monday, the first day of the week. By creating two "Mondays," job sharing boosts productivity. But most surprising is the evidence that under certain conditions a shorter workday will not necessarily reduce output and can even raise it. When the Kellogg Company made their historic switch to a six-hour day on 1 December 1930, they were searching for a strategy to cope with the unemployment of the Depression. To their surprise, they found that workers were more productive, on the order of 3 percent to 4 percent. In some departments, the pace had picked up even more. According to one observer, "eighty-three cases of shredded whole wheat biscuit used to be packed in an hour (under the eight-hour day). At the time of my visit, the number was 96." The workers were pleased, preferring the quicker pace but shorter hours. And management was pleased as well. According to W. K. Kellogg, "the efficiency and morale of our employees is [*sic*] so increased, the accident and insurance rates are so improved, and the unit cost of production is so lowered that we can afford to pay as much for six hours as we formerly paid for eight."[21]

Contemporary evidence tells a similar story. When the Medtronic Corporation in Minneapolis decided to give its employees forty hours' pay for thirty-six hours of work, it hired no additional personnel but found that output increased. On balance, the company saved money. Ideal Industries, a small family-owned business, shifted to a four-day, thirty-eight-hour week—also at forty hours' pay. Again, productivity did not decline, but absenteeism did. At the United Services Automobile Association insurance company in Texas, sales were up, even though personnel hours were down. Efficiency and morale improved. Turnover and error rates declined. These experiences have been repeated in other American companies and in foreign firms as well. A British study of a variety of companies reached similar conclusions. Far from being costly, nearly all these workweek reductions paid for themselves, even when workers' incomes were held steady.[22]

Part of the reason is that the workday gets compressed. At its summer peak, the medieval day stretched from sunup to sundown. But over such a long period, frequent and extended breaks were required. Modern workdays, being shorter, have far less time off within them. But they do have unproductive time, either scheduled (such as official break and meal times) or unscheduled (such as gatherings around the water cooler). As Australian economist Chris Nyland has argued, when management cuts the workweek the difference is often made up by these idle periods. In some cases the tradeoff is explicit and before the fact. Management agrees to shorter hours if workers guarantee to make it up in higher production. In other companies, higher production has been an unexpected result. Such accommodations are part of why shortening the workday has been a disappointing strategy for creating employment. The pace of work also rises for another reason, as the Kellogg Corporation found. When hours are shorter, workers can physically and mentally sustain more intense effort. This has traditionally been an important side effect of the reduction of daily hours.[23]

There may seem to be some contradiction between the fact that businesses do not like shorter hours because they lower the employment rent and, by implication, productivity (see chapter 3), and my claim here that in many real situations the shorter workday is not costly. But consider what has actually happened to the employment rent in places like Kellogg, Medtronic, and Ideal. Each company reduced hours without reducing pay. Therefore the *hourly* wage went up, thereby maintaining the original employment rent. That's why productivity didn't fall. In cases where workers are paid by the hour, where the company raises the hourly wage, and where the changes are incremental (on the order of one to two hours a day), a shorter workday has been shown to pay for itself.[24]

The changes also improved morale. Workers appreciated the company's willingness to schedule fewer hours and raise pay. As a result they conducted more personal business on their own time and showed up for work more regularly. If a workplace reform is done right, a company can gain loyalty and productivity from its employees at no cost. In other words, the employment rent/ productivity relationship can shift upward (see figure 3.2, page 63). At every employment rent, productivity is higher. It is clear that money can be saved if people are managed better. Study after study shows that reforms that humanize the work environment, respect employees, or give them more latitude turn out to be very profitable.[25]

Yet most companies fail to institute these reforms. Inertia, myopia, fear of the unknown, and a climate of conservatism pervade many U.S. corporations. According to one young clerical worker who requested a job-share, "they gave us a very hard time." Eventually the company agreed to the scheme on a trial basis. Now, "we've discovered that both of us are a lot more effective and the work actually gets done better than before . . . but they're still asking us all the time to prove ourselves, and I think they're going to call off the experiment soon." Change could be profitable, but companies do not change. Management is often mistrustful of its workers, and is reluctant to follow the example of a Medtronic or an Ideal. Often one particular group within an organization is sufficient to block change; and in the case of workplace reforms, middle management has frequently been that group.[26]

Many economists do not agree that there are profitable workplace reforms that companies do not introduce, and believe that management is all-knowing or that competition will always force companies to do what is most profitable. But considerable evidence contradicts this view. Historically, the working day has been "too long" in the sense that fatigue impaired effectiveness. Each time the workday was reduced—first to ten hours and then to eight—productivity rose. Even now, the improvement in morale and a faster pace of work which would occur with a shift to six or seven hours could have a similar effect. The problem is that companies have always been resistant to lowering hours, despite this historical experience. Management is opposed to a shorter workweek on the grounds of cost. But its calculus is too narrow.[27]

Some of my proposals do, of course, have short-term costs, such as the prorating of benefits, guaranteed vacations and parental leave, and the standardization of hours for salaried workers. But others will save money, such as the substitution of comp time for overtime or, possibly, the shorter working day. The proposal to trade off future income is at worst "cost-neutral"—it merely asks for free time in lieu of already scheduled wage increases—and might even partly pay for itself (depending on the form of time off). Even so, business will no doubt claim that America cannot afford less working time—an objection that has been raised to every proposal to reduce hours throughout our history. This objection has been overcome before, and will be again.

OVERCOMING CONSUMERISM

Economic feasibility is an important condition for gaining leisure. So is breaking the automatic translation of productivity into income. But for many Americans escaping the trap of overwork will also entail stepping off the consumer treadmill, which requires altering a way of life and a way of thinking. The transformation must be not only economic and social but cultural and psychological.

The first step is practical—to put oneself in a financial position where a fixed or smaller income is sufficient. For example, one California environmental planner spent three years preparing to cut back his work hours. He had to "grind down the charge cards," pay off his car, and convince his partner that life with less money would be okay: "There are two ways to get through. You either have to make the money which will buy you the kind of life that you think you have to have, or you can change those expectations and you don't need the money anymore. And that's what I've done."[28]

Being able to change expectations depends on understanding the psychological and cultural functions that material goods fulfill. They can be the means to an identity or a way to create self-esteem. Things fill up empty spaces in our lives. Many couples concentrate on owning a house or filling it with nice furnishings, when what they really crave is an emotional construction—home. Some women turn to fashion to create a fantasy self that compensates for what they are consciously or unconsciously missing. Materialism can even be an altruistic vice. Men pursue the pot of gold to give it to their wives or children—to provide the "best that life can offer" or "what I never had." But in the process everyone is cheated: "I thought I was doing the right thing making money at work all the time. But I was never home." Realization often comes too late: "Now that I'm older, I can see . . . what I was missing."[29]

Involuntary reductions in income caused by a company shutdown or an inability to work can be painful, often devastating. But those who willingly reject the quest for affluence can find themselves perfectly satisfied. One public employee, currently on a four-fifths schedule, swears that only a financial disaster could get her back to full-time: "The extra twenty percent just isn't worth it." Even at the California company where employees were forced to take a ten-percent reduction in pay and hours, reactions were positive: only 22 percent of the workforce rated the program negatively, and half were positive about it.[30]

For many, opting out of the rat race has transformed their lives: "In the last four years, I went from upper middle class to poor, but I am a lot richer than most people, and I'm happier too." A divorced father raising three young children rejected the long hours, high-income route. He's at home with his children in the evenings, and has learned that "less is more." A career woman gave up her job, and along with it designer clothes, hair and nail appointments,

lunching out and a second car: "I adopted a whole new set of
values and put aside pride, envy, competitiveness and the need for
recognition."[31]

What?

THE VALUE OF LEISURE TIME

Some people are skeptical of Americans' need for leisure time.
Work may be bad, but perhaps leisure isn't all it's cracked up to be
either. According to economist Gary Burtless, "Most Americans
who complain they enjoy too little leisure are struggling to find
a few extra minutes to watch Oprah Winfrey and 'L.A. Law.' "[32]
Will free time be "wasted," in front of the tube or at the mall? What
will we do with all that leisure? Won't people just acquire second
jobs? These are serious questions, embodying two main assumptions. The first is that people prefer work or, if they don't, they
should. The second is that leisure time is wasted time that is neither
valued nor valuable.

One possibility is that work is irrepressible. The Akron rubber
workers immediately come to mind. After they won the six-hour
day, many of the men who worked at Firestone started driving cabs,
cutting hair, and selling insurance. While no one knows exactly
what percentage of the workers took on extra jobs, during the
1950s it was thought to be between one in five and one in seven.[33]
Some observers concluded from this experience that American
workers do not want, or cannot handle, leisure time. If they are
right, so be it. My aim is not to force leisure on an unwilling
population but to provide the possibility of a real choice. If the
chance to work shorter hours—when fairly presented—is not appealing, then people will not take it. But before we take the Akron
experience as definitive, let's ask a few more questions.

Why did so many take a second job? The male rubber workers
were reasonably well paid by the blue-collar standards of the day,
and many of their wives worked. They did not labor out of sheer
economic necessity. I suspect that their behavior was dictated more
by a cultural imperative—the same imperative that drove the operatives in the shoe factory, or the colleagues of the machinist quoted
earlier. The imperative that says that men with leisure are lazy. It is

significant that women rubber workers did not seek a second pay-check.

Today there are signs that this cultural imperative is becoming less compelling. Perhaps most important is the transformation of sex roles. Women have taken up responsibility for breadwinning. And men are more at home around the house. Increasing numbers of fathers want to parent. In a recent poll of men between the ages of eighteen and twenty-four, nearly half said they would like to stay home and raise their children. The ethos of "male sacrifice" is disappearing: a declining portion of the population believes that being a "real man" entails self-denial and being the family provider.[34]

The traditional work ethic is also undergoing transformation. Commitment to hard work retains its grip on the American psyche. But young people are moving away from "the frenzied work ethic of the 1980s to more traditional values." In addition, ideas of what work is and what it is for are being altered. The late 1960s and 1970s witnessed the rise of what some have called "post-materialist values"—desires for personal fulfillment, self-expression, and meaning. Throughout the industrialized world, a culture shift occurred as young people especially began demanding satisfying work. Although there was a burst of old-style materialism during the 1980s, it did not permanently dislodge what now looks more and more like a long-term trend. People are expecting more from work than a paycheck and more from life than what 1950s culture offered.[35]

People *will* work on their time off. They will work hard and long in what is formally designated as leisure time. But where the Akron example leads us astray is the quest for the second paycheck. Americans need time for unpaid work, for work they call their own. They need the time to give to others. Much of what will be done was the regular routine in the days when married women were full-time housewives. And it is largely caring work—caring for children, caring for sick relatives and friends, caring for the house. Today many haven't got the time to care. If we could carve the time out from our jobs, we could prevent the current squeeze on caring labor. And this time around, the men should share the load. The likelihood is good that unpaid work would occupy a significant fraction of any "leisure" gained in the market. At the California company that gave its employees two days off a month, nearly as much time was devoted to household and volunteer work as to leisure itself. Predictably, women did more of this labor. But times are changing.[36]

Other productive activities would take up uncommitted time as well. Many people would like to devote more time to their churches, get involved in their children's schools, coach a sports team, or help out at a soup kitchen. But the time squeeze has taken a toll on volunteer activities, which have fallen considerably since the rise in hours began. Time out of work would also be used for schooling. Education remains a primary factor in economic success. And continual training and retraining are projected to be increasingly important in the economy of the twenty-first century, as job skills become obsolete more rapidly. A survey at two large Boston corporations found that over 20 percent of full-time employees were also enrolled in school.[37]

The unpaid work—at home and in the community—that will fill free time is vital to us as individuals and as a society—as should be clear from the mounting social problems attendant upon its decline. Still, if we were to gain free time only to fill it up again with work, the battle will be only half won. There is also a pressing need for more true leisure. For the first time in fifteen years, people have cited leisure time as the "more important" thing in their lives than work.[38] The nation needs to slow down, unwind, and recover from its ordeal of labor. But can we handle leisure time?

The skeptics, who cite heavy television viewing or excessive shopping, have a point. It may be, however, that work itself has been eroding the ability to benefit from leisure time. Perhaps people are just too tired after work to engage in active leisure. Evidence from the Gallup Poll suggests this may be the case. Today, the most popular ways to spend an evening are all low-energy choices: television, resting, relaxing, and reading. Although it certainly isn't proof, it is suggestive that the globe's only other rich, industrialized country with longer hours than the United States—namely, Japan—is also the only nation to watch more television.[39]

The issue goes beyond the physical capacity to use free time. It is also true that the ability to use leisure is not a "natural" talent, but one that must be cultivated. If we veer too much toward work, our "leisure skills" will atrophy. At the extremes are workaholics like

Sheila Mohammed. After sixteen-hour days—two full-time shifts—
as a drug rehabilitation counselor, Sheila finds herself adrift outside
the job: "I'm so used to . . . working and then when I have the time
off, what do I do, where do I go?"[40] But even those with moderate
working habits are subject to a milder version of this syndrome.
Many potentially satisfying leisure activities are off limits because
they take too much time: participating in community theater, seriously taking up a sport or a musical instrument, getting involved
with a church or community organization. In the leisure time available to us, there's less of interest to do. To derive the full benefits
of free time, we just may need more of it.

A final impediment to using leisure is the growing connection
between free time and spending money. Private corporations have
dominated the leisure "market," encouraging us to think of free
time as a consumption opportunity. Vacations, hobbies, popular
entertainment, eating out, and shopping itself are all costly forms of
leisure. How many of us, if asked to describe an ideal weekend,
would choose activities that cost nothing? How resourceful are we
about doing things without spending money? A successful movement to enhance free time will have to address this dynamic head
on. Governments and communities will need to subsidize more
affordable leisure activities, from the arts to parks to adult education. We need a conscious effort to reverse "the commodification
of leisure."

Whatever the potential problems associated with increasing leisure time, I do not think they are insurmountable. A significant
reduction in working hours will by itself alleviate some of the
difficulties. And if we can take positive steps to enhance the value
of leisure time, we will be well rewarded. The experience of the
Kellogg workers calls for optimism: "The visitor sees . . . a lot of
gardening and community beautification . . . athletics and hobbies
were booming . . . libraries well patronized . . . and the mental
background of these fortunate workers . . . becoming richer."[41]

RECLAIMING LEISURE

While leisure holds great appeal, it is difficult to be confident that
the next century will bring us more of it. It is possible that the future

holds yet another episode in the nation's saga of work-and-spend. Of course, some observers continue to believe that work will disappear, as robots, computers, and micro-electronic technology replace human labor. Others see a more sinister side to leisure, in which the little work that remains is monopolized by a fraction of the population. Society will split into two great classes—those with jobs (and income) and those without. Economic inequality, already on the rise, will mount.[42]

Then there are those, as we have seen, who think America *needs* more work, to compete against the Japanese. But having already gone through two decades of rising hours, this "Japanese solution" is truly daunting. If current U.S. trends in work continue for another twenty years, the average person would be on the job sixty hours a week, fifty weeks a year—for an annual total of three thousand hours.[43] If it sounds like Dickens's England, that's because it would be. If hours rise again, how can we solve the parenting deficit, marital problems, or the adverse health effects of stress and overwork? And then there's the ecology: another round of work, produce, and spend may put the human habitat beyond the point of no return.

I have already chronicled the many barriers to becoming a more leisured society. Corporations remain the most significant obstacle. Most will be vociferous opponents to my ideas. At last count, the Conference Board reports that fewer than fifty firms nationwide have comprehensive programs for work and family issues. But, as always, enlightened, forward-looking companies do exist. Wells Fargo gives personal-growth leaves, Xerox offers social-service sabbaticals. Job sharing is possible at a growing number of companies, including Hewlett Packard, Black & Decker, TRW Vidar, and Levi-Strauss. Control Data has a vibrant part-time program which includes benefits. Anna Roddick, founder of the rapidly expanding Body Shop, gives her employees a half-day off each week with pay to engage in volunteer activities. While the number of innovative corporations is still small, it is growing. And apparently awareness of time-related personnel problems is increasing as well. In the last few years, at least some corporate executives have been waking up to the realities of their employees' lives.[44]

None of this is to say that increased leisure is impossible. Certainly not. It is only to remind ourselves that it will not come about through automatic market forces, the munificence of technology, or as a natural consequence of postindustrial society. Long hours are a hallmark of the market; labor-saving technology frequently does not save labor; and it is capitalism, not industry, that has been responsible for expanding work schedules. There will be more leisure only when people become convinced that they must have it.

On some parts of the landscape, the signs are hopeful. There is growing public awareness of the need for change. For the first time since such surveys have been systematically conducted, a majority of Americans report that they are willing to relinquish even current income to gain more family and personal time. In a 1989 poll, almost two-thirds said they would prefer to give up some of their salary, by an average amount of 13 percent; fewer than one-quarter were unwilling to give up any money at all.[45] Despite this survey's limited scope and its variance with previous results, its findings are intriguing. Have we entered a new era, in which Americans have begun to rebel against their demanding worklives?

Other trends in public opinion also bode well for leisure. The "greening" of public consciousness is forcing us to take stock of the American life style. The crisis of the family—the problem of child care and the strains of marriage—is also intruding onto the social agenda. Both men and women, particularly young ones, are adopting new expectations about family and career. They are overturning the assumptions that men are responsible for breadwinning and women must take the second shift—trends that point in the direction of more balance between work and family. Although still only a trickle, the stream of "downshifters"—those who reject high-powered, demanding jobs in order to gain more control over their lives—may be the latest trendsetters.[46] But as I have stressed throughout this book, public opinion on its own is not an effective force for change. To organize and mobilize it, we will need to look to environmental and women's organizations, the children's lobby, and even the trade-union movement. The few labor organizations that have been expanding in recent years—public and service sector unions with heavily female membership—are already in the forefront on work and family issues. And government will need to play a major role, as should be clear from the failures of the market in this area.

If we are to have a chance at leisure, we'll need to resurrect the public debate that ended in the 1920s. For despite the major transformations our nation has gone through since then, the basic alternatives remain surprisingly the same. On the one hand, commitment to an expanding material standard of living for everyone—or what Galbraith has called the "vested interest in output"—entails our continuing confinement in the "squirrel cage" of work and holds the potential for ecological disaster.[47] Or, we can redirect our concern with material goods toward redressing the inequalities of their distribution—and realize the promise of free time which lies before us. This time, let's make the choice for leisure.

Appendix

A. THE STABILITY OF POSTWAR HOURS, 1948–1968

Total annual hours were calculated from the *National Income and Product Accounts of the United States.* (Hours are for all full-time and part-time employees for all domestic industries.) These data were then converted to a per capita basis, using the total population aged sixteen and over. They were converted to a labor force basis by deflating by the labor force minus self-employment. These calculations yielded the following estimates:

	1948	1969
Hours per capita	1069	1124
Hours per labor force participant	1968	1944

It is often thought that hours declined during this period because weekly hours (calculated from establishment data) fell and because paid time off rose. The former is overstated, because it does not account for the growth in moonlighters. Paid time off did rise slightly during this time, but it was offset by other factors, such as moonlighting and perhaps a growth in weeks worked per year, which do not show up in the weekly hours.

SOURCES: Hours and self-employed persons are from *National Income and Product Accounts of the United States, 1929–1982*, U.S. Department of Commerce, Bureau of Economic Analysis, (Washington, D.C.: Government Printing Office, 1986). Hours from Table 6.11, p. 287; self-employment from Table 6.9B, p. 282. Population and labor force are from Council of Economic Advisers, *Economic Report of the President*, (Washington, D.C.: Government Printing Office, 1989), Table B-32, p. 344.

B. COMPARISON OF OUR RESULTS WITH ESTIMATES FROM THE UNIVERSITIES OF MICHIGAN AND MARYLAND

As we noted in the text, researchers who administer the time-use surveys at the Universities of Michigan (1965, 1975, and 1981 surveys) and Maryland (1985 survey) claim that since 1965 work time in the United States has fallen and leisure time has risen. In my view, their inference is unwarranted and stems from particularities of their samples. The Michigan researchers, F. Thomas Juster and Frank P. Stafford, compare 1965 and 1981. However, both the 1965 and 1981 surveys have a variety of problems which have not been addressed in their comparison. For example, Juster and Stafford have corrected for only two shortcomings of the 1965 sample—age and city size. Furthermore, their method, which truncates the 1981 sample to be identical to the 1965 sample on these two dimensions, produces an estimate of hours changes among an unrepresentative sample, rather than a sample which can be said to be representative of the U.S. population in 1981. (Among other things, the 1965 sample is whiter, more affluent, and more employed than the actual population.) There are other serious problems with the 1965 and 1981 comparison which they have not addressed. First, the 1965 and 1981 samples are limited to employed heads of households and their spouses (where head of household is defined as the male in the case of male-female households). Second, 1965 and 1981 are incomparable points in the business cycle. The former is in the midst of a vigorous expansion and the latter is during a deep recession, which biases hours upward during 1965 and downward during 1981. Furthermore, the researchers have not corrected for the upward trend in unemployment and underemployment during this period. Third, the estimates of women's household labor have been shown to be artificially inflated in the 1965 sample. A study of the purported decline in household labor between the 1965 and 1975 samples (from which the 1981 sample is drawn) found that half the decline was a statistical artifact, due to the peculiarities of the 1965 sample. The 1965–1981 comparison is also plagued by this false decline in household labor, which the researchers have not corrected. Finally, the Michigan and Maryland samples estimate only weekly hours, yet we found that the bulk of the hours increase occurred because weeks per year rose. These surveys are too small to adequately pick up this increase. John Robinson's 1985 Maryland survey reported results that leisure rose between 1965 and 1985, with the bulk of the change coming between 1965 and 1975. Robinson says that he has corrected the 1965 samples, but he provides no information on the corrections. In any case, the best he can do with respect to the lack of nonemployed household heads in the 1965 sample is to compare two unrepresentative samples, which renders his claim that the average American is gaining leisure unsupported. In the first reports of his survey, he finds a decline in free time between 1975 and 1985. Once the data are rendered more comparable with the 1965 survey, there is a one- to two-hour increase in free time in this period. This appears to be due to imposing the characteristics of the 1965 survey on the data. The claim that the average American is enjoying more leisure cannot be supported.

SOURCES: F. Thomas Juster and Frank P. Stafford, "The Allocation of Time: Empirical Findings, Behavioral Models, and Problems of Measurement," working paper, Institute for Survey Research, University of Michigan, February 1990. John P. Robinson, "Time's Up," *American Demographics,* 11(7): 32–35. John P. Robinson, "Trends in Americans' Use of Time: Some Preliminary 1965–1975–1985 Comparisons," 1986 mimeo, University of Maryland Survey Research Center, Table 5, p. 36. John P. Robinson, "Household Technology and Household Work," in Sarah Fenstermaker Berk, ed., *Women and Household Labor* (Beverly Hills: Sage Publications, 1980).

C. METHOD FOR ESTIMATING
MARKET HOURS*

Annual hours are calculated between 1969 and 1987 from the March Current Population Surveys. In contrast to many hours estimates, these are annual. They are corrected for the rise in unemployment and underemployment, and allow for yearly variation in schedules—which has become more common in recent years. The estimates were done for 1969, 1973, 1979, and 1987, all years which are business cycle peaks, with the exception of 1987, which was the latest available year. Because the upward trend in hours occurred throughout the entire period 1968–87, I have only included the endpoints in the tables presented in chapter 2. Hours data include all hours at work plus paid leave (paid holidays, vacations, sick leave, and so on). Separate estimates of paid leave have been made in chapter 2. The annual hours estimate is calculated as the product of weekly hours and weeks worked per year. More precisely, it is: HOURSLW × WEEKSLY, where HOURSLW is actual hours worked during a week in March of year $t+1$ ($t = 1969$, 1987), and WEEKSLY is number of weeks worked during year t. Unfortunately, estimates of "usual weekly hours" rather than "hours last week" are not available for 1969. An estimate of hours per week is used instead of HOURSLW in the following cases:

1. If a person's 1-digit occupation or industry changed between year t and March in year $t+1$.
2. If a person's full-time/part-time status changed between year t and March in year $t+1$.
3. If WEEKSLY > 0 but HOURSLW $= 0$.
4. If HOURSLW < 35 but it is indicated that this is not a usual schedule and the person usually works full-time.

---

*All estimates of hours were carried out jointly with Laura Leete-Guy of Harvard University. For more detail on estimates, see our paper "Assessing the Time Squeeze Hypothesis: Estimates of Market and Non-Market Hours in the United States, 1969–1987," unpublished mimeo, Harvard University, June 1990.

In these cases, hours per week is estimated as the average for persons of the same part-time/full-time status in the same industry and occupation, if industry and occupation are available. If industry and occupation are not available for year t, as in the case of someone who had positive weeks looking for work, but no job, then hours per week are taken as the average of persons of the same age, race, and gender.

D. ESTIMATES OF HOUSEHOLD HOURS

1. Time Use Studies—Modeling Household Hours

Our estimates are based on the 1975–76 and 1980–81 Michigan Time Use Studies. (We have excluded the 1965 study because, as discussed in appendix B, it was not representative and the 1985 Maryland survey because it was not available at the time.) We have calculated household hours by constructing estimates of hours for relevant demographic/economic groups from the Michigan surveys and applying them to the Current Population Survey in order to get the benefits of a large, representative sample.

The 1975–76 study was close to being a nationally representative, random draw of individuals aged eighteen and over. The 1980–81 study interviewed only a subset of these same individuals, including only those who were household heads or their spouses. Since the individuals in the first sample were six years older by the time the second survey was conducted, in theory the 1980–81 sample will include no one under age twenty-three. In practice it actually contains no one aged eighteen to twenty-four. We used these data to estimate regression equations which we then used to construct the demographic/economic group estimates.

In order to eliminate any spurious changes due to changes in the sample, our main regression equations are estimated only for those individuals who were included in both samples. This restricted sample, however, only includes household heads and their spouses and underrepresents people of color. Since the effects of race and household head status cannot be adequately estimated from the restricted sample, coefficients for these variables were estimated for the entire 1975–76 sample and then added to the otherwise complete equations estimated on the restricted 1975–76 and 1980–81 samples shown below. Finally, since the 1980–81 sample includes no one aged eighteen to twenty-four, the coefficients for the dummy variable for those aged eighteen to twenty-four and its interaction terms were estimated on the full 1975–76 sample and included with the equation on the restricted 1980–81 sample. The constant terms for the restricted sample equations were adjusted for the addition of these other slope coefficients.

The full set of regression coefficients used is presented below.* All variables are dummy variables except the square root of the number of children over and under age 3, family income, and market hours worked. Dummy variables are set equal to one for the characteristic named.

The dependent variable is total household hours per week, which included the following activities: *Indoor Household Activities* (meal preparation, meal cleanup, laundry and clothes care, indoor cleaning and chores, repairs and maintenance, care of houseplants); *Outdoor Household Activities* (gardening, outdoor cleaning and chores, repairs and maintenance, home improvements); *Child Care* (general child care, help with homework, helping/teaching children, reading to/conversations with children, playing with children, medical care to children, babysitting [unpaid], travel related to child care); *Obtaining Goods and Services* (shopping, apartment/house hunting, obtaining services [except personal care], travel while obtaining goods and services); *Miscellaneous Household* (pet care, car care and maintenance, household paperwork, care of other friends or relatives).

---

*The coefficients applied to the 1970 CPS and the 1974 CPS are slightly different from one another; the 1970 CPS does not include race categories that matched those available in the time-use studies or the later CPS's. Thus, the coefficients used for the 1970 CPS were calculated leaving out the 'other race' variable.

2. Regression Coefficients

Women: Dependent Variable Is Household Hours per Week
(Standard errors in parentheses)

From: Applied to:	1975–76 Time-use		1980–81 Time-use
	1970 CPS	1974 CPS	1980 and 1988 CPS
Constant	27.7	27.8	32.2
Age 18–24	−3.8	−3.8	−3.6*
	(3.4)	(3.4)	(2.3)
Age 45–64	2.7	2.7	1.8
	(2.3)	(2.3)	(2.4)
Age 65+	−.94	−.94	−5.7**
	(3.2)	(3.2)	(3.1)
SQRT (No. of children	13.3***	13.3***	7.7***
<3)	(3.0)	(3.0)	(3.3)
SQRT (No. of children	3.9***	3.9***	3.8***
>3)	(1.4)	(1.4)	(1.6)
Market Hours	−.44***	−.44***	−.46***
	(.06)	(.06)	(.06)
Marital Status	3.7***	3.7***	4.2***
	(1.9)	(1.9)	(2.1)
Housewife	3.8**	3.8**	1.8
	(2.1)	(2.1)	(2.1)
Head of Household	3.7*	3.6*	3.6*
(or spouse of)	(2.5)	(2.5)	(2.5)
Head of Subfamily	5.4	5.3	5.3
(or spouse of)	(5.6)	(5.6)	(5.6)
Family Income	.0001	.0001	−.0001*
(in 1975 or 1980 $s)	(.0001)	(.0001)	(.0001)
Black	−1.8	−1.9	−1.9
	(3.2)	(3.2)	(3.2)
Other Race	—	−1.9	−1.9
		(3.7)	(3.7)
BLACK*SQRT	−13.1***	−13.3***	−13.3***
(children <3)	(5.7)	(5.7)	(5.7)
BLACK*SQRT	−3.7	−3.6	−3.6
(children >3)	(3.0)	(3.0)	(3.0)
AGE1824*SQRT	−6.9**	−7.8***	−7.8***
(children <3)	(4.0)	(4.0)	(4.0)
adjusted R²	.49	.49	.39

*significant at the .20 level
**significant at the .10 level
***significant at the .05 level

Men: Dependent Variable Is Household Hours per Week
(Standard errors in parentheses)

From: Applied to:	1975–76 Time-use 1970 CPS	1974 CPS	1980–81 Time-use 1980 and 1988 CPS
Constant	14.8	14.6	21.1
Age 18–24	−1.6	−1.6	−.29
	(2.6)	(2.6)	(2.0)
Age 45–64	1.5	1.5	1.3
	(1.8)	(1.8)	(1.9)
Age 65+	−.42	−.42	−2.4
	(2.9)	(2.9)	(3.0)
SQRT (No. of children <3)	3.5**	3.5**	2.7
	(1.9)	(1.9)	(2.5)
SQRT (No. of children >3)	2.0**	2.0**	1.8*
	(1.0)	(1.0)	(1.2)
Market Hours	−.29***	−.29***	−.34***
	(.05)	(.05)	(.05)
Marital Status	.72	.72	3.5**
	(1.8)	(1.8)	(2.1)
Head of Household	5.6***	5.7***	5.7***
	(2.5)	(2.5)	(2.5)
Family Income	.0001*	.0001*	−.0001**
	(.0001)	(.0001)	(.00004)
Black	2.6	2.7	2.7
	(3.1)	(3.1)	(3.1)
Other Race	—	3.4	3.4
		(2.7)	(2.7)
Black*Age 18–24	−7.1	−7.1	−7.1
	(5.9)	(5.9)	(5.9)
Black*SQRT (children >3)	−6.4***	−6.1***	−6.1***
	(2.7)	(2.7)	(2.7)
adjusted R^2	.22	.22	.27

*significant at the .20 level
**significant at the .10 level
***significant at the .05 level

These regression coefficients were then used to calculate an average estimate of weekly household hours for each person in the Current Population Survey (based on their characteristics). Annual hours were weekly hours times fifty-two.

Notes

Preface

1. Robert Levine, "The Pace of Life," *Psychology Today* (October 1989): 42–46.
2. E. P. Thompson, "Time, Work-Discipline and Industrial Capitalism," *Past and Present,* 38 (December 1967): 61.

Chapter 1. The Overworked American

1. Nine hours figure from author's calculations. See Chapter 2.

   Median leisure hours were 16.6 in 1987. Louis Harris, *Americans and the Arts;* Study 871009, January 1988 (New York: Louis Harris and Associates), 60, table 1. On the decline of leisure, also see: Decision Research Corporation, *Decision Research Corporation's 1990 Leisure Study: Trends in America's Leisure Time and Activities* (Lexington, Mass.) February 1990.

   The calculation on present trends is made on the basis of John D. Owen's figures for per capita labor input between 1920 and 1977. He finds a net decline of 10 percent. Between 1979 and 1987 per capita hours rose 4.5 percent (my estimates). If this rate of increase continues until the year 2000, the entire 1920–77 decline will be eliminated. John D. Owen, *Working Lives: The American Work Force Since 1920* (Lexington, Mass.: Lexington Books, 1986), 23 and table 2–7.
2. Author's estimates, 1988, from Bureau of Labor Statistics, Office of Productivity and Technology, "Underlying Data for Indexes of Output per Hour, Hourly

Compensation, and Unit Labor Costs in Manufacturing, Twelve Industrial Countries, 1950–1988," June 1989.

3. I am using the term *productivity* as a shorthand for "labor productivity," which is, strictly speaking, measured as output per hour of labor input. Official statistics assume that productivity growth for government workers is always zero. Also, productivity figures are calculated only for the "market" economy and exclude unpaid work in the home.

4. Figures are from *Economic Report of the President (ERP)* (Washington, D.C.: Government Printing Office, 1991), 338–39, tables B–46 and B–47. They are for the business sector.

5. These are from my calculations of total working hours per capita and per labor force from the National Income and Product Accounts. Between 1948 and 1969, per-capita hours rose from 1,069 to 1,124, or 55 hours. Annual hours per labor force participant fell slightly—from 1,968 to 1,944 hours. See the appendix for the methods used in calculating these figures.

    On a per-person basis, gross national product went from $9,060 in 1948 to $19,900 at the end of 1988 (measured in constant 1988 dollars). See *ERP*, 1989 ed., 308, table B–1 and 344, table B–32.

6. Full citations for these claims can be found in note 38, chap. 5, p. 210.

7. Current GNP per capita is $21,953 per year. Calculated from *ERP*, 286, table B–1 and 321, table B–31. Income figures for other countries can be found in the annual *World Development Report* (Washington, D.C.: World Bank).

8. The major exception on days off is for the 18 percent of the workforce covered under collective bargaining agreements.

9. Russell Lynes, "Time on Our Hands," in Eric Larrabee and Rolf Meyerson, eds., *Mass Leisure* (Glencoe, Ill.: Free Press, 1958), 346.

    Predictions on current worktime are from 1967 Testimony from a Senate Subcommittee, cited in Nancy Gibbs, "How America Has Run Out of Time," *Time,* 24 April 1989, p. 59.

10. Reuel Denney, "The Leisure Society," *Harvard Business Review* 37, 3 (May–June 1959): 47, 60, on boredom.

    See Lynes, "Time on Our Hands," for discussion of these efforts.

    See David Riesman, with Reuel Denney and Nathan Glazer, *The Lonely Crowd: A Study of the Changing American Character* (New Haven: Yale University Press, 1950); or "Leisure and Work in Post-Industrial Society," Riesman's contribution to Larrabee and Meyerson, *Mass Leisure.*

11. The most prominent voice on the stability of postwar hours has been economist John D. Owen, whose books include *Working Lives, Working Hours: An Economic Analysis* (Lexington, Mass.: Lexington Books, 1979), and *Reduced Working Hours: Cure for Unemployment or Economic Burden?* (Baltimore: Johns Hopkins University Press, 1989).

    See, for example, Sar A. Levitan and Richard S. Belous, *Shorter Hours, Shorter Weeks: Spreading the Work to Reduce Unemployment* (Baltimore: Johns Hopkins University Press, 1977).

Frank Levy, *Dollars and Dreams: The Changing American Income Distribution* (New York: W. W. Norton, 1988).

12. This is not to say there has been no attention paid lately to working hours. Historians have recently produced some new and excellent works. These include Benjamin Hunnicutt's *Work Without End: Abandoning Shorter Hours for the Right to Work* (Philadelphia: Temple University Press, 1988); Gary Cross, *A Quest for Time* (Berkeley, Calif.: University of California Press, 1989), *Worktime and Industrialization: An International History* (Philadelphia: Temple University Press, 1988), and his forthcoming *Time and Money: The Making of Consumerist Modernity* (London: Routledge, forthcoming); and David Roediger and Phillip S. Foner, *Our Own Time: A History of American Labor and the Working Day* (London: Verso, 1989). Among sociologists, the work of Carmen Sirianni is exemplary and includes his "Economies of Time in Social Theory: Three Approaches Compared," *Current Perspectives in Social Theory*, vol. 8 (Greenwich, Conn.: JAI Press, 1987), 161–95, and *Working Time in Transition*, jointly edited with Karl Hinrichs and William Roche (Philadelphia: Temple University Press, 1991). Europeans have done far more on this issue, although most of it from the perspective that work is disappearing. A prominent example is André Gorz, whose recent book, *A Critique of Economic Reason* (London: Verso, 1989), is oriented to the issue of working time. See also the work of Claus Offe.

13. Examples include André Gorz, *Critique of Economic Reason* (London: Verso, 1989); Fred Block, *Post-Industrial Possibilities: A Critique of Economic Discourse* (Berkeley: University of California, 1990), 205–6; Theresa Diss Greis, *The Decline of Annual Hours Worked in the United States Since 1947* (Philadelphia: Industrial Relations Unit, Wharton, University of Pennsylvania, 1984); F. Thomas Juster and Frank P. Stafford, "The Allocation of Time: Empirical Findings, Behavioral Models, and Problems of Measurement," Working Paper Institute for Social Research, University of Michigan, February 1990; and John P. Robinson, "Time's Up," *American Demographics*, 11, 7 (July 1989): 32–35.

    Gary Burtless, "Are We All Working Too Hard? It's Better Than Watching Oprah," *Wall Street Journal*, 4 January 1990. Burtless missed the fact that paid time off has fallen substantially in the last decade.

    John P. Robinson, "Time's Up," *American Demographics*, 11 (1989): 34. For the same conclusion based on a shorter period of time, but essentially similar data, see Juster and Stafford, "The Allocation of Time," p. 8.

    My estimates, which are both more comprehensive and representative of the U.S. population than those of previous researchers, reveal a clear and dramatic trend to more work. For discussion of the differences among estimates, see the appendix. A few economists, particularly those on the left, have alluded to a rise in worktime. See, for example, publications of the Economic Policy Institute.

14. Some, although not all, of these conclusions are presented in Laura Leete-Guy and Juliet B. Schor, "Assessing the Time Squeeze Hypothesis: Estimates of Market and Non-Market Hours in the United States, 1969–1987," unpublished

mimeo, Harvard University, June 1990, as well as an updated forthcoming version in *Industrial Relations*.

15. The phrase "time poverty" was used by Clair Vickrey in an important article entitled "The Time-Poor: A New Look at Poverty," *Journal of Human Resources*, 12, 1 (1977): 27–48.

Harris, *Americans and the Arts*, 60, table 1, on the decline of leisure time.

On sleep, see note 22, Chapter 1. Eating figures were calculated from John P. Robinson, "Trends in Americans' Use of Time: Some Preliminary 1965–1975–1985 Comparisons," 1986 mimeo, University of Maryland, Survey Research Center, calculated from table 5, p. 36.

On children see Victor Fuchs, *Women's Quest for Economic Equality* (Cambridge, Mass.: Harvard University Press, 1988); and Sylvia Ann Hewlett, *When the Bough Breaks: The Cost of Neglecting Our Children* (New York: Basic Books, 1991).

16. For evidence see chapter 3.

17. See chapter 3 for a discussion of why Western Europe is a relevant area for comparison.

On holidays in ancient Greece and Rome, see Hutton Webster, *Rest Days: A Study in Early Law and Morality* (New York: The Macmillan Company, 1926), 394. Gustave Glotz concludes that Greek masons were with certainty "idle for at least one fifth of the year and probably much more." See Glotz, *Ancient Greece at Work: An Economic History of Greece from the Homeric Period to the Roman Conquest* (New York: Knopf, 1927), 283.

18. Marshall Sahlins, *Stone Age Economics* (New York: Aldine, 1972), 4.

19. For a critique of the idea of progress, see Juliet B. Schor, "Why I Am No Longer a Progressive," *Zeta*, April 1990.

20. Sahlins, *Stone Age Economics*, 2.

For these estimates, see Leopold Pospisil, *Kapauku Papuan Economy* (New Haven, Conn.: Yale University Publication in Anthropology 67, 1963), 144–45 on Kapauku; Richard Lee, "What Hunters Do for a Living or How to Make Out on Scarce Resources," in Richard B. Lee and Irven DeVore, eds., *Man the Hunter* (Chicago: Aldine Publishing Company, 1968), 30–48 on !Kung; C. S. Stewart on the Sandwich Islands (cited in Sahlins, *Stone Age Economics*, p. 56); Frederick D. McCarthy and Margaret McArthur, "The Food Quest and the Time Factor in Aboriginal Economic Life," reprinted from *Records of the American-Australian Scientific Expedition to Arnhem Land*, vol. 2 (Melbourne: Melbourne University Press, 1960), on Australia.

21. On stress, see Louis Harris, *Inside America* (New York: Vintage, 1987), 8–10. Fifty-nine percent have great stress at least once or twice a week, and 89 percent report experiencing high stress. These polls were taken in 1985–86.

John P. Robinson, "The Time Squeeze," *American Demographics*, 12, 2 (February 1990): 30–33. The question asked was whether respondents "always," "sometimes," or "almost never" feel rushed to do the things they have to do.

Robert Karasek and Töres Theörell, *Healthy Work: Stress, Productivity and the Reconstruction of Working Life* (New York: Basic Books, 1990), 166, on workers' compensation claims and "working to death."

According to the 9 to 5 national stress survey, which was conducted in 1983, just over two-thirds of respondents reported that in the previous year there was an increase in the amount of work required or a speedup. These women also reported increased levels of insomnia, pain, chest pain, tension, anger, depression, and exhaustion. See *The 9to5 National Survey on Women and Stress* (Cleveland, Ohio: 9to5, 1984), 35–38. See also Amanda Bennett, *The Death of the Organization Man* (New York: William Morrow, 1990), which chronicles speed-up in large corporations.

Karasek and Theörell, *Healthy Work,* on stressful workplaces.

22. Natalie Angier, "Cheating on Sleep: Modern Life Turns America Into the Land of the Drowsy," *New York Times,* 15 May 1990. Recent research by economist Daniel Hamermesh finds a relationship between employment and sleep in "Sleep and the Allocation of Time," *Journal of Political Economy,* 98, 5 (October 1990): 922–43.

23. MassMutual Family Values Study. (Washington, D.C.: Mellman & Lazarus, 1989), 3, on families and time.

Diane S. Burden and Bradley Googins, *Boston University Balancing Job and Homelife Study* (Boston University: mimeo, 1987), 26, on women and stress.

"When I'm at home," from Harris, *Inside America,* 95.

Paul Williams Kingston and Steven L. Nock, "Time Together Among Dual-Earner Couples," *American Sociological Review,* 52 (June 1987): 391–400. See also Arlie Hochschild, *The Second Shift: Working Parents and the Revolution at Home* (New York: Viking Penguin, 1989).

Harriet Presser, "Shift Work and Child Care Among Young Dual-Earner American Parents," *Journal of Marriage and the Family* 50, 1 (February 1988): 133–48. This figure is for couples in which the wife works full time. Among part-timers, the proportion is over one-half.

Quote from Parents United for Child Care (PUCC) survey comments, mimeo, Boston, Massachusetts, 1989.

24. Hochschild, *Second Shift,* 212.

25. Sylvia A. Hewlett, *When the Bough Breaks: The Cost of Neglecting Our Children* (New York: Basic Books, 1991), 1.

John J. Sweeney and Karen Nussbaum, *Solutions for the New Work Force* (Washington, D.C.: Seven Locks Press, 1989), 209, *n.* 15, for 7 million figure.

Burden and Googins, *Balancing Job and Homelife,* 21, table 12, for the local study.

Preschoolers figure cited in Fern Schumer Chapman, "Executive Guilt: Who's Taking Care of the Children?" *Fortune,* 16 February 1987, p. 37.

Quote from PUCC, "Survey comments."

26. Ibid.

Victor Fuchs, *Women's Quest for Economic Equality* (Cambridge, Mass.: Harvard University Press, 1988), 111.

Hewlett, *When the Bough Breaks*.

Expert is Edward Zigler, Yale University, cited in Nancy Gibbs, "How America Has Run Out of Time," *Time,* 24 April 1989, pp. 61–64.

27. See Chris Rojek, *Capitalism and Leisure Theory* (London: Tavistock Publications, 1985), chap. 1. Other discussions can be found in Michael R. Marrus, ed., *The Emergence of Leisure* (New York: Harper Torchbooks, 1974), and the classic work by Sebastian de Grazia, *Of Time, Work and Leisure* (New York: Twentieth Century Fund, 1962). A feminist discussion can be found in Rosemary Deem, *All Work and No Play? The Sociology of Women and Leisure* (Milton Keynes: Open University Press, 1986).

28. Keith Thomas, "Work and Leisure in Pre-Industrial Society," *Past and Present,* 29 (December 1964): 53.

On usage of these terms, see de Grazia, *Time, Work and Leisure,* 193.

For a classic article, see E. P. Thompson, "Time, Work-Discipline, and Industrial Capitalism," *Past and Present,* 38 (December 1967). On the instrumentality of work, see Stephen A. Marglin, "Losing Touch: The Cultural Conditions of Worker Accommodation and Resistance," in Frédérique Apffel-Marglin and Stephen A. Marglin, eds., *Dominating Knowledge: Development, Culture, and Resistance* (Oxford: Clarendon Press, 1990).

Thomas, "Work and Leisure," 54.

Chapter 2. Time Squeeze: The Extra Month of Work

1. "All Work, No Play," on "Real Life with Jane Pauley," NBC, 17 July 1990.

"Overworked and Out of Time," on "Our Times," WHDH-TV, Boston, 14 April 1990.

Transcript of "Fast Times," Show 97, "48 Hours," CBS News, 8 March 1990. All these examples are from the script.

2. Nancy Gibbs, "How America Has Run Out of Time," *Time,* 24 April 1989, p. 59.

3. Anne B. Fisher, *Wall Street Women: Women in Power on the Street Today* (New York: Alfred A. Knopf, 1990), 152, 150.

4. Quoted in Brian O'Reilly, "Is Your Company Asking Too Much?" *Fortune,* 12 March 1990, p. 39.

5. See Amanda Bennett, *The Death of the Organization Man* (New York: William Morrow, 1990).

On downsizings, see O'Reilly, "Is Your Company," 41.

6. Evidence on the increased commitment in what she calls "post-entrepreneurial" firms can be found in Rosabeth Moss Kanter's *When Giants Learn to Dance* (New York: Simon & Schuster, 1989), chap. 10, p. 275. The quote is from Thomas Bolger, CEO of Bell Atlantic.

Kanter, *When Giants Dance,* 273.

Dolores A. Kordek, personal interview, 5 January 1991. Kordek followed this schedule for twelve years, rarely seeing her family, eating either in the office or the car, and eventually "burning out."

7. A poll by Korn/Ferry International in 1985 found that among Fortune 500 and Service 500 companies, senior executives' hours rose from 53 to 56 between 1979 and 1985; vacation days fell from 16 to 14. A poll of CEOs by Heidrick and Struggles found that the percentage who worked more than 60 hours per week rose between 1980 and 1984, from 44 percent to 60 percent. Cited in Ford S. Worthy, "You're Probably Working Too Hard," *Fortune,* 27 April 1987, p. 136. The Harris Poll reports consistent findings for managers. Sixty-two percent of CEOs also report that their subordinates are putting in longer hours. See Sally Solo, "Stop Whining and Get Back to Work," *Fortune,* 12 March 1990, p. 49.

8. See Bennett, *Death,* and Kanter, *When Giants Dance,* for evidence from case-study research on individual companies.

9. Labor force participation rate of adult women from Current Population Survey, author's estimates. Rates of labor force participation for mothers (of own children under eighteen) from "Marital and Family Characteristics of the Labor Force from the March 1990 Current Population Survey," unpublished Bureau of Labor Statistics mimeo, October 1990, p. 4, table 15.

10. These quotes are from Ann Landers's column, *Boston Globe,* 26 February 1990. "Busy every waking hour" is from Laurie Sheridan, "Interviews on Working Hours," unpublished mimeo.

Arlie Hochschild, *The Second Shift: Working Parents and the Revolution at Home* (New York: Viking Penguin, 1989), 9.

11. Boston study is Dianne S. Burden and Bradley Googins, *Boston University Balancing Job and Homelife Study,* mimeo (Boston University, 1987), 18, table 10.

Shelley Coverman, using the Quality of Employment Survey, found an average workweek of 87.4 hours for white, currently married, employed women. See "Gender, Domestic Labor Time, and Wage Inequality," *American Sociological Review,* 48 (October 1983): 623–37, table 1, p. 629. A second study, based on the Panel Survey of Income Dynamics, found that in white, married couples, mothers who worked full-time had a workweek ranging from 76 hours (if the oldest child was 4 to 13 years old) to 89 (oldest child 0 to 3 years). See Cynthia Rexroat and Constance Shehan, "The Family Life Cycle and Spouses' Time in Housework," *Journal of Marriage and the Family,* 49, 4 (November 1987): 737–50, fig. 1, p. 746. A nationwide magazine survey by the 9to5 union found that women respondents had an average workweek of 84.3 hours. See *The 9to5 National Survey on Women and Stress* (Cleveland, Ohio: 9to5, 1984), estimates calculated from appendix C; however, this was not a statistically representative survey.

12. Anna Quindlen, "Men at Work" in "Public and Private," *New York Times,* 18 February 1990, p. 19, on "endangered species" and 50-plus hours.

Weekend data from Harriet Presser, "Can We Make Time for Children? The Economy, Work Schedules, and Child Care," *Demography,* 26 (November 1989): 523–44, table 1.

13. Sheridan, "Interviews."

14. One-third figure calculated from table 3.5 in Lawrence Mishel and David M. Frankel, *The State of Working America,* 1990–91 ed. (Armonk, N.Y.: M. E. Sharpe); hourly wage figure for 1988, p. 77.

Valerie Connor (pseud.), personal interview, 23 December 1990.

Bill Meyerson, Service Employees International Union, Hartford, Connecticut, personal interview, 30 November 1990.

Dominic Bozzotto, personal interview, December 1990.

I. N. Yazbek, personal interview, 11 December 1990.

15. The Harris Poll question on leisure is the following: "About how many hours each week do you estimate you have available to relax, watch TV, take part in sports or hobbies, go swimming or skiing, go to the movies, theater, concerts, or other forms of entertainment, get together with friends, and so forth?" Louis Harris, *Americans and the Arts,* Study 871009 (New York: Louis Harris and Associates), January 1988, Appendix C. The Decision Research Corporation question is: "Compared to a few years ago do you feel you have more leisure time, less leisure time or the same amount of leisure time?" Decision Research Corporation, *Decision Research Corporation's 1990 Leisure Study: Trends in America's Leisure Time and Activities* (Lexington, Mass.: D.C. Heath, February 1990), 6, table 1.

For the Harris Poll, the most serious problem is that it reportedly has a very low response rate. A second issue, for both the Harris and Decision Research Corporation polls, is the accuracy of estimates that are based on respondent recall. For a critique of this method, see John P. Robinson, "The Validity and Reliability of Diaries versus Alternative Time Use Measures," in F. Thomas Juster and Frank P. Stafford, eds., *Time, Goods, and Well-Being* (Ann Arbor: Institute for Social Research, University of Michigan, 1985), 63–91. Because time diaries are expensive to administer, most surveys of time use are based on the recall method; therefore, it is difficult to avoid reliance on it altogether.

16. Jeremy Rifkin, *Time Wars* (New York: Henry Holt, 1987), 14–15.

On Nintendo, ibid., 26.

Alstedt quote from Trish Hall, "Why All Those People Feel They Never Have Enough Time," *New York Times,* 2 January 1988, p. 1.

17. John P. Robinson, "The Time Squeeze," *American Demographics,* 12, 2 (February 1990): 30–33. Results from Robinson's 1985 survey show that rising numbers of people feel rushed in other age groups besides the "baby boomers." The walking résumé quote is from Geoffrey Godbey of Pennsylvania State University, in Hall, "Why All Those People."

18. Gary Becker, "A Theory of the Allocation of Time," *Economic Journal,* 75, 299 (1965): 493–517; and Staffan B. Linder, *The Harried Leisure Class* (New York: Columbia University Press, 1970).

19. Trish Hall, "The Dinner Party Quietly Bows to More Casual Alternatives," *New York Times*, 24 February 1988, p. C1.

    Linder, following standard neoclassical economic theory, has no prediction about whether a wage increase will lead to more or less leisure time. There is also a logical question about Linder's theory: If the income effect for leisurely activities is large, demand for them may increase. See William J. Baumol, "Income and Substitution Effects in the Linder Theorem," *Quarterly Journal of Economics*, 87 (1973): 629–33.

20. One-fourth from Bureau of Labor Statistics, *Labor Force Statistics Derived from the Current Population Survey, 1948–1987* (Washington, D.C.: Government Printing Office, 1988), 801, table C–12, 804, table C–14. The percentage was rising over this period; one-quarter is a rough figure.

    Bureau of Labor Statistics, "Marital and Family Characteristics," 4, table 15.

21. Bruce D. Butterfield, "Long Hours, Late Nights, Low Grades: In Labor-Short Towns Across America, Teen-agers Are Overworked," *Boston Globe*, Children at Work series, 24 April 1990.

22. Bruce D. Butterfield, "The New Harvest of Shame: For Farm Workers' Children, Cycle of Poverty and Work Unbroken," *Boston Globe*, Children at Work series, 26 April 1990.

23. Bureau of Labor Statistics, *Labor Force Statistics Derived from the Current Population Survey, 1948–1987*, 153, table A–10.

24. One study of older male (aged 45–65) nonparticipants indicates that these men have relatively little income that suggests voluntary retirement—namely, pensions, rental income, interest, or dividends. Instead, their support comes much more from government disability payments, indicating that physical and mental impairments are preventing them from working. The inability to find jobs is also correlated with disability rates. For white men, disability payments alone made up about 30 percent of total family income; for black men, these payments were roughly half. Donald O. Parsons, "The Decline in Male Labor Force Participation," *Journal of Political Economy*, 88, 11 (1980): 117–34. Since these data were collected before the Reagan administration's attack on disability programs, the figures may be lower during the 1980s.

    1990 survey is in The Commonwealth Fund, *Americans Over 50 at Work Program*, Research Reports 1 and 2 (New York: The Commonwealth Fund, 25 January and 8 March 1990).

    See Bennett, *Death*, for a discussion of pressures to take early retirement among white-collar workers. For evidence on the effects of plant closings or job loss on older workers, see Paul O. Flaim and Ellen Sehgal, "Displaced Workers of 1979–83: How Well Have They Fared?" *Monthly Labor Review* (June 1985): 3–16. Their figures show that 34 percent of males aged fifty-five and above dropped out of the labor force after being displaced (calculated from table 1, p. 4).

    African-American men face rates of unemployment more than twice those of white men. They have also been disproportionately hit by plant closings, industrial decline, and suburbanization. Once they suffer job displacement,

African-Americans have a 42-percent chance of becoming unemployed, nearly twice the rate for whites, and are more likely to drop out of the labor force altogether. Data on job displacement are from a special Bureau of Labor Statistics survey for 1979–83. See Flaim and Sehgal, "Displaced Workers," p. 4, table 1. For a discussion of the long-term picture, see William J. Wilson, *The Truly Disadvantaged: The Inner City, the Underclass, and Public Policy* (Chicago: University of Chicago Press, 1987), 100–101.

25. More information on these categories can be found in Laura Leete-Guy and Juliet B. Schor, "Is There a Time Squeeze? Estimates of Market and Non-Market Hours in the United States, 1969–1987," *HIER Working Paper* 1525, Harvard University, November 1989. The occupational data are difficult to construct due to changes in the occupational codes between 1969 and 1987; however, a rough test confirmed the generality of the rise. The results for industries are also likely to be somewhat correlated with those for occupations.

26. Earl F. Mellor and William Parks II, "A Year's Work: Labor Force Activity from a Different Perspective," *Monthly Labor Review* (September 1988): 13–18.

27. The decline in average weekly hours registered in the establishment data is spurious because it double-counts moonlighters and excludes the informal sector and many of the self-employed.

Figures on long schedules are from Bureau of Labor Statistics, *Employment and Earnings,* August 1990, p. 32, table A-27, calculated as a percentage of full-time workers only, all industries (49+ hours are 25 percent, 60+ hours are 11 percent).

28. See Leete-Guy and Schor, "Assessing the Time Squeeze Hypothesis: Estimates of Market and Non-Market Hours in the United States, 1969–1987," unpublished mimeo, Harvard University, June 1990.

29. Bureau of Labor Statistics Press Release, "Multiple Jobholding Reached Record High in May 1989," 89–529, 6 November 1989.

See Sar A. Levitan and Richard S. Belous, *Shorter Hours, Shorter Weeks: Spreading the Work to Reduce Unemployment* (Baltimore: Johns Hopkins University Press, 1977), 12 on under-reporting.

See Bureau of Labor Statistics News release, 89–529, 6 November 1989, table 6; and Daniel E. Taylor and Edward S. Sekscenski, "Workers on Long Schedules, Single and Multiple Jobholders," Research Summary, *Monthly Labor Review,* 105, 5 (May 1982): 47–53 for data on reasons for multiple jobholding and the differences between 1980 and 1989.

30. Average annual overtime hours per job were 204.5 in 1987:4, which on the basis of a 40-hour week is equivalent to five weeks. Overtime data are from Ray Fair, of Yale University, whose original source is *Employment and Earnings.* They are the variable HO, as defined in his *Specification, Estimation, and Analysis of Macroeconomic Models* (Cambridge, Mass.: Harvard University Press, 1984), table A–4. Data are not available outside the manufacturing sector.

Quotes from Sheridan, "Interviews."

31. Bennett, *Death,* 140–41, on DuPont and other large corporations.

Illness data from author's calculations from Current Population Survey data. Absences from Bruce W. Klein, "Missed Work and Lost Hours, May 1985," *Monthly Labor Review,* 109, 11 (November 1986): 26–30.

32. Max L. Carey, "Occupational Tenure in 1987: Many Workers Have Remained in Their Fields," *Monthly Labor Review,* 111, 10 (October 1988): 3–12.

33. "Gradual erosion" quote from Theresa Diss Greis, *The Decline of Annual Hours Worked in the United States Since 1947* (Philadelphia: Industrial Relations Unit, Wharton, University of Pennsylvania, 1984), 1.

I have used two methods to estimate paid time off. The first used unpublished Bureau of Labor Statistics estimates of hours paid relative to hours worked. The drawback to these data is that they are only available for the manufacturing sector earlier than 1981. Therefore, I have relied on manufacturing sector data for the period 1969 to 1981. These data show a rise in time off of three days. After 1981, I have all-economy data to 1989, which indicate a decline equivalent to three and a half days per year. There is, therefore, a net decrease in total paid time off between 1969 and 1989 of one-half day, or about four hours. If I calculate these figures only until 1987, the year my data end, I get a net increase in paid time off of one and a half days, or about twelve hours. (The difference is due to the decline in paid time off between 1987 and 1989.)

A second method is to use direct estimates of the major forms of paid time off—vacations, holidays, and sick leave. Because the Current Population Survey does not provide the information to enable me to calculate vacations and holidays, I have used BLS estimates. They calculate that in 1968 paid vacation and holidays totaled seventeen days per year. In 1983–86, they estimate 19.5 days per year, or an increase of 2.5 days (or 20 hours). Against this, I have calculated sick leave from the Current Population Survey (the variable is available only for full-time workers). Total hours lost to illness for full-time workers fell between 1969 and 1987 from 58 per year to 41, a decline of 17 hours. (Notably, between 1969 and 1979 there was little change; all of the decline happened after 1979.) Combining the vacation, holiday, and sick leave yields a net figure of 3 hours per year in additional paid time off. For Bureau of Labor Statistics estimates, see Janice Hedges and Daniel E. Taylor, "Recent Trends in Worktime: Hours Edge Downward," *Monthly Labor Review,* 103, 3 (1980): 3–11; and John E. Buckley, "Variations in Holidays, Vacations, and Area Pay Levels," *Monthly Labor Review,* 112, 2 (February 1989): 24–30.

34. Commuting times calculated from John P. Robinson, "Trends in Americans' Use of Time: Some Preliminary 1965–1975–1985 Comparisons," mimeo, 1986 University of Maryland, Survey Research Center, p. 36, table 5.

A development my calculations do not fully capture is the growth of the underground economy. The underground economy consists of economic production that is not reported to the government and does not show up in official statistics—either because the activity itself is illegal (drugs, prostitution, gambling) or because those engaging in it wish to avoid paying taxes on the income it generates. It is difficult to know exactly how these considerations affect people's responses to the CPS; however, it is probable that some percentage will not acknowledge hours of work that are "underground." The fact that the underground economy has increased tremendously over the period I am considering means that my calculations are biased downward. In effect, I am counting a shrinking percentage of the total economy. It is impossible to calculate with any accuracy how much it is shrinking and how many hours I am missing. This problem is common to all estimates of worktime.

35. There is no single, convenient term for unpaid work done in the home. Some terms commonly in use are *domestic labor, unpaid labor, household work,* and *work done in the home.* The latter is somewhat confusing because some work for pay is physically located in the home and some domestic labor occurs outside the home (transporting family members, purchasing food, etc.). *Domestic labor* and *unpaid labor* are somewhat arcane. The economist's preferred terminology is *market* and *nonmarket work,* but these have little meaning in common parlance. I try to avoid these terminological minefields by using most of these terms interchangeably. Some readers may have their doubts about whether such household activities as food preparation, child care, and house cleaning should be considered work. This issue is discussed in chapter 4.

Officers of the Association for the Advancement of Women wrote to the U.S. Congress in 1878, requesting changes in Census procedures that would allow enumeration of household workers. See Nancy Folbre and Marjorie Abel, "Women's Work and Women's Households: Gender Bias in the U.S. Census," *Social Research,* 56, 3 (Autumn 1989): 545–69.

The diary studies originating at the University of Michigan are biased upward in terms of income and the percentage of whites, two factors that raise domestic hours. A second problem is that the Michigan surveys were done during recessions (1975–76 and 1980–81), which distorts their estimates of market work.

36. For more discussion, see the appendix. A simple description is the following: My colleague, Laura Leete-Guy, and I predicted hours of domestic labor for our CPS sample based on a multiple regression model using data from the University of Michigan surveys in 1975–76 and 1980–81. The independent variables included marital status, number of children, age, number of hours worked in paid employment, and so forth. The 1975–76 survey was used to predict hours for 1969 and 1973. The 1980–81 follow-up survey was used for 1979 and 1987. See Victor Fuchs, "His and Hers: Differences in Work and Income, 1959–79," *Journal of Labor Economics,* 4, 3 (1986): pt. 2, S245–72, for an earlier example of this methodology. One drawback to this method is that we cannot pick up any post-1981 trends occurring due to excluded factors, such as men's increased willingness to do work around the house. A more recent survey was carried out in 1985; however, these data were not available except in summary form.

37. In the contemporary United States, hours per working-age person is a superior

measure to a second, often-cited statistic—namely, hours per capita, which includes children and teenagers. There are at least two reasons for this. First, since child labor has been legally restricted and for some ages prohibited, including children as part of the potential labor force is somewhat suspect. Inclusion of child labor would also be hampered by the lack of adequate data, given that it is often illegal. (As noted earlier, however, child labor is on the rise.) Second, there has been a sharp decline in the number of children per adult during the last twenty years, which artificially inflates the hours-per-capita figure.

The standard of living will also be affected by the extent to which income flows in and out of the country on the basis of assets held abroad by U.S. citizens and domestic assets owned by foreigners. The hours-per-capita measure also does not account for consumption that occurs by running down stocks of previously produced goods and services, or for the labor of children.

38. I am here defining leisure time as whatever is left over after household and market work are accounted for. The uncorrected figures show a more modest decline of 25 hours per year. See Leete-Guy and Schor, "Assessing the Time Squeeze."

39. Researchers have not yet provided an estimate of how much domestic production is being replaced by marketed goods and services, however there is no doubt that this substitution is taking place.

40. John P. Robinson, "Who's Doing the Housework?" *American Demographics,* 10, 12 (December 1988): 24–28.

41. See James P. Smith and Michael Ward, "Time-Series Growth in the Labor Force," *Journal of Labor Economics,* 3, 1 (January 1985): S59–S90, and Elaine McCrate, "Trade, Merger, and Employment: Economic Theory on Marriage," *Review of Radical Political Economics,* 19 (1987): 73–89.

42. For a comprehensive discussion of the decline of macroeconomic performance and the resulting unemployment, the reader is referred to Stephen A. Marglin and Juliet B. Schor, eds., *The Golden Age of Capitalism: Reinterpreting the Postwar Experience* (Oxford: Clarendon Press, 1990). For more on changes in unemployment itself, see Jukka Pekkarinen, Matti Pohjola, and Bob Rowthorn, *Social Corporatism: A Superior System?* (Oxford: Clarendon Press, 1991). Both these volumes were produced by the Macroeconomic Policies Project of the World Institute for Development Economics Research.

43. See, among others, Levitan and Belous, *Shorter Hours;* Martin J. Morand and Ramelle Macoy, eds., *Short-time Compensation: A Formula for Work Sharing* (New York: Pergamon Press, 1984); and William McGaughey, Jr., *A Shorter Workweek in the 1980s* (White Bear Lake, Minn.: Thistlerose Publications, 1981).

These proposals also overestimated the impact workweek reductions were likely to have on the demand for labor. As we argue in chapter 6, there is strong evidence that workweek reductions are accompanied by rising productivity, which largely negates the positive employment effect. Recent European experience provides strong support for this conclusion. See Wouter van Ginneken, "Employment and the Reduction of the Work Week: A Comparison of Seven European Macro-economic Models," *International Labour Review,* 123, 1 (January/February 1984): 35–52.

Chapter 3. "A Life at Hard Labor": Capitalism and Working Hours

1. For example, see Gary Burtless, "Are We All Working Too Hard? It's Better Than Watching Oprah," *Wall Street Journal,* 4 January 1990.
2. One group for whom incomes did not rise were slaves in the New World.
3. See Barbara A. Hanawalt, who argues that women's hours were longer than men's. "Peasant Women's Contribution to the Home Economy in Late Medieval England," in Barbara A. Hanawalt, ed., *Women and Work in Pre-industrial Europe* (Bloomington, Ind.: Indiana University Press, 1986), 3–19.

   Because there is no significant "precapitalist" American past—for those of either European or African descent—we have to look back at the area of origin. In the African case, there is little doubt that American slavery entailed a massive expansion of work effort. Africans had been forcibly uprooted from their homes and labor traditions; the plantation was a veritable workhouse in comparison. By the time European settlers arrived in America, their work patterns had already been significantly altered by capitalism. Therefore, I make the comparison to medieval Europe, rather than early America. I have chosen to concentrate on England, both because the English made up the bulk of the settlers, and because the literature on England is most extensive.

4. The Bishop Pilkington is cited in Keith Thomas "Work and Leisure in Preindustrial Society," *Past and Present,* 29 (December 1964): 61.

   An important piece of evidence on the working day is that it was very unusual for servile laborers to be required to work a whole day for a lord. One day's work was considered half a day; and if a serf worked an entire day, this was counted as two "days-works." See H. S. Bennett, *Life on the English Manor* (Cambridge: Cambridge University Press, 1960), 104–6. The Statutes of Artificers passed between 1495 and 1563 set work at an average of nine and a half hours per day (author's calculations). However, these laws were passed in a period when worktime was falling, as an attempt to elicit more effort from laborers. There is evidence of widespread violations. For the Statutes, see B. W. Clapp, H. E. S. Fisher, A. R. J. Jurica, eds., *Documents of English Economic History: England from 1000 to 1760,* vol. 1 (London: G. Bell and Sons, 1977), 489–98. On violations see Bertha Haven Putnam, *Enforcement of the Statutes of Laborers* (New York: Longmans, Green, 1908). Detailed accounts of artisans' workdays are available. Knoop and Jones' figures for the fourteenth century work out to a yearly average of 9 hours (exclusive of meals and breaktimes). See Douglas Knoop and G. P. Jones, *The Medieval Mason* (New York: Barnes and Noble, 1967), 105. Brown, Colwin, and Taylor's figures for masons suggest an average workday of 8.6 hours. See R. Allen Brown, H. M. Colvin, and A. J.

Taylor, *The History of the King's Works,* vol. I, The Middle Ages (London: Her Majesty's Stationery Office, 1963).

James E. Thorold Rogers, *Six Centuries of Work and Wages* (London: Allen and Unwin, 1949), 542–43.

5. Jacques Le Goff, *Time, Work and Culture in the Middle Ages* (Chicago: Chicago University Press, 1980), 44.

Nigel Thrift, "Owners' Time and Own Time: The Making of a Capitalist Time Consciousness, 1300–1880," *Lund Studies in Human Geography,* 48 (1981): 58. See also David Landes, *Revolution in Time: Clocks and the Making of the Modern World* (Cambridge, Mass.: Harvard University Press, 1983). On the United States, see Michael O'Malley, *Keeping Watch: A History of American Time* (Viking: New York, 1990). Monasteries had more precise scheduling and a different consciousness of time than did rural areas, where the vast majority of the population resided.

6. See Fernand Braudel, *The Structures of Everyday Life: The Limits of the Possible* (London: Collins, 1981), 90, 112. According to standard texts, the range of contemporary requirements for average male farmers is from 3,420 to 4,000. In the past, people were considerably smaller, so their needs would be lower; however, their farmwork was also less mechanized and therefore more energy-intensive. Studies of food consumption indicate that both calories and effort levels have been increasing through the twentieth century. See O. G. Edholm, "The Society's Lecture," Ergonomics Research Society, *Ergonomics,* 13, 6 (1970): 625–43; and J. L. Hersch, "Allocation of Time and Human Energy and Its Effects on Productivity," *Applied Economics,* 17 (1985): 867–84. See also Chris Nyland's discussion in *Reduced Worktime and the Management of Production* (Cambridge: Cambridge University Press, 1989).

7. Edith Rodgers, *Discussion of Holidays in the Later Middle Ages* (New York: Columbia University Press, 1940), 10–11. See also C. R. Cheney, "Rules for the Observance of Feast-Days in Medieval England," *Bulletin of the Institute of Historical Research,* 34, 90 (November 1961): 117–29.

Bennett, *Life on the English Manor,* 265.

Estimates of holiday time vary. In P. Boissonade, *Life and Work in Medieval Europe* (New York: Dorset Press, 1987), the estimate is one-quarter of the year; in Aron Gurevich, *Categories of Medieval Culture* (London: Routledge & Kegan Paul, 1985), it is one-third. Walter of Henley's estimate of one-sixth is widely cited, but apparently it has been misinterpreted because of its treatment of Sundays, which, if included, raise his estimate of leisure time to slightly over one-quarter. His estimate is for the thirteenth century only, after which time holidays increased. See Rodgers on Walter of Henley in *Discussion of Holidays,* 14. Other relevant sources on worktime include Bennett, *Life on the English Manor;* Nathaniel J. Hone, *The Manor and Manorial Records* (New York: E. P. Dutton, 1906), 923; George Homans, *English Villagers of the Thirteenth Century* (New York: Russell and Russell, 1960), 365; Nora Ritchie, "Labour Conditions in Essex in the Reign of Richard II," in E. M. Carus-Wilson, ed., *Essays in Economic History,* vol. II (London: Edward Arnold, 1962), 91–107;

Christopher Hill, *Society and Puritanism in Pre-Revolutionary England*
(New York: Schocken Books, 1964); Nigel Thrift, "Owner's Time"; M. A.
Bienefeld, *Working Hours in British Industry: An Economic History*, London
School of Economics Research Monograph (London: Weidenfeld and Nicol-
son, 1972); and Knoop and Jones, *Medieval Mason.*

On the *ancien régime*, see Sebastian de Grazia, *Of Time, Work and Leisure*
(New York: Twentieth Century Fund, 1962), 119. G. G. Coulton cites an
estimate for fourteenth-century France of 200 days per year worked for un-
skilled laborers in *The Medieval Village* (London: Cambridge University Press,
1925), 311.

On Spain, see Hill, *Puritanism*, 148–49. High as it seems, Hill believes the
Spanish estimate is not "wildly out."

8. Quote from Ritchie, "Labour Conditions," 93. This complaint was a frequent
refrain of employers through the centuries. See also D. C. Coleman, "Labour
in the English Economy of the Seventeenth Century," *Economic History Review,* new series, 111, 3 (April 1956): 280–95.

The 120 figure is from Ritchie, "Labour Conditions," 94.

Thirteenth-century figure is from Gregory Clark, "Impatience, Poverty, and
Open Field Agriculture," mimeo, 1986. Clark concurs with my characterization of work patterns: "The poverty of the peasants thus seems to have
stemmed more from too many rest days or very leisurely work, rather than
from any constraint from agricultural technique" (pp. 23–24).

Manorial records indicate that virgaters worked "137 days in winter and
summer and 38 during the harvest, on a basis of a 5-day week, four weeks'
holiday at Christmas, Easter, and Whitsun, and 61 saints' days in winter and
summer, and 4 in the harvest season." Ritchie, "Labour Conditions," 94.

Farmer-miners' figure is from Ian Blanchard, "Labour Productivity and
Work Psychology in the English Mining Industry, 1400–1600," *Economic
History Review,* 31, 1 (1978): 23, table B2–1. This figure is for 1600. The
farming year (135 days) is consistent with Gregory Clark's figure; the remainder was spent in mining.

9. See Coleman, "Labour in the Seventeenth Century."

10. Precise estimates are hard to come by. Coleman in "Labour in the Seventeenth Century" notes that in seventeenth-century England, there might ordinarily be employment for only half the year. See also Krishnan Kumar,
"From Work to Employment and Unemployment: The English Experience,"
in R. E. Pahl, *On Work: Historical, Comparative and Theoretical Approaches* (Oxford: Basil Blackwell, 1988), 138–64. Robert N. Whapples,
"The Shortening of the American Work Week: An Economic and Historical
Analysis of its Context, Causes and Consequences" (Ph.D. dissertation, University of Pennsylvania, 1990), argues that the regularity of employment increased in the United States in the nineteenth century. The U.S. case also has
evidence for a backward-bending supply of labor. See Herbert Gutman,
*Work, Culture and Society in Industrializing America: Essays in American
Working-Class and Social History* (New York: Vintage, 1977), and the clas-

sic work by Paul Douglas, *The Theory of Wages* (New York: Macmillan 1934), 310–14.

11. Le Goff, *Time, Work and Culture,* 43–52. See also Landes, *Revolution in Time,* who argues that clocks were introduced when they were economically valuable.

12. E. P. Thompson, "Time, Work-Discipline and Industrial Capitalism," *Past and Present,* 38 (December 1967): 61.

Quote on "owner's time" from Nigel Thrift, "Owner's time," 61.

Quote on "objective force" from Francis Hearn, *Domination, Legitimation, and Resistance: The Incorporation of the Nineteenth Century English Working Class* (Westport, Conn.: Greenwood Press, 1978), 149.

13. There is a debate on English working hours. See Thompson, "Time, Work-Discipline"; Eric Hopkins, "Working Hours and Conditions During the Industrial Revolution: A Re-Appraisal," *Economic History Review,* 35 (February 1982): 52–66; and Douglas A. Reid, "The Decline of St. Monday: 1766–1876," *Past and Present,* 71 (May 1976): 76–101. However, this debate is about a small percentage of workers—mainly skilled, male craft workers. There is no question about the rise in hours if we include agricultural laborers and domestic servants.

The timing differs between the two countries. Hours rose earlier in England as capitalism developed earlier. The United States started off with longer hours, and hours rose in the first half of the nineteenth century. On the United States, see Robert E. Gallman, "The Agricultural Sector and the Pace of Economic Growth: U.S. Experience in the Nineteenth-Century," in David C. Klingaman and Richard K. Vedder, eds., *Essays in Nineteenth Century Economic History: The Old Northwest* (Athens, Ohio: Ohio University Press, 1975).

A classic estimate suggests that at its peak, the workweek climbed to 70 hours in Britain and just under 80 in the United States. This is probably an overestimate for the United States. See W. S. Woytinsky, "Hours of Labor," in *Encyclopedia of the Social Sciences,* vol. III (New York: Macmillan, 1935). Manufacturing hours were lower than hours in agriculture and domestic service, the two largest occupational groups in each country in the nineteenth century. A serious flaw in most discussions of hours has been the exclusion of domestic servants.

14. On decline of holidays, see Hill, *Puritanism;* and Bienefeld, *Working Hours.* On nineteenth-century agricultural laborers' schedules, see James Obelkovich, *Religion and Rural Society: South Lindsey 1825–1875* (Oxford: Clarendon Press, 1976), 62–70. Of course, the decline of holidays did not yet imply year-round work; during the winter, labor was still minimal.

The United States had fewer official holidays to begin with; however, regularity of employment increased throughout the nineteenth century.

15. The one exception was night work, which was generally prohibited, but apparently not absolutely prevented. See Le Goff, *Time, Work and Culture,* 44.

16. This occurred in England, but not all European countries.

17. "Lose control" quote from comments of Christopher Hill, who stressed that hostility to wage labor had deep "ideological roots," cited from the discussion in Thomas, "Work and Leisure," 63.

    On "commodification of labor," see Gareth Stedman Jones, *Languages of Class: Studies in English Working Class History 1832–1982* (Cambridge: Cambridge University Press, 1983).

    Thompson, "Time, Work-Discipline," 78.

    On poverty, see Coleman, "Labour in the Seventeenth Century." See also Hill, *Puritanism*.

    Quote on "hunger" cited in Thomas, "Work and Leisure," 62.

18. Karl Marx, *Capital* (New York: Vintage, 1976), vol. I, chap. 10, p. 389. See also J. L. and Barbara Hammond, *The Town Labourer 1760–1832* (London: Longman, Green, 1919). The aptly-named "Hell's Bay" mill provides a grim example. Regular hours were 5 A.M. to 9 P.M., and twice a week the children were scheduled to work all through the night.

19. Quotes from Marx, *Capital*, vol. 1, chap. 10, p. 352.

20. Cited in Thompson, "Time, Work-Discipline," 86.

21. From Alfred [S. Kydd], *History of the Factory Movement*, cited in ibid., 86.

22. David R. Roediger and Philip S. Foner, *Our Own Time: A History of American Labor and the Working Class* (London: Verso, 1989), 26.

23. Ibid., 26.

24. From reports of the inspectors of factories, cited in Marx, *Capital*, 352.

25. On the occupational distribution, for England, see J. D. Chambers, *The Workshop of the World* (London: Oxford University Press, 1961), 21–22. In 1851, agricultural laborers (not all farm servants, of course) were 1,790,000 and domestic servants 1,039,000, more than double the workers in manufacturing and mining. (By contrast, there were only half a million textile workers.) For the United States, see David Montgomery, *Beyond Equality: Labor and Radical Republicans 1862–1872* (New York: Knopf, 1976); and David M. Katzman, *Seven Days a Week: Women and Domestic Service in Industrializing America* (New York: Oxford University Press, 1978). According to Katzman, in 1870, 50 percent of all women wage-earners in the United States were domestic servants.

    Quote is from Katzman, *Seven Days,* 111.

    Schedule of servants is from ibid., 113–15. In the South, conditions were generally better.

26. Jacqueline Jones, *Labor of Love, Labor of Sorrow: Black Women, Work and the Family from Slavery to Present* (New York: Vintage Books, 1985), 16.

    Ibid., 13.

    One estimate puts slaves' annual hours at 2,798; however, this does not rely on direct evidence on the length of the workday. See Robert W. Fogel and Stanley L. Engerman, "Explaining the Relative Efficiency of Slave Agriculture in the Antebellum South," *American Economic Review,* 67, 3 (June 1977): 275–95. They also cite 3,130 hours as the early twentieth-century annual average for Northern farmers.

27. Cited from Alfred P. Wadsworth and Julia DeLacy Mann in Sidney Pollard, "Factory Discipline in the Industrial Revolution," *Economic History Review,* 26, 2 (December 1963): 257.

28. J. D. Chambers, "The Domestic Rural Industries," cited in Maxine Berg, *The Age of Manufactures, 1700–1820* (Totowa, N.J.: Barnes and Noble, 1985), 103. See also Ivy Pinchbeck, *Women Workers and the Industrial Revolution* (London: Frank Cass, 1930), 174–82, table, p. 142, who cites hours of 5 or 6 A.M. to 8 P.M. for England.

    On New York, see Christine Stansell, *City of Women: Sex and Class in New York* (New York: Alfred A. Knopf, 1986), 113–14.

    Berg, *Age of Manufactures,* 130–33.

    Pinchbeck, *Women Workers,* 232–33.

29. Cited in Stansell, *City of Women,* 262, *n.* 34.

30. Quotes from William Foote Whyte, *Money and Motivation: An Analysis of Incentives in Industry* (Westport, Conn.: Greenwood Press, 1977), 15, 23.

31. This dynamic operates with piece-rate workers as well. A recent study makes the point: although employees were permitted to schedule their breaks whenever they pleased, they were obliged to be on the floor a total of eight hours per day. See Hersch, "Allocation of Time," 872.

    If there are fixed costs of hiring and firing, such as personnel costs, training costs, severance pay, and so forth, then firms have an interest in longer hours. Fringe benefits are currently the most important cause of such a bias, as I will argue later. An early treatment of the fixed-cost argument was made by H. G. Lewis in his 1969 unpublished paper, "Employer Interests in Employee Hours of Work."

32. Roediger and Foner, *Our Own Time,* 230–36. Twin relics quote from William Brown Dickson, a U.S. Steel vice-president, on p. 232.

33. The "contract" which exchanges a worker's time for an hourly wage is "incomplete" in that the actual amount of labor to be done, the quality of that labor, and the precise nature of the tasks to be carried out are left unspecified. From the employer's point of view this ambiguity is often necessary. There are too many uncertainties, too many contingencies, to write a fully specified contract beforehand. Ambiguity also serves another purpose: it would be far more difficult for labor and capital to come to a mutually-agreed-upon definition of exactly what the work process consists of than it is to complete the straightforward transaction of dollars per hour. Economists have recently explored the effects of these contracts. See the collection by George Akerlof and Janet Yellen, *Efficiency Wage Models of the Labor Market* (Cambridge: Cambridge University Press, 1986).

34. Quotes cited in Pollard, "Factory Discipline," 255, 261.

35. Cited in Thrift, "Owner's Time," 65.

36. The annual turnover rate was 370 percent in 1913. See Daniel M. G. Raff, "Wage Determination Theory and the Five-Dollar Day at Ford," *Journal of Economic History,* 48, 2 (June 1988): 387–99, table 1, p. 389.

37. Ford denied women eligibility for the pay increase on the grounds that they were not breadwinners. An alternate interpretation is that women were excluded because they presented fewer discipline problems: they did not drink as much and were more punctual.

38. "Absolutely docile" from Arnold and Faurote, cited in Daniel M. G. Raff and Lawrence H. Summers, "Did Henry Ford Pay Efficiency Wages?" *Journal of Labor Economics,* 5, 4, pt. 2 (1987): S81.

    See Juliet B. Schor, "Does Work Intensity Respond to Macroeconomic Variables? Evidence from British Manufacturing, 1970–1986," Harvard Institute for Economic Research, Discussion Paper 1396, April 1988.

    See Juliet B. Schor and Samuel Bowles, "Employment Rents and the Incidence of Strikes," *Review of Economics and Statistics,* 49, 4 (November 1987): 584–92.

    Of course, employment rents were not the only effective strategy used by firms. A substantial literature has detailed a variety of other mechanisms, such as management's monopoly on technical expertise, the use of bureaucratic "rules" to control behavior, and tactics of divide-and-conquer. Furthermore, it would be wrong to think that capitalists "solved" the problem of labor discipline. Even a passing acquaintance with the labor relations debates of the 1980s should put the lie to that idea. My claim is much more modest: that development of employment rents played a major role in stabilizing and containing problems of labor discipline in twentieth-century America.

39. So far, I have been deliberately vague about the exact definition of the employment rent. Although a variety of alternatives are possible, a standard formulation is the following: annual employment rent = annual income in original job minus [(weeks unemployed × weekly unemployment income) + (weeks at new job during year × weekly earnings in new job)].

    Bert Johnson (pseud.), personal interview, 24 March 1991.

40. In Johnson's case, this will be true as long as some period of unemployment is anticipated, or alternative jobs do not offer a comparable wage rate.

41. For the argument that reductions in daily hours can pay for themselves if the employment rent is not reduced, see Chapter 6, pages 152–57. The second argument put forward here is an "evolutionary" one: once a long hours equilibrium is established, there will be forces to perpetuate it. This will especially be the case if a shorter hours equilibrium is not more profitable than a long hours one.

42. Some readers may object to this analysis, pointing out that in recent years, employers have been eager to hire part-time workers. This development does not vitiate my point. In the first place, the lack of benefits can make these workers cheaper. (Part of the reason management is unwilling to pay benefits to part-time workers may be that they are, *ceteris paribus,* less profitable, for the reasons I have argued.) Second, I suspect that the substantial increase in employment rents during the 1980s (due to the rise of unemployment rates) has increased employers' room for maneuver, and that the growth of part-timers is one consequence.

43. Quote from Raff and Summers, "Did Henry Ford?" S81.

    Chris Nyland, *Reduced Worktime and the Management of Production* (Cambridge: Cambridge University Press, 1989), 57. Edward Denison, a well-known productivity expert, has also reached this conclusion in *Why Growth Rates Differ: Postwar Experience in Nine Western Countries* (Washington, D.C.: Brookings Institution, 1967), 59.

44. Quote from a forty-one-year-old automobile worker, in Laurie Sheridan, "Interviews on Working Hours," unpublished mimeo.

45. A classic work is Josephine Goldmark's *Fatigue and Efficiency: A Study in Industry* (New York: Charities Publication Committee, 1912). For a recent test of this hypothesis, which supports it, see Jeremy Atack and Fred Bateman, "How Long Did People Work in 1880?" mimeo, University of Illinois, 1989.

    This discussion raises a number of complex issues surrounding our analysis of the employment rent and its effect on hours. If the employment rent is defined purely in income terms, then the employer will prefer to raise hours until physical constraints begin to impair productivity. If the estimated value of the employment rent also includes a value for leisure time, it may begin to fall after some level of hours, which limits employers' desired hours. The actual role of the value of leisure time is empirically unclear, given the difficulties involved in measuring it. A second issue involves the neoclassical claim that on the margin employers will offer workers just that combination of pay and hours that maximizes their utility. In the neoclassical world, employers' preferences for long hours will have no particular effect, as employees choose their optimal level of hours. My approach is different, and implies that employers do not optimize on the hours margin, but rather set hours that employees adapt to. (The reasons for this are somewhat obscure, but I suspect that employers' preference for long hours is the underlying cause.) While this view is at variance with neoclassical theory, there is now a growing empirical literature to support it, which I discuss in chapter 5. Institutional labor economists have long denied that firms optimize on the hours margin. For more discussion of these issues, see Juliet B. Schor, "The Underproduction of Leisure: The Economics of Output Bias," mimeo, Harvard University, November 1990.

46. I have not found any evidence on why fringe benefits have taken this form.

47. U.S. Chamber of Commerce, *Employee Benefits, 1988 Edition: Survey Data from Benefit Year 1987* (Washington, D.C.: U.S. Chamber of Commerce, 1988), 33, table 17.

48. Ronald G. Ehrenberg and Paul L. Schumann, *Longer Hours or More Jobs?* (Ithaca: Cornell University Press, 1982).

49. H. G. Lewis, "Employer Interests."

50. Martin Morand, Indiana University of Pennsylvania, private communication, July 1987, on USX.

    Solidarity, June 1990, p. 11, on auto industry.

51. Ford S. Worthy, "You're Probably Working Too Hard," *Fortune,* 27 April 1987, p. 138.

52. Earl F. Mellor and Steven E. Haugen, "Hourly Paid Workers: Who They Are and What They Earn," *Monthly Labor Review,* 109, 2 (February 1986): 20–26.
53. Diane Rothbard Margolis, *The Managers: Corporate Life in America* (New York: William Morrow, 1979), 58–59.
54. Rosabeth Moss Kanter, *Men and Women of the Corporation* (New York: Basic Books, 1977), 64–65.

    On the California corporation, see Victor R. Fuchs and Joyce P. Jacobsen, "Employee Response to Compulsary Short-Time Work," National Bureau of Economic Research Working Paper 2089, 1986, p. 10, table 2.
55. Kanter, *Men and Women,* 65.
56. Sheridan, "Interviews."
57. Quote from ibid.

    For a discussion of the fact that small firms face higher costs, see Charles Brown, James Hamilton, and James Medoff, *Employers Large and Small* (Cambridge, Mass.: Harvard University Press, 1990), 40–42.
58. Estimates are my own from the Current Population Survey. Weekly hours for men in the professional, technical, executive, and managerial categories rose from 47.0 to 47.8 from 1979 to 1987. Women's hours rose from 43.4 to 44.3 over that period. Annual hours also rose—by roughly 30 for men and 112 for women.

    Rosabeth Moss Kanter, *When Giants Learn to Dance* (New York: Simon and Schuster, 1989), 268.
59. On Massachusetts, see Hill, *Puritanism,* 141. See also Daniel T. Rodgers, *The Work Ethic in Industrial America 1850–1920* (Chicago: University of Chicago Press, 1978). Although it was a powerful force, it is important to remember that the work ethic was mainly a white bourgeois Northeastern ideology.

    "Elevation of work" from ibid., 7.

    "Never penetrated very far" is from ibid., 15.

    Quote from engineer is from Fred Moody, "When Work Becomes an Obsession," *Baltimore City Paper,* 23 October 1987.

    None of this is to deny that for some, work is an addiction. The problems of "workaholics" cannot be solved solely with structural changes, but require personal transformation.
60. On occupational satifaction, see Louis Harris, *Inside America* (New York: Vintage Books, 1987), 52.

    See also Robert Karasek and Töres Theörell, *Healthy Work: Stress, Productivity and the Reconstruction of Working Life* (New York: Basic Books, 1990). The desire to escape authority and attain control in one's job is very strong.
61. The workweek is estimated at 70 hours for 1850. See Joseph S. Zeisel, "The Workweek in American Industry 1850–1956," *Monthly Labor Review,* 81 (1958): 23–29, chart 1, p. 24. For the range of estimates in manufacturing, which are lower, see Whapples, *Shortening the Work Week,* 33, table 2.1. In the postwar period the full-time workweek (for nonagricultural workers) has generally stood at 43 hours, and for all workers (all industries, all schedules)

is now in the neighborhood of 39 hours. See Bureau of Labor Statistics, *Employment and Earnings* and unpublished data.

62. Roediger and Foner, *Our Own Time,* 7, 56.

63. Quote from Helen L. Sumner, "Causes of the Awakening," in John R. Commons et al., *History of Labor in the United States* (New York: Macmillan, 1918).

    For a discussion of changing attitudes toward leisure, see Rodgers, *Work Ethic;* and Hunnicutt, *Work Without End: Abandoning Shorter Hours for the Right to Work* (Philadelphia: Temple University Press, 1988).

64. Whapples, *Shortening the Work Week.*

65. Roediger and Foner, *Our Own Time,* 22, 57, 141.

    On NAM and Saturday work, see Hunnicutt, *Work Without End,* 40. One prominent executive proclaimed that "any man demanding the forty-hour week should be ashamed to claim citizenship in this great country."

66. Bienefeld, *Working Hours,* 177.

67. Michal Kalecki, "Political Aspects of Full Employment," in *Selected Essays on the Dynamics of the Capitalist Economy 1933–1970* (Cambridge: Cambridge University Press, 1971), 140–41.

68. The correlation of low employment and high inflation has been a second factor in explaining business opposition to full employment. See Gerald A. Epstein and Juliet B. Schor, "Corporate Profitability as a Determinant of Restrictive Monetary Policy: Estimates for the Postwar United States," in Thomas Mayer, ed., *The Political Economy of American Monetary Policy* (Cambridge: Cambridge University Press, 1990).

    The "real" rate of unemployment roughly doubled during the 1980s, if one includes discouraged workers (those who have given up looking for a job but still want work) and those who are involuntarily working part-time. The government collects data on these categories, but excludes them from the unemployment rate. More ambitious measures would also include involuntary part-year workers and involuntary early retirees, and would drive the jobless totals up even more.

    Despite economists' pronouncements to the contrary, joblessness is not inevitable. Many European countries have managed to sustain, for long periods, true full employment. The key is to curtail effectively the opposition of business, something that U.S. workers have never managed to do. For discussion of the conditions and possibilities for full employment see Juliet B. Schor, "The Economics and Politics of Full Employment," *Socialist Review,* 81 (May 1985): 65–92; and Jukka Pekkarinen, Matti Pohjola, and Bob Rowthorn, *Social Corporatism: A Superior System?* (Oxford: Clarendon Press, 1991).

69. Hunnicutt, *Work Without End,* 310. William McGaughey, Jr., "The International Dimensions of Reduced Hours," *Society for the Reduction of Human Labor Newsletter,* 1 (1).

    Sally Solo, "Stop Whining and Get Back to Work," *Fortune,* 12 March 1990, p. 49.

70. Roediger and Foner, *Our Own Time,* 259.

71. For more discussion of this period, see Daniel Cantor and Juliet B. Schor, *Tunnel Vision: Labor, the World Economy, and Central America* (Boston: South End Press, 1987).

    Machinists' newspaper quoted in Roediger and Foner, *Our Own Time,* 269.

72. Comment by Katherine P. Ellickson, Assistant Director, Social Security Department, AFL-CIO, cited in Public Affairs Press, *The Shorter Work Week* (Washington, D.C.: Public Affairs Press, 1957), 89.

    For a discussion of the postwar growth consensus, see Alan Wolfe, *America's Impasse: The Rise and Fall of the Politics of Growth* (New York: Pantheon Books, 1981).

73. George Brooks, Paper Mill Workers, "Historical Background," in *Shorter Week* (Washington, D.C.: Public Affairs Press, 1957), 18.

    Second quote by Sylvia Gottlieb, Research Director, Communications Workers of America, cited in *Shorter Week* (Public Affairs Press), 20.

74. This phrase is from Hunnicutt, "The End of Shorter Hours," *Labor History,* 25 (Summer 1984): 373–404.

75. See Stephen A. Marglin and Juliet B. Schor, eds., *The Golden Age of Capitalism: Reinterpreting the Postwar Experience* (Oxford: Clarendon Press 1990).

76. Nonstudent male hours from John D. Owen, *Reduced Working Hours: Cure for Unemployment or Economic Burden?* (Baltimore: Johns Hopkins University Press, 1989), 16.

    Bureau of Labor Statistics data on total paid time off relative to time worked are available only for the manufacturing sector during this period. This measure is probably overly generous for our purposes because it includes time off during which the employee must remain at work, such as short breaks within the day. The provisions for paid time off are also considerably more generous within the manufacturing sector than the remainder of the economy, so the manufacturing estimates are an upper bound. (During the 1980s, manufacturing workers had from 3 to 5 additional days off per year.) These data show that paid time off rose from 16 days in 1948 to 20 in 1969, a gain of only four days a year. Source: unpublished Bureau of Labor Statistics data. This finding contradicts the views of researchers such as Theresa Diss Greis, *The Decline of Annual Hours Worked in the United States Since 1947* (Philadelphia: Industrial Relations Unit, Wharton, University of Pennsylvania, 1984). For those readers who are interested in a more detailed discussion of the derivation of these figures and of the various worktime statistics available for the 1950s and 1960s, please consult the appendix.

77. A study by the Economic Policy Institute calculates what would have happened to family incomes since 1979 had wives' labor supply not risen. It shows that only the top 40 percent of families in the income distribution would have had any income growth at all, had wives' hours stayed at their 1979 levels. The lower the income group, the more extra work wives have been doing. A final implication of this study is that wives' labor supply may be rising because husbands' wages are falling. Between 1979, husbands'

wages declined in all but the very top income group. For this 80 percent of American families, the modest goal of maintaining a constant level of income is likely to have required increases in work effort. See Stephen Rose and David Fasenfest, "Family Incomes in the 1980s: New Pressures on Wives, Husbands, and Young Adults," Working Paper 103, November 1988.

Seventy-nine percent of those polled believe that "it is getting to be impossible to support a family on just one income." Half (52 percent) agree strongly with that statement. See MassMutual Family Values Study (Washington, D.C.: Mellman & Lazarus, 1989), 36. In the words of one Chicago housewife: "You either buy a home, both of you work and your kids suffer, or one of you works and you live in a rental. Paying rent feels like digging a hole and crawling right in." Cited in Sylvia Ann Hewlett, "Running Hard Just to Keep Up," *Time,* Special Issue entitled *Women: The Road Ahead* (Fall 1990): 54.

78. Author's calculations from the changes in average hourly earnings of production and nonsupervisory workers, *Economic Report of the President* (Washington, D.C.: Government Printing Office, 1991), 336, table B–44. In constant 1990 dollars, the 1973 wage rate was $11.31 and the 1990 wage rate was $10.03. At the 1973 level of 1,919 annual hours, the difference in annual incomes is $2,456. At $10.03 an hour, it requires 245 additional hours to make up this amount.

79. See Lawrence Mishel and Jacqueline Simon, *The State of Working America* (Washington, D.C.: Economic Policy Institute, 1988), 13, table 24. These figures show that among salaried employees, real hourly wages have risen slightly since 1973.

Chapter 4. Overwork in the Household

1. The Michigan studies, on which my estimates are based, yield much lower estimates of household work, and especially child care, than virtually all the others for at least two reasons. First, recall methods typically yield higher hours than diary methods. Second, Michigan uses a restrictive definition of child care. According to Joseph Pleck, the higher estimates are more consistent with small-scale studies. My estimates should be seen as conservative, lower bounds. See Joseph H. Pleck, *Working Wives, Working Husbands* (Beverly Hills: Sage, 1985), 48–49.

2. For a fascinating discussion of this point, see Nancy Folbre and Heidi Hartmann, "The Rhetoric of Self-interest and the Ideology of Gender," in Arjo Klamer, Donald McCloskey, and Robert Solow, eds., *The Consequences of Economic Rhetoric* (Cambridge: Cambridge University Press, 1988), 184–206.

3. Nancy Folbre, "The Unproductive Housewife: Her Evolution in Nineteenth-Century Economic Thought," *Signs,* 6, 3 (Spring 1991): 463–84. Statistical conventions have helped to define and perpetuate this devaluation of domestic labor. According to Folbre, in the early federal censuses, families were considered as entities, and allocated to specific sectors of the economy. It was not until 1850 that individuals' occupations were requested by enumerators, and

those individuals were only men. In the next census, women were allowed to have occupations, but housewife was not one of them; however, there was a distinct (nonoccupational) category for "keeping house." By 1900, the census adopted the terms *breadwinners* and *dependents* and relegated housewives to the latter. Interestingly, the 1875 Massachusetts Census did classify housewives in the occupational category of domestic service, and specifically argued that they were productive, but by 1905 this New England rebellion was put down.

4. On the complexities of defining employment, see Amartya Sen, *Employment, Technology and Development* (Oxford: Clarendon Press, 1975), chaps. 1–3. The argument that the accounts are sexist is made in Marilyn Waring, *If Women Counted: A New Feminist Economics* (New York: Harper & Row, 1988).

5. Specifically, Leeds's families had somewhat higher incomes than those in subsequent studies, and income tends to be positively correlated with housewives' hours. Only four of the women in Leeds's study earned any outside income at all, and the amount was very small. Leeds's families were defined as "earning enough for decency." The Leeds study is discussed in Ruth Schwartz Cowan, *More Work for Mother: The Ironies of Household Technology from the Open Hearth to the Microwave* (New York: Basic Books, 1983), 154–60.

6. Joann Vanek's work is summarized in "Time Spent in Housework," *Scientific American,* 231, 5 (November 1974): 116–20. The 1920s studies were done under a series of guidelines developed by the U.S. Bureau of Home Economics. They allow for comparable sets of tasks between urban and rural women, and distinguish between full-time homemakers and those who are also employed. Comparable studies also exist for the 1940s, 1950s, and 1960s. Most of Vanek's estimates are from the compilation of local studies. These studies show that when the metric is housework proper (rather than farm tasks), rural women do no more than urban women. Hildegarde Kneeland reports that the 1920s study of 1,000 homes yields an average of 51 hours per week. See Kneeland's "Woman's Economic Contribution in the Home," *The Annals of the American Academy of Political and Social Science* 143, 232 (May 1929): 34, 38.

   My estimates are derived from a combination of the University of Michigan Time-Use study done in 1975–76 and the Current Population Survey. On account of limitations of the 1975–76 study, I have not relied on its estimates alone. I have used middle-class women with three children to provide maximum comparability with the earlier studies. See the appendix for a detailed discussion of my methods.

7. Leeds's families had electricity and gas, but many 1920s families did not, particularly those in rural areas. For discussions of the adoption of new household technologies, see Siegfried Giedion, *Mechanization Takes Command: A Contribution to Anonymous History* (New York: Oxford University Press, 1948); and Susan Strasser, *Never Done: A History of American Housework* (New York: Pantheon, 1982).

8. According to Maxine Margolis, the amount of capital in the household increased more than seven times between 1920 and 1950. See *Mothers and Such* (Berkeley: University of California Press, 1984), 166.

9. Alexander Szalai, *The Use of Time: Daily Activities of Urban and Suburban Populations in Twelve Countries* (The Hague: Mouton, 1972), 125.

John P. Robinson, "Household Technology and Household Work," in Sarah Fenstermaker Berk, *Women and Household Labor* (Beverly Hills: Sage Publications, 1980), 62–64, and table 3. These studies use cross-section data: that is, they compare different people at one point in time. Confirmation of the result would be strongest with longitudinal studies, which look at the same women before and after machinery is introduced. To my knowledge, such studies have not been done.

10. Vanek, "Time Spent," 119.

Cowan, *More Work.*

11. See Vanek, "Time Spent," p. 119. After a promising existence in the early part of the century, the neighborhood laundry was wiped out by competition from do-it-yourself. Heidi Hartmann has argued that commercial laundries lost this competition because the companies that made the washing and drying machines were large and monopolized, hence more powerful than the small retail establishments that dominated the field. See Hartmann's Ph.D. thesis, "Capitalism and Women's Work in the Home, 1900–1930" (Yale University, 1974).

12. On the colonial period, see Alice Morse Earle, *Home Life in Colonial Days* (Middle Village, N.Y.: Jonathan David, 1975), 255.

Until the 1920s and 30s, most households lacked indoor plumbing. All water brought in had to be taken out. Laundry was done once a week and was an arduous, all-day task. See Cowan, *More Work;* or Strasser, *Never Done.*

13. John P. Robinson, Vladimir G. Andreyenkov, and Vasily D. Patrushev, *The Rhythm of Everyday Life* (Boulder, Colo.: Westview Press, 1988), 76, table 4.11. The actual estimate is for one city only—Jackson, Michigan, but is representative of nationwide levels.

14. Gove Hambridge and Dorothy Cooke Hambridge, "Leisure to Live," *Ladies' Home Journal,* 46 (May 1930), 30. Cited in Margolis, *Mothers and Such,* 161.

15. Lawrence Stone, *The Family, Sex, and Marriage in England 1500–1800* (New York: Harper & Row, 1977), 77, 257.

"Waste of time" from Michelle Perrot, ed., *A History of Private Life IV: From the Fires of Revolution to the Great War* (Cambridge, Mass.: Belknap Press, Harvard University Press, 1990), 484–85. According to Perrot, the turning point for cleanliness was as late as 1900.

16. "Once a year" from Margolis, *Mothers and Such,* 115.

Mary Beth Norton, *Liberty's Daughters: The Revolutionary Experience of American Women 1750–1800* (Glenwood, Ill.: Scott, Foresman 1980), 11. See also Barbara Ehrenreich and Deirdre English, *For Her Own Good: 150 Years of the Experts' Advice to Women* (Garden City, N.Y.: Anchor Press/Doubleday, 1978), 129; and Glenna Matthews, *"Just A Housewife": The Rise and Fall of Domesticity in America* (New York: Oxford University Press, 1987), chap. 1.

Cowan, *More Work,* 24.

17. Jacqueline Jones, *Labor of Love, Labor of Sorrow: Black Women, Work and the Family* (New York: Vintage Books, 1985), 86.

18. Christine Stansell, *City of Women: Sex and Class in New York* (New York: Alfred A. Knopf, 1986), 47–49.

19. Harvey Green, *The Light of the Home: An Intimate View of the Lives of Women in Victorian America* (New York: Pantheon, 1983), 75–76.

20. Cowan, *More Work,* 21, on one-pot dishes.

    Laura Shapiro, *Perfection Salad: Women and Cooking at the Turn of the Century* (New York: Farrar, Straus & Giroux, 1986), 3.

21. Historian Phillipe Aries goes so far as to argue that parents were "indifferent" to their children. See his *Centuries of Childhood: A Social History of Family Life* (New York: Alfred A. Knopf, 1962).

    Neglect by wetnurses is believed to be responsible for the fact that an infant's chance of survival with a wetnurse was only half as great as with its biological mother. A major cause of wetnursing was apparently husbands' demands for the sexual services (which were prohibited during lactation) of their wives. See Stone, *Family, Sex and Marriage,* 81, 427.

    Ibid; see especially chaps. 2 and 5.

    Quote on rocking of infants cited in Ann Dally, *Inventing Motherhood: The Consequences of an Ideal* (New York: Schocken Books, 1983), 65.

    Historians have also argued that sadistic behavior by adults was far more common and socially acceptable than today. Beatings were common, as were psychological abuses, such as locking children in closets. For a chilling description of the "nightmare" of the history of childhood, see Lloyd deMause, "The Evolution of Childhood," in deMause, ed., *The History of Childhood* (New York: The Psychohistory Press, 1974), 1–74. See also Stone, *Family, Sex and Marriage,* 666–71; Dally, *Inventing Motherhood;* and Margolis, *Mothers and Such.* Not surprisingly, these conclusions remain controversial.

22. See Stone, *Family, Sex and Marriage,* 473–76.

23. Quoted in P. E. Razzell and R. W. Wainwright, *The Victorian Working Class: Selections from Letters to the Morning Chronicle* (London: Frank Cass, 1973). Quoted from a letter on the condition of the rural poor, 1849–50.

24. Joseph E. Illick, "Child-Rearing in Seventeenth-Century England and America," in deMause, ed., *History of Childhood,* 324–25. See also Stone, *Family, Sex and Marriage,* 70.

    See Dally, *Inventing Motherhood.*

25. See Illick, "Child-Rearing," and Stone, *Family, Sex and Marriage,* 427, 430. For a critique of the oft-repeated view that wetnursing was not practiced in the United States, see John F. Walzer, "A Period of Ambivalence: Eighteenth-Century American Childhood," in deMause, *History of Childhood,* 352–57.

    "Motherhood" quote from Jessie Bernard, *The Future of Motherhood* (New York: Dial Press, 1974), 7.

26. Ruth Schwartz Cowan, "Two Washes in the Morning and a Bridge Party at Night: The American Housewife between the Wars," *Women's Studies,* 3 (1976): 166–67. Improved sanitation contributed to well-being for adults as

well. While not all this additional housekeeping had a hygienic purpose, the general improvement in standards had clear consequences: death and disease were kept at bay more effectively in the new, cleaner environment.

27. C. Northcote Parkinson, *Parkinson's Law and Other Studies in Administration* (Boston: Houghton-Mifflin, 1957), 2. Parkinson's book actually begins with the example of a woman who takes all morning to write a simple note. He does not discuss housework, but see Margolis, *Mothers and Such*, who does.

  See Maxine Margolis's study of hints from Heloise. Margolis finds that the hints are all time using, not saving. See Margolis, "In Hartford, Hannibal, and (New) Hampshire, Heloise Is Hardly Helpful," *Ms.*, 9 (June 1976): 28–36.

28. Claudia Goldin, *Understanding the Gender Gap: An Economic History of American Women* (New York: Oxford University Press, 1990), 162, table 6.1.

29. On the family, or male breadwinner wage, see Wally Seccombe, "Patriarchy Stabilized: The Construction of the Male Breadwinner Wage Norm in Nineteenth-Century Britain," *Social History*, 2, 1 (January 1986): 53–76; and Jonathan Hacker, "Interpreting the Dual Oppression of Women Workers: The Women's Trade Union League and the Development of the Family Wage Economy," unpublished thesis, Harvard College, April 1990.

30. A study of one city found that 56 percent of families had kept boarders in either 1851 or 1861. An 1855 New York state census found that 40 percent of working women sampled in two poor districts were employed as "outside" seamstresses. Many were married women. See Stansell, *City of Women*, 114, and 225, table 1. See also Marjorie Abel and Nancy Folbre, "A Methodology for Revising Estimates: Female Market Participation in the U.S. Before 1940," *Historical Methods*, 23 (Fall 1990): 167–76.

31. Robert S. Lynd and Helen Merrell Lynd, *Middletown in Transition: A Study in Cultural Conflicts* (New York: Harcourt, Brace, 1929), 27, 181.

  "Pardoxical expectations" from Daniel T. Rodgers, *The Work Ethic in Industrial America 1850–1920* (Chicago: University of Chicago Press, 1978), 202–8.

32. Participation rates from Winifred Wandersee, *Women's Work and Family Values, 1920–1940* (Cambridge, Mass.: Harvard University Press, 1981), 68, table 4.1.

  Strasser, in *Never Done*, discusses the progressive elimination of opportunities for women to earn income inside the home.

33. A comparison with market wages does not eliminate the artificial devaluation of women's time: discrimination in the labor market (again by reducing its opportunity cost) has the effect of undervaluing their labor at home.

34. See, for example, the works previously cited by Ehrenreich and English, Margolis, Strasser, Matthews, Shapiro, and Dally. Ruth Cowan is a prominent exception, as she focuses much more heavily on technological change itself. This literature has slighted the question of whether the experts were successful in their mission. Were floors washed more frequently because women's magazines warned of germs? Did ordinary women follow the elab-

orate instructions of a Lillian Gilbreth on time-saving in the home? (Lillian Gilbreth was a leading follower of Frederick Winslow Taylor, who attempted to apply his principles, *tout court*, to the home.) Or was the fate of domestic science similar to that of "scientific management" itself? Despite a great deal of attention scientific management had a limited impact on U.S. workplaces.

35. "Lysol" and "Grapenuts" from Stuart Ewen, *Captains of Consciousness: Advertising and the Social Roots of the Consumer Culture* (New York: McGraw-Hill, 1976), 170, 173–74.

   Floor polish from Roland Marchand, *Advertising the American Dream: Making Way for Modernity 1920–1940* (Berkeley: University of California Press, 1985), 171.

36. See Daniel Rodgers for a discussion of the work ethic. Paradoxically, feminism may have also undermined the value of the housewife's work and leisure. Middle-class feminists who were suffocating in domestic settings attacked the banality, superfluity, and irrelevancy of their lives. They demanded productive work—that is, the kind men did. See Rodgers, *Work Ethic,* chap. 7.

   Arlie Hochschild's *The Second Shift: Working Parents and the Revolution at Home* (New York: Viking Penguin, 1989), catalogues the resentment created by the fact that employed women's total hours tend to be longer than their husbands'.

   Strasser, *Never Done,* 240, on the moral obligation.

   In the 1920s males aged twenty-five to sixty-four worked about 53 hours a week. John D. Owen, *Working Lives: The American Work Force Since 1920* (Lexington, Mass.: Lexington Books, 1986), 13, table 2–2. These figures are not strictly comparable because they are for all males, not husbands only.

37. For the view that women act as "unpaid domestic servants," see Heidi Hartmann, "Capitalism, Patriarchy, and Job Segregation by Sex," *Signs,* 1, 3 (Spring 1976): 137–69.

38. At the margin, the additional services had no cost to the husband. He "pays" only a lump sum, the fraction of his income consumed by his wife, which does not vary with the services she produces.

   Some would argue that housework was unpaid because women's labor has been less valued and less appreciated than men's. Many scholars have argued that this devaluation was exacerbated by the growth of industrial capitalism. By this account, the colonial economy operated with a more palpable symmetry between men and women, as they toiled together on family farms. The wife's contribution to the family was socially recognized as valuable—indeed, necessary for survival. Her work was physically demanding and produced tangible products such as clothing and food. Although she was not directly remunerated for her efforts, neither was her husband paid for much of what he did. Both would typically orient a portion of their labor to the market; the remainder was consumed by the family. As men moved out into the market economy, the status of women who were left behind sank markedly. For this interpretation, see Strasser, *Never Done.*

In this account, the household is seen as a vestigial institution, whose essential productive functions have been taken over by the capitalist core of the economy. Women once made clothing, butter, buttons, candles, soap, and medicines; they grew and prepared food. Today the market economy does virtually all these things. The housewife is involved at only the last stages, if at all. Butchering an animal in order to make the family supper appears far more productive, and *economic,* than popping a store-bought meal in and out of the microwave. On the other hand, a plausible case can be made that women's labor had been held in low esteem for centuries, and that the growth of the market merely transformed the conditions under which she worked. Whichever version one chooses, the general import is similar: household labor received no wage because it was socially devalued.

39. Dolores Hayden, *The Grand Domestic Revolution: A History of Feminist Designs for American Homes, Neighborhoods, and Cities* (Cambridge, Mass.: The MIT Press, 1981). *Ladies' Home Journal* quotation on frontispiece, chap. 1; Gilman quote, p. 16.

   Quoted in Hayden, *Domestic Revolution,* 195–96, from Gilman, "Why Cooperative Housekeeping Fails," *Harper's Bazaar,* 41 (July 1907): 629.

40. And then again, business may not have preferred this outcome. Advocates of this view generally fail to recognize that private housekeeping put whole areas of service production out of the reach of business. On the other hand, they have argued that the sale of appliances and products was more profitable than commercialization of services would have been. For the view that the needs of capitalism dominated these choices, see Strasser, *Never Done.*

   On privacy, see Cowan, *More Work,* 149–50.

41. Margolis, *Mothers and Such,* 174–75, on appliances.

   Giedion, *Mechanization*, on kitchen design.

42. This result is not exactly comparable because it does not correct for the number of children or include only married women, but is just for employed women. My nonemployed category has a four-hour-a-week decline from 1973 to 1987; Robinson's has a six-hour decline. See John P. Robinson, "Trends in American's Use of Time: Some Preliminary 1965–1975–1985 Comparisons," mimeo, 1986, University of Maryland, Survey Research Center, p. 36, table 5.

43. For earlier studies, see Heidi Hartmann, "The Family as a Locus of Gender, Class and Political Struggle: The Example of Housework," *Signs,* 6, 3 (1981): 366–94.

   Quotes from Martin Meissner et al., "No Exit for Wives: Sexual Division of Labour and the Cumulation of Household Demands in Canada," in R. E. Pahl, ed., *On Work: Historical, Comparative and Theoretical Approaches* (Oxford: Basil Blackwell, 1988), 493–94.

   On father's child-care time, see Harriet Presser, "Can We Make Time for Children? The Economy, Work Schedules, and Child Care," *Demography,* 26, 11 (November 1989): 523–44.

   John P. Robinson, "Who's Doing the Housework?" *American Demographics,* 10, 12 (December 1988): 24–28.

44. This is according to a mid-1980s poll. Among all women, 41 percent reported they do all household chores, 41 percent say they do a lot and their husbands help some, 15 percent report equal division and 2 percent say husbands do more. Among employed wives, 24 percent do all, 42 percent say they do the bulk but the husbands help some, 28 percent report equal sharing, and 5 percent say husbands do more. Greater sharing is more common among those who are under thirty and college-educated. See Louis Harris, *Inside America* (New York: Vintage, 1987), 98–99.

Chapter 5. The Insidious Cycle of Work-and-Spend

1. Data from the comprehensive international survey of time use. John P. Robinson, Philip E. Converse, and Alexander Szalai, "Everyday Life in Twelve Countries;" and Alexander Szalai, ed., *The Use of Time: Daily Activities of Urban and Suburban Populations in Twelve Countries* (The Hague: Mouton, 1972). My comparison is among Western European countries (Belgium, France, and West Germany) and the United States, for which daily shopping minutes are 6, 6, 3, and 18, respectively. Shopping excludes food marketing. See p. 114, table 1.
2. Popularity of shopping from Decision Research Corporation, "1990 Leisure Study: Trends in America's Leisure Time and Activities" (Lexington, Mass., February 1990), 8.

    Data on shopping centers from *Statistical Abstract of the United States,* U.S. Department of Commerce (Washington, D.C.: Government Printing Office, 1990), 775, table 1368.
3. Quote on South Street Seaport from W. S. Kowinski, "A Mall Covers the Waterfront," *The New York Times Magazine,* 13 December 1981, 112.

    Ronald L. Krannich et al., *Shopping in Exciting Australia and Papua New Guinea* (Virginia: Impact, 1989).
4. Quote on credit card debt from Katy Butler, "The Great Boomer Bust," *Mother Jones,* 14, 5 (June 1989): 35.

    Linda Weltner, "Once a Shopping Addict, She's Got a Brand New Bag," *Boston Globe,* 16 November 1990, 50.
5. Figures calculated from *Statistical Abstract of the United States,* U.S. Department of Commerce (Washington, D.C.: Government Printing Office, 1989), 748, table 1321.
6. For the argument that personal consumption was not unusually high during the 1980s relative to earlier decades, see Robert A. Blecker, *Are Americans on a Consumption Binge? The Evidence Reconsidered* (Washington, D.C.: Economic Policy Institute, 1990). A key difference from earlier postwar decades is that consumption has been more highly concentrated among high-income groups.

    On the long-term change, consider that, in 1947, the bottom quintile of the income distribution for families ended at roughly $5,000 (in 1984 dollars); in

1984, the figure was $12,500. For comparisons of the two income distributions, see Frank Levy, *Dollars and Dreams: The Changing American Income Distribution* (New York: W. W. Norton, 1988), 20, table 2.3, and 40, table 3.5.

7. Data on housing size from Witold Rybczynski, "Living Smaller," *Atlantic Monthly* (February 1991): 67–68.

Rooms per person from Stanley Lebergott, *The American Economy: Income, Wealth and Want* (Princeton, N.J.: Princeton University Press, 1976), 94–95.

8. Data on running water and flush toilets from Lebergott, *American Economy,* 98–99; on number of bathrooms, see Rybczynski, "Living Smaller," 68.

Refrigerator data for 1940 from Lebergott, *American Economy,* 101. Other data (for 1953) are from *Statistical Abstract,* 1971, 677, table 1117; and *Statistical Abstract,* 1989, 723, table 1280. These data exclude homes without electricity.

9. Home ownership statistics for 1940 and 1950 from *Statistical Abstract,* 1990, 720, table 1274. Data for 1989 from Lawrence Mishel and David M. Frankel, *The State of Working America* (Armonk, N.Y.: M. E. Sharpe, 1990–91), 224, table 8.1.

Ownership rates for two-person households are calculated from United States Department of Labor Press Release, no. 90–96, "Consumer Expenditures in 1988," November 1990, 13, table 6. The exact figure is 70.5 percent.

Families with automobiles in 1935 from Lebergott, *American Economy,* 103. Current figure from *Statistical Abstract,* 1990, 723, table 1280. This is the fraction of households with motor vehicles. Average vehicles per household is from USDL Press Release 90–96, p. 2, table A.

VCR data are from Decision Research Corporation, *Decision Research Corporation's 1990 Leisure Study: Trends in America's Leisure Time and Activities* (Lexington, Mass., 1990), 13. Television data from *Statistical Abstract,* 1990 edition, 723, table 1280.

Services expenditures calculated from *Economic Report of the President* (Washington, D.C.: Government Printing Office, 1988), tables B–2 and B–32.

10. Isabel Wilkerson, "Middle-Class Blacks Try to Grip a Ladder While Lending a Hand," *New York Times,* 26 November 1990.

Figure of 37 percent of Americans with college education from *Statistical Abstract,* 1990, 134, table 217.

11. George Gallup, *The Gallup Poll,* 28 June 1989, pp. 146–51.

12. On recent inequality, see Barry Bluestone and Bennett Harrison, *The Great U-Turn* (New York: Basic Books, 1988).

Gallup, *The Gallup Poll,* 1989.

13. A number of polls ask identical questions, yet give different levels of happiness. For example, the General Social Survey polls yield consistently higher results than the Survey Research Center or the National Opinion Research Corporation. SRC and NORC polls end in the 1970s; the GSS poll continues through the 1980s. The conclusion that "very happy" has not recovered is based on the GSS poll, which begins in 1972 and is the only poll still being

taken during the 1980s. The GSS peaks in 1973 and does not recover throughout the 1980s. See Richard G. Niemi, John Mueller, and Tom W. Smith, *Trends
in Public Opinion: A Compendium of Survey Data* (New York: Greenwood
Press, 1989), 290, table 15.1.

14. Louis Harris, *Inside America* (New York: Vintage, 1987), 148.

15. Paul S. Hewitt, "Something's Gone Terribly Wrong with Being 'Rich'," *Los
Angeles Herald Tribune*, 7 January 1989.

   Hollywood executive from Andrew Tobias, "Getting By on $100,000 a
Year," *Esquire* (23 May 1978): 24.

   New Yorker from ibid., 21

   Brooke Kroeger, "Feeling Poor on $600,000 a Year," *New York Times*, 26
April 1987.

16. Obeys' position in income distribution calculated from Mishel and Frankel,
Working America, 25, table 1.10.

   Quote from Tom Coakley, "One Couple's Lament Captures Anti-tax Mood,"
Boston Globe, 2 February 1990, p. 1.

17. Butler, "Great Boomer Bust," 34, 37.

18. See the discussion in chap. 3.

   On the United States, see Herbert Gutman, *Work, Culture and Society in
Industrializing America* (New York: Vintage, 1977). See also the discussion
of the 1925 Consumer League of New York study in Benjamin Hunnicutt,
Work Without End: Abandoning Shorter Hours for the Right to Work (Philadelphia: Temple University Press, 1988), 68–69, where respondents displayed
strong preferences for leisure.

   On the anthropological evidence, see Marshall Sahlins, *Stone Age Economics* (New York: Aldine, 1972).

19. See Neil McKendrick, John Brewer, and J. H. Plumb, *The Birth of a Consumer
Society: The Commercialization of Eighteenth-Century England* (London:
Europa Publications, 1982); and Arjun Appadurai, "Technology and the Reproduction of Values in Rural Western India," in Frédérique Apffel-Marglin
and Stephen A. Marglin, eds., *Dominating Knowledge: Development, Culture,
and Resistance* (Oxford: Clarendon Press, 1990), 185–216.

20. Winifred D. Wandersee, *Women's Work and Family Values, 1920–1940*
(Cambridge, Mass.: Harvard University Press, 1981), 7–8.

21. On the Yale study, see ibid., 10, table 1.1, and 21–22.

   On the Berkeley study, see Jessica Peixotto, *Getting and Spending at the
Professional Standard of Living* (New York: Macmillan, 1927). Data from
chapter 6.

22. Roland Marchand, *Advertising the American Dream: Making Way for Modernity* (Berkeley: University of California Press, 1985), 4, 5.

23. Ibid.

24. John Kenneth Galbraith, *The Affluent Society*, 4th ed. (Boston: Houghton
Mifflin, 1984), 127.

   Marchand, *Advertising the American Dream*, chap. 5.

25. Hunnicutt, *Work Without End,* 38.

   Allen quoted in ibid., 45.

26. The "savior" phrase is Thomas Cochran's, cited in Hunnicutt, *Work Without End,* 44.

   Charles F. Kettering, "Keep the Consumer Dissatisfied," *Nation's Business,* January 1929; "organized creation," Marchand, *Advertising the American Dream,* 156.

   Marchand, *Advertising the American Dream,* 158, and Hunnicutt, *Work Without End,* chap. 2.

27. From an ILGWU pamphlet cited in Hunnicutt, *Work Without End,* 75.

28. Ibid., 94.

29. Galbraith, *Affluent Society,* 127.

30. This conclusion is from John Owen, *Working Lives: The American Work Force Since 1920* (Lexington, Mass.: Lexington Books, 1986), 23.

31. On "mesmerization," see Stuart Ewen and Elizabeth Ewen, *Channels of Desire: Mass Images and the Shaping of American Consciousness* (New York: McGraw-Hill, 1982).

   From a Steinway ad cited in Marchand, *Advertising the American Dream,* 142.

32. John Maynard Keynes, "Economic Possibilities for Our Grandchildren," in *Essays in Persuasion* (New York: Harcourt, Brace, 1932), 365.

   The classic statement of the importance of relative consumption was made in 1949 by Harvard economist James Duesenberry in *Income, Saving and the Theory of Consumer Behavior* (Cambridge, Mass.: Harvard University Press, 1949). Unfortunately, the ideas put forward in this pioneering work have not been adequately tested and pursued. For further discussion of these issues, in addition to Duesenberry, see the works of Tibor Scitovsky, Richard Easterlin, Fred Hirsch, and Robert Frank.

   Investment banker from Brooke Kroeger, "Feeling Poor," p. 8.

33. In a Prisoner's Dilemma, both partners would be made better off if they cooperated, but failure to do so leads both to be worse off. This point has been made by Robert H. Frank in *Choosing the Right Pond* (New York: Oxford University Press, 1985), 133–35.

34. Galbraith calls this "the dependence effect"; Scitovsky, the difference between "pleasure" (what one gets at first) and "comfort" (the sensation after habituation).

35. This passage from Jonathan Freedman, the author of a book on happiness, describes the syndrome: "As a student, I lived on what now seems no money at all, but I lived in a style which seemed perfectly fine . . . As my income has grown since then, I have spent more . . . but it has always seemed to be just about the same amount of money and bought just about the same things. The major change is that I have spent more on everything, and I consider buying more expensive items. None of this has had an appreciable effect on my life or on my feelings of happiness or satisfaction. I imagine that if I earned five

times as much, the same would be true—at least it would once I got used to the extra money. This is not to say that I would turn down a raise—quite the contrary. But after a while everything would settle down, the extra money would no longer be 'extra,' and my life would be the same as before." From *Happy People* (New York: Harcourt, Brace, Jovanovich, 1978), 140.

36. Paul Wachtel, *The Poverty of Affluence: A Psychological Portrait of the American Way of Life* (Philadelphia: New Society Publishers, 1989), 39.

37. George H. Gallup, *The Gallup Poll: Public Opinion* (New York: Random House, 1989), 55–58.

Second survey is MassMutual American Family Values Study (Washington, D.C.: Mellman & Lazarus, 1989), 20.

"Less emphasis" poll from George H. Gallup, *The Gallup Poll*, 1988, 180–81.

38. *Economic Report of the President* (Washington, D.C.: Government Printing Office), 1991 ed., p. 316, table B–26, 1990 figure. My interpretation suggests that the U.S. savings rate is low at least in part because of the consumerism I have described. The international data are consistent with this view: household savings rates in the United States are low by comparative international standards. See Katri Kosonen, "Saving and Economic Growth in a Nordic Perspective," in Jukka Pekkarinen, Matti Pohjola, and Bob Rowthorn, *Social Corporatism: A Superior System?* (Oxford: Clarendon Press, 1991). For a discussion of theories of saving, including a perspective that is a counterpart to my arguments, see Stephen A. Marglin, *Growth, Distribution, and Prices* (Cambridge, Mass.: Harvard University Press, 1984), chaps. 17–18.

39. In neoclassical theory there is no alternative notion of well-being than preferences.

40. Although the idea of adjusting, or endogenous, preferences is not new, almost no economists have pursued it. A prominent exception is Herbert Gintis. See his "Welfare Criteria with Endogenous Preferences: The Economics of Education," *International Economic Review*, 15, 4 (June 1974): 415–30, which examines the implications of this idea for standard conclusions of welfare economics.

41. In the first study, 27 percent said they could work less but not more, 15 percent could work more but not less, and 43 percent could work neither more nor less. Shulamit Kahn and Kevin Lang, "Constraints on the Choice of Work Hours: Agency vs. Specific-Capital," National Bureau of Economic Research Working Paper 2238, May 1987, p. 14.

The second study is by Robert Moffitt, "The Tobit Model, Hours of Work, and Institutional Constraints," *Review of Economics and Statistics*, 64, 3 (August 1982): 510–15. Moffitt's sample is low-income, married, prime-aged males with children. This is a recent literature, and to date most of it looks at men.

For other evidence, see John Ham, "Estimation of a Labour Supply Model with Censoring Due to Unemployment and Underemployment," *Review of*

Economic Studies, 49, 3 (July 1982): 335–54; Joseph Altonji and Christina H. Paxson, "Labor Supply Preferences, Hours Constraints, and Hours-Wage Tradeoffs," *Journal of Labor Economics,* 6, 2 (1988): 254–76, "Labor Supply, Hours Constraints and Job Mobility," Working Paper 271, Industrial Relations Section, Princeton University, September, 1990, and "Hours-Wage Tradeoffs and Job Mobility," Working Paper 199, Industrial Relations Section, Princeton University, 1985; Alan L. Gustmann and Thomas L. Steinmeier "Minimum Hours Constraints and Retirement Behavior," *Contemporary Policy Issues,* a supplement to *Economic Inquiry,* 3 (April 1982): 77–91, and "Partial Retirement and the Analysis of Retirement Behavior," *Industrial and Labor Relations Review,* 37, 3 (April 1984): 403–15; M. Arellano and C. Meghir, "Labour Supply and Hours Constraints," Applied Economics Discussion Paper 26, (1987), Institute of Economics and Statistics, Oxford University. Neoclassical theory assumes that a wide range of schedules will be available if workers desire them. One study (again of men) tested this assumption by predicting the hours that workers would choose in the absence of constraints. According to the predictions, there should be a substantial number of jobs at every level of hours. But the actual distribution is very different: workers are clustered in the range of 35 to 45 hours per week. In fact, the market offers little else. Particularly in the area of 20 to 35 hours, desires are not accommodated. See William Dickens and Shelly J. Lundberg, "Hours Restrictions and Labor Supply," Working Paper 1638, National Bureau of Economic Research, 1985.

42. The Altonji and Paxson papers show that job changes are associated with changes in hours. See citations in note 41.

Samuelson quote from Chicago Tribune, 9 December 1971, section 1A, p. 7, quoted in Sar A. Levitan and Richard S. Belous, *Shorter Hours, Shorter Weeks* (Baltimore: Johns Hopkins University Press, 1977), 26–27.

There is a large literature, from a variety of perspectives, on the point that labor markets favor employers. For a classic statement, see John Maynard Keynes's *The General Theory of Employment, Interest and Money* (London: Macmillan, 1936). More recent treatments take a different perspective, but reach similar conclusions. The reader may consult Herbert Gintis, "The Nature of the Labor Exchange," *Review of Radical Political Economics,* 8 (1976), 36–54; and Samuel Bowles, "The Production Process in a Competitive Economy: Walrasian, Neo-Hobbesian, and Marxian models," *American Economic Review,* 75 (1985): 16–36.

In the end, common sense may provide the strongest case against the neoclassicals. And common sense points to the vigorous resistance of business to reductions in hours. This resistance is just not consistent with the neoclassical story. If firms do the adjusting, why do they oppose requests for shorter hours? What can account for such a high degree of conflict—the strikes, the violence, the bitterness—that accompanied the century of declining hours? Why did advocates of shorter hours find it necessary to petition the state for legislation to accomplish their goals?

The neoclassical claim that workers were really fighting for wage increases is not a satisfactory one, for a number of reasons. First, even when workers were prepared to accept less pay for less work, employers have often been unwilling to go along. Second, and more important, the history of conflict over hours has been fraught with ambiguity on the question of pay. Far from advocating increased wages, workers often undertook these struggles without knowing what would happen to their incomes. Even after settlements had been reached or legislation had been passed, the issue of payment was often left unresolved. In the eight-hour-day struggle, very few workers gained reduced hours without loss in earnings. While some campaigns were crystal clear (the 1930s cry for thirty hours for forty hours pay), others (the ten- and eight-hour-day movements) were comparatively mute on the question of remuneration.

This ambiguity suggests a final objection to the neoclassical claim that workers were really interested in money, and not time: Why did they go through such a convoluted process? Why couldn't they just ask for what they wanted, instead of demanding what they did not want, in hopes that it might lead to what they actually desired? Especially within the confines of neoclassical theory, where workers choose and firms respond, this explanation ultimately makes little sense. It is difficult to avoid the conclusion that the struggles over working hours occurred *because* the market did not deliver what workers wanted. The very thing that firms refused to do was accommodate. It was only when workers left the market and took to the streets that they were able to get their employers to respond. Recent claims that hours struggles were a result of heterogeneity of workers' preferences are also unconvincing. If this had been the case, it should have resulted in different firms operating different schedules, rather than the high degree of uniformity that is observed.

43. Susan E. Shank, "Preferred Hours of Work and Corresponding Earnings," *Monthly Labor Review* (November 1986): 41, table 1. The survey asked the following question: "If you had a choice, would you prefer to work: (1) the same number of hours and earn the same money? (2) fewer hours at the same rate of pay and earn less money? or (3) more hours at the same rate of pay and earn more money?" Sixty-five percent chose the first option. The remainder were split four to one toward longer worktime, but it must be remembered that many of those who desired more hours were underemployed. Earlier polls by Louis Harris and George Katona yielded similar results.

44. See Wachtel, *Poverty of Affluence*. On adaptation theory, see Harry Helson, *Adaptation Level Theory: An Experimental and Systematic Approach to Behavior* (New York: Harper & Row, 1964).

45. These findings have been supported by psychologists. For example, Professors Daniel Kahneman of the University of California at Berkeley and Amos Tversky of Stanford University have found that people exhibit a strong aversion to the *loss* of income, which is not replicated in the case where they are presented with the forfeiture of income gains. Whether loss aversion extends

beyond income to "goods" such as leisure is as yet unknown (personal communication).

46. Robert Half International, "Family Time Is More Important Than Rapid Career Advancement: Survey Shows Both Men and Women Support Parent Tracking," San Francisco, 28 June 1989, p. 4.

   European workers have similar preferences about future income tradeoffs. In a 1977 survey, when given a choice between increased pay and shorter working time, half opted for time and 36 to 45 percent for income. But unlike their American counterparts, European workers have actually received increases in free time. A key difference is that European workers are much more unionized and their unions are more powerful. They have also made reduced worktime a priority—and lobbied hard with employers and governments. See Daniel Yankelovich et al., *The World at Work* (New York: Octagon Books, 1985), 310, table III–46.

47. For a discussion of this disillusionment, see Amy Saltzman, *Downshifting: Reinventing Success on a Slower Track* (New York: HarperCollins, 1991).

48. MassMutual Family Values Study. Forty-six percent of the respondents in this study reported that they "spend too little time with their families," 3.

49. Rate of part-timers calculated from Current Population Survey data.

   In the Panel Survey of Income Dynamics 58 percent of males say that they cannot reduce their hours at all. See Kahn and Lang, "Constraints," 14.

50. Median wage rate from Mishel and Frankel, *Working America,* 79, table 3.6.

   Eighty percent of part-timers are paid by the hour. Earl F. Mellor and Steven E. Haugen, "Hourly Paid Workers: Who They Are and What They Earn," *Monthly Labor Review* (February 1986): 21–22, tables 1 and 2.

   Health insurance data pertain to those who work 19 or fewer hours a week. Diane S. Rothberg and Barbara Ensor Cook, *Employee Benefits for Part-Timers,* 2nd ed. (McLean, Va.: Association of Part-Time Professionals, 1987), 6, table 4. Among workers at 20 to 29 hours, 49 percent have medical benefits.

51. Quoted in Peter T. Kilborn, "For Many Women, One Job Just Isn't Enough," *New York Times,* 15 February 1990.

52. For the most part, economists have considered utility in terms of material goods and services, and this is typically the context in which *homo economicus* is discussed. In theory, a utility function can be defined over anything—not only material goods, but also "nonpecuniary" ones. However, because these are often nonmeasurable, these predictions can become unfalsifiable. At times, recourse to these nonpecuniary goods has bordered on the tautological.

53. On the "Zen" path see such writers as Mohandas K. Gandhi, E. F. Schumacher, and Marshall Sahlins.

   Sahlins, *Stone Age Economics,* 2.

   Edward F. Schumacher, *Small Is Beautiful: Economics as If People Mattered* (New York: Harper & Row, 1973), 57.

54. These are original meanings from the *Oxford English Dictionary*. This point was originally made by Raymond Williams. The reader will also recall that

"consumption" was a common term for tuberculosis. An eventual meaning of "consumer" distinguishes between producer and consumer. *Oxford English Dictionary*, compact ed. (Oxford: Oxford University Press, 1971), 532.

55. Weltner, *Shopping Addict*.

For an explanation of how and why global inequality can be better addressed, see my "Working Hours and Global Inequality," *World Development*, 19, 1 (January 1991): 73–84.

Chapter 6. Exiting the Squirrel Cage

1. Jacques Le Goff, "The Crisis of Labor Time," in *Time, Work and Culture in the Middle Ages* (Chicago: Chicago University Press, 1980), 44. Time consciousness also contributed to the development of capitalism. There was a two-way causality between economic advancement and time consciousness. See E. P. Thompson, "Time, Work-Discipline and Industrial Capitalism," *Past and Present*, 38 (December 1967): 56–97; Nigel Thrift, "Owner's Time and Own Time: The Making of a Capitalist Time Consciousness, 1300–1880," *Lund Studies in Human Geography*, 48 (1984): 56–84; and Christopher Hill, *Society and Puritanism in Pre-Revolutionary England* (New York: Schocken Books, 1964).

2. In his classic article, British historian Edward Thompson summarized the transformation that occurred with the growth of capitalism. At first workers struggled against time; they resisted the idea that they were selling their time. Eventually "the workers begin to fight, not against time, but about it. . . . They had accepted the categories of their employers and learned to fight back within them. They had learned their lesson, that time is money, only too well." Thompson, "Time, Work-Discipline," 85–86.

3. Neoclassical economics equates time and money.

4. See David R. Roediger and Philip S. Foner, *Our Own Time: A History of American Labor and the Working Class* (London: Verso, 1989), 3–4.

5. Victor Fuchs and Joyce P. Jacobsen, "Employee Response to Compulsory Short-Time Work," National Bureau of Economic Research Working Paper 2089, December 1986, 10, table 2.

6. Laurie Sheridan survey, "Interviews on Working Hours," unpublished mimeo.

7. Stephen J. Trejo, "Compensating Differentials and Overtime Pay Regulation," Working Paper 2–89, Department of Economics, University of California at Santa Barbara, January 1989.

8. Ann Harriman, *The Work/Leisure Trade Off: Reduced Work Time for Managers and Professionals* (New York: Praeger, 1982), 78, 98–99.

9. Sheridan, "Interviews."

10. This analysis abstracts from inflation. The firm's pay increase is in real terms. If there were inflation, the numbers would be adjusted upward to account for it.

Linda Weltner, "Once a Shopping Addict, She's Got a Brand New Bag," *Boston Globe*, 16 November 1990, p. 50.

11. Barbara Moorman and Barney Olmsted, "V-Time: A New Way to Work" (San Francisco: New Ways to Work, 1985).

Of those surveyed in the 1978 survey, 47.3 percent said they would trade all of a 10-percent pay raise for additional free time; 11.6 percent wanted to trade 70 percent; 25.4 percent chose 40 percent; and 15.4 percent were unwilling to trade off any future income. See Fred Best, *Exchanging Earnings for Leisure: Findings of an Exploratory National Survey on Work Time Preferences* (Washington, D.C.: United States Employment and Training Administration, 1980), 77, table 6 (reproduced here as table 5.3).

1989 poll is Robert Half International, "Family Time Is More Important than Rapid Career Advancement: Survey Shows Both Men and Women Support Parent Tracking," San Francisco, 28 June 1989, 4–5.

12. Sheridan, "Interviews."

13. Cited in André Gorz, *A Critique of Economic Reason* (London: Verso, 1989), 117–18.

14. Quote cited in William McGaughey, Jr., "The International Dimensions of Reduced Hours," *Society for the Reduction of Human Labor Newsletter,* 1 (1): 6.

Sally Solo, "Stop Whining and Get Back to Work," *Fortune,* 12 March 1990, p. 49.

15. Roediger and Foner, *Our Own Time,* 23. The quote is from *The Working Man's Advocate,* 7 April 1832.

16. Japanese hours in 1987 were 2,111, compared with my estimate for U.S. workers of 1,949. Hideo Takahashi, "The Long Workweek in Japan: Difficult to Reduce," *Japan Economic Institute Report,* 11A (Washington, D.C., 1990), 2, table 1, and 6–7.

For manufacturing, author's estimates from Bureau of Labor Statistics, Office of Productivity and Technology, "Underlying Data for Indexes of Output per Hour, Hourly Compensation, and Unit Labor Costs in Manufacturing, Twelve Industrial Countries, 1950–1988," unpublished, June 1989.

17. Bureau of Labor Statistics, Office of Productivity and Technology, "Hourly Compensation Costs for Production Workers, 40 Manufacturing Industries, 34 Countries, 1975 and 1979–89," unpublished data, September 1990. Even U.S. and Japanese wages are converging: in 1975, Japanese wages were 48 percent of U.S. wages; now they are 88 percent.

18. David Sanger, "Tokyo Tries to Find Out If 'Salarymen' Are Working Themselves to Death," *New York Times,* 19 March 1990.

19. Ibid.

20. Productivity study and 1,800 figure from Takahaski, "Long Workweek," 4, 9.

The 1985 poll is cited in Narumi Yamada, "Working Time in Japan: Recent Trends and Issues," *International Labour Review,* 124, 6 (November–December 1985): 704–5

The quotation is from Michael J. Barrett, "The Case for More School Days," *Atlantic Monthly* (November 1990): 80.

21. On job-sharing, see Nan McGuire et al., "Survey of Private Sector Work and Family Policy" (San Francisco: New Ways To Work, 1986), 14.

   On Kellogg, see Benjamin Hunnicutt, "The Short Life of Kellogg's Six-Hour Day—The Death of a Vision," mimeo, University of Iowa. Productivity figure from p. 21; quote from Chapin Hoskins, managing editor of *Forbes,* from a *Forbes* report cited in Hunnicutt on p. 23.

   Kellogg quote from Hunnicutt, "Short Life," p. 33.

22. U.S. cases are from Maureen E. McCarthy and Gail S. Rosenberg, *Work Sharing: Case Studies* (Kalamazoo, Mich.: W. E. Upjohn Institute, 1981). British evidence is from a study of 400 firms reported in Michael White, *Case Studies of Shorter Working Time,* 597 (London: Policy Studies Institute, 1981).

23. Chris Nyland, *Reduced Worktime and the Management of Production* (Cambridge: Cambridge University Press, 1989).

   On management-worker tradeoffs, see the cases in White, *Case Studies.*

   See Nyland, *Reduced Worktime,* on the growing pace of work. Of course, where the pace is already too demanding, an increase is not to be desired because it accelerates an already overaccelerated work environment and can transform time off the job into necessary recuperation. There are workplaces in which a ratcheting down of the pace is called for.

24. Improvements in effort vary with the form of hours reductions—for example, extended periods of time off yield less of an increase.

25. See David I. Levine and Laura D'Andrea Tyson, "Participation, Productivity, and the Firm's Environment," in Alan Blinder, ed., *Paying for Productivity* (Washington, D.C.: Brookings Institution, 1990), 183–244.

26. Sheridan, "Interviews."

   On management attitudes, see Richard Edwards, *Contested Terrain* (New York: Basic Books, 1979); and Shoshanna Zuboff, *In the Age of the Smart Machine* (New York: Basic Books, 1988).

27. Among economists, Herbert Simon's work on bounded rationality is a prominent exception. So are theories that emphasize conflicting interests within the firm—for example, the ability of middle management to block profitable reforms.

   The argument that the length of the workday was inefficient was given by Louis Brandeis and Josephine Goldmark in the debate over Oregon's ten-hour law for women. See also Goldmark's *Fatigue and Efficiency: A Study in Industry* (New York: Charities Publication Committee, 1912), and a recent statistical confirmation of this view in Jeremy Atack and Fred Bateman, "How Long Did People Work in 1880?" mimeo, University of Illinois.

28. Quoted in Harriman, *Work/Leisure Tradeoff,* 107–8.

29. Sheridan, "Interviews."

30. Quote from Harriman, *Work/Leisure Tradeoff,* 109.

   Fuchs and Jacobsen, "Employee Response," 22.

31. All quotes from Ann Landers, *Boston Globe,* 26 February 1990, 37.

32. Gary Burtless, "Are We All Working Too Hard? It's Better Than Watching Oprah," *Wall Street Journal,* 4 January 1990.

33. Harvey Swados, "Less Work—Less Leisure," *The Nation* (22 February 1958): 153–58.

34. Dana Kennedy, "Sexes Agree: Women Face Too Much Pressure," *Boston Globe*, 26 October 1990. Results are from a *Time* magazine/Yankelovich Clancy Shulman poll.

    On "real men," see Daniel Yankelovich, *The World at Work* (New York: Octagon Books, 1985), 139.

35. "Frenzied work ethic" conclusion is from the *Time* magazine/Yankelovich Clancy Shulman poll cited in note 34. See Kennedy, "Sexes Agree," 62.

    On the long-term shift, see Yankelovich, *World at Work;* and Ronald Inglehart, *Culture Shift in Advanced Industrial Society* (Princeton, N.J.: Princeton University Press, 1990).

36. Fuchs and Jacobsen, "Employee Response," 10, table 2.

37. Bureau of Labor Statistics News Release, "Thirty-Eight Million Persons Do Volunteer Work," 29 March 1990. The rate of volunteering fell from 24 percent in 1974 to 20 percent in 1989. An increase in leisure will almost certainly result in a rise of volunteering, given that workers on part-time schedules have much higher rates of volunteering than any other group.

    Boston study is Dianne S. Burden and Bradley Googins, *Boston University Balancing Job and Homelife Study,* mimeo, Boston University, 1987, p. 55.

38. "The Public Perspective: A Roper Center Review of Public Opinion Polling," 1, 4 (May/June 1990): 118.

39. Choices from *The Gallup Report,* 248, May 1986, p. 8.

    On television viewing, see F. Thomas Juster and Frank P. Stafford, "The Allocation of Time: Empirical Findings, Behavioral Models, and Problems of Measurement," Working Paper, Institute for Social Research, University of Michigan, February 1990, p. 9, table 2. Television viewing is higher in the USSR than the United States, but working hours are also higher. The USSR is significantly less well off than other Western industrialized countries, however.

40. Mohammed was interviewed by Katie Abel for a Boston documentary, "Overworked and Out of Time," which aired on "Our Times," WHDH-TV Boston, 14 April 1990.

41. Quote from Henry Goddard Leach, editor of *The Forum and Century,* cited in Hunnicutt, "Kellogg," p. 47.

42. See Gorz, *Critique.*

43. Total hours (market plus nonmarket) for the fully employed labor force were 2,837 in 1987, up 162 hours from 1969. Addition of another 162 would yield 2,999 hours, or 60 per week in a 50-week year (author's estimates).

44. Conference Board estimate cited in Amy Saltzman, *Downshifting: Reinventing Success on a Slower Track* (New York: HarperCollins, 1991), 63.

    Most of these examples are from McCarthy and Rosenberg, *Work Sharing.*

    On corporate executives, Sylvia Ann Hewlett, *When the Bough Breaks: The Cost of Neglecting Our Children* (New York: Basic Books, 1991), preface.

45. Robert Half International, "Family Time," pp. 2, 4. The use of the word salary

may have been problematic. Although the poll did not explicitly target sala-ried, rather than hourly workers, the wording of the question may have imparted a bias to the answers.

46. Saltzman, *Downshifting*.
47. John Kenneth Galbraith, *The Affluent Society*, 4th ed. (Boston: Houghton Mifflin, 1984), chap. 12.

Bibliography

ABEL, MARJORIE, AND FOLBRE, NANCY. "A Methodology for Revising Estimates: Female Market Participation in the U.S. Before 1940." *Historical Methods* 23 (Fall 1990): 167–76.

AKERLOF, GEORGE, AND YELLEN, JANET. *Efficiency Wage Models of the Labor Market.* Cambridge: Cambridge University Press, 1986.

ALTONJI, JOSEPH, AND PAXSON, CHRISTINA H. "Hours-Wage Tradeoffs and Job Mobility." Working Paper 199, Industrial Relations Section, Princeton University, 1985.

———. "Labor Supply Preferences, Hours Constraints, and Hours-Wage Tradeoffs." *Journal of Labor Economics* 6, 2 (1988): 254–76.

ANGIER, NATALIE. "Cheating on Sleep: Modern Life Turns America into the Land of the Drowsy." *New York Times,* 15 May 1990.

APPADURAI, ARJUN. "Technology and the Reproduction of Values in Rural Western India." In Frédérique Apffel-Marglin and Stephen A. Marglin, eds., *Dominating Knowledge: Development, Culture, and Resistance,* pp. 185–216. Oxford: Clarendon Press, 1990.

ARELLANO, M., AND MEGHIR, C. "Labour Supply and Hours Constraints." Applied Economics Discussion Paper, no. 26, Institute of Economics and Statistics, Oxford University, 1987.

ARIES, PHILLIPE. *Centuries of Childhood: A Social History of Family Life.* New York: Alfred A. Knopf, 1962.

ATACK, JEREMY, AND BATEMAN, FRED. "How Long Did People Work in 1880?" University of Illinois. Mimeographed, 1989.

BARRETT, MICHAEL J. "The Case for More School Days." *Atlantic Monthly,* November 1990: 78–106.

BAUMOL, WILLIAM J. "Income and Substitution Effects in the Linder Theorem." *Quarterly Journal of Economics* 87 (1973): 629–33.

BECKER, GARY. "A Theory of the Allocation of Time." *Economic Journal* 75 (1965): 493–517.

BENNETT, AMANDA. *The Death of the Organization Man.* New York: William Morrow, 1990.

BENNETT, H. S. *Life on the English Manor.* Cambridge: Cambridge University Press, 1960.

BERG, MAXINE. *The Age of Manufactures, 1700–1820.* Totowa, New Jersey: Barnes & Noble, 1985.

BERNARD, JESSE. *The Future of Motherhood.* New York: Dial Press, 1974.

BEST, FRED. *Exchanging Earnings for Leisure: Findings of an Exploratory National Survey on Work Time Preferences.* Washington, D.C.: United States Employment and Training Administration, 1980.

BIENEFELD, M. A. *Working Hours in British Industry: An Economic History,* London School of Economics Research Monograph. London: Weidenfeld and Nicolson, 1972.

BLANCHARD, IAN. "Labour Productivity and Work Psychology in the English Mining Industry, 1400–1600." *Economic History Review* 31, 1 (1978): 1–24.

BLECKER, ROBERT A. *Are Americans on a Consumption Binge? The Evidence Reconsidered.* Washington, D.C.: Economic Policy Institute, 1990.

BLOCK, FRED. *Post-Industrial Possibilities: A Critique of Economic Discourse.* Berkeley: University of California, 1990.

BLUESTONE, BARRY, AND HARRISON, BENNETT. *The Great U-Turn.* New York: Basic Books, 1988.

BOISSONADE, P. *Life and Work in Medieval Europe.* New York: Dorset Press, 1987.

BOWLES, SAMUEL. "The Production Process in a Competitive Economy: Walrasian, Neo-Hobbesian, and Marxian Models." *American Economic Review* 75 (1985): 16–36.

BRAUDEL, FERNAND. *The Structures of Everyday Life: The Limits of the Possible.* London: Collins, 1981.

BROWN, ALAN; COLVIN, H. M.; AND TAYLOR, A. J. *The History of the King's Works, vol. I, The Middle Ages.* London: H. M. Stationery Office, 1963.

BROWN, CHARLES; HAMILTON, JAMES; AND MEDOFF, JAMES. *Employers Large and Small.* Cambridge, Mass.: Harvard University Press, 1990.

BUCKLEY, JOHN E. "Variations in Holidays, Vacations, and Area Pay Levels." *Monthly Labor Review* 112 (February 1989): 24–30.

BURDEN, DIANE S., AND GOOGINS, BRADLEY. *Boston University Balancing Job and Homelife Study.* Boston University, 1987, Mimeographed.

BUREAU OF LABOR STATISTICS. Office of Productivity and Technology. "Underlying Data for Indexes of Output Per Hour, Hourly Compensation, and Unit Labor Costs in Manufacturing, Twelve Industrial Countries, 1950–1988," June 1989.

————. *Labor Force Statistics Derived from the Current Population Survey, 1948–1987.* Washington, D.C.: Government Printing Office, August 1988.

————. "Marital and Family Characteristics of the Labor Force from the March 1990 Current Population Survey." October 1990. Unpublished.

————. *Employment and Earnings.* Washington, D.C.: Government Printing Office, August 1990.

————. "Multiple Jobholding Reached Record High in May 1989." Press release 89–529, 6 November 1989.

————. Office of Productivity and Technology. "Hourly Compensation Costs for Production Workers, 40 Manufacturing Industries, 34 Countries, 1975 and 1979–89." September 1990. Unpublished.

————. "Thirty-Eight Million Persons Do Volunteer Work." News release, 29 March 1990.

BURTLESS, GARY. "Are We All Working Too Hard? It's Better Than Watching Oprah." *Wall Street Journal,* 4 January 1990.

BUTLER, KATY. "The Great Boomer Bust." *Mother Jones* 14 (June 1989): 32–38.

BUTTERFIELD, BRUCE D. "Long Hours, Late Nights, Low Grades: In Labor-Short Towns across America, Teen-agers Are Overworked." *Boston Globe* Children at Work series, 24 April 1990.

————. "The New Harvest of Shame: For Farm Workers' Children, Cycle of Poverty and Work Unbroken." *Boston Globe* Children at Work series, 26 April 1990.

CANTOR, DANIEL, AND SCHOR, JULIET B. *Tunnel Vision: Labor, the World Economy, and Central America.* Boston: South End Press, 1987.

CAREY, MAX L. "Occupational Tenure in 1987: Many Workers Have Remained in Their Fields." *Monthly Labor Review* 111, 10 (October 1988): 3–12.

CHAMBERS, J. D. *The Workshop of the World.* London: Oxford University Press, 1961.

————. "The Domestic Rural Industries." Cited in Maxine Berg, *The Age of Manufactures 1700–1820,* p. 103. Totowa, New Jersey: Barnes & Noble, 1985.

CHAPMAN, FERN SCHUMER. "Executive Guilt: Who's Taking Care of the Children?" *Fortune,* 16 February 1987: 30–37.

CHENEY, C. R. "Rules for the Observance of Feast-Days in Medieval England." *Bulletin of the Institute of Historical Research* 34 (November 1961): 117–29.

CLAPP, B. W.; Fisher, H.E.S.; and Jurica, A.R.J.; eds., *Documents of English Economic History: England from 1000 to 1760,* vol. 1. London: G. Bell and Sons, 1977.

CLARK, GREGORY. "Impatience, Poverty, and Open Field Agriculture." 1986. Mimeographed.

COAKLEY, TOM. "One Couple's Lament Captures Anti-tax Mood." *Boston Globe,* 2 February 1990, p. 1.

COLEMAN, D. C. "Labour in the English Economy of the Seventeenth Century." *Economic History Review* New Series, 111 (April 1956): 280–95.

COMMONWEALTH FUND. *Americans Over 50 at Work Program,* Research Reports 1 and 2. New York: The Commonwealth Fund, 25 January and 8 March 1990.

COULTON, G. G. *The Medieval Village.* London: Cambridge University Press, 1925.

COVERMAN, SHELLEY. "Gender, Domestic Labor Time, and Wage Inequality." *American Sociological Review* 48 (October 1983): 623–37.

COWAN, RUTH SCHWARTZ. "Two Washes in the Morning and a Bridge Party at Night: The American Housewife between the Wars." *Women's Studies* 3 (1976): 147–72.

―――. *More Work for Mother: The Ironies of Household Technology from the Open Hearth to the Microwave.* New York: Basic Books, 1983.

CROSS, GARY. *Worktime and Industrialization: An International History.* Philadelphia: Temple University Press, 1988.

―――. *A Quest for Time: the Reduction of Work in Britain and France 1840–1940.* Berkeley: University of California Press, 1989.

―――. *Time and Money: The Making of Consumerist Modernity.* London: Routledge, forthcoming.

DALLY, ANN. *Inventing Motherhood: The Consequences of an Ideal.* New York: Schocken Books, 1983.

DE GRAZIA, SEBASTIAN. *Of Time, Work and Leisure.* New York: Twentieth Century Fund, 1962.

DECISION RESEARCH CORPORATION. *Decision Research Corporation's 1990 Leisure Study: Trends in America's Leisure Time and Activities.* Lexington, Mass.: D.C. Heath, February 1990.

DEEM, ROSEMARY. *All Work and No Play? The Sociology of Women and Leisure.* Milton Keynes: Open University Press, 1986.

DEMAUSE, LLOYD. "The Evolution of Childhood." In Lloyd deMause, ed., *The History of Childhood,* pp. 1–74. New York: Psychohistory Press, 1974.

DENISON, EDWARD. *Why Growth Rates Differ: Postwar Experience in Nine Western Countries.* Washington, D.C.: Brookings Institution, 1967.

DENNEY, REUEL. "The Leisure Society." *Harvard Business Review* 37 (3): 47.

DICKENS, WILLIAM, AND LUNDBERG, SHELLY J. "Hours Restrictions and Labor Supply." Working Paper 1638, National Bureau of Economic Research, 1985.

DOUGLAS, PAUL. *The Theory of Wages.* New York: Macmillan, 1934.

DUESENBERRY, JAMES. *Income, Saving and the Theory of Consumer Behavior.* Cambridge, Mass.: Harvard University Press, 1949.

EARLE, ALICE MORSE. *Home Life in Colonial Days.* Middle Village, New York: Jonathan David, 1975.

Economic Report of the President. Washington, D.C.: Government Printing Office, 1989 and 1991.

EDHOLM, O. G. "The Society's Lecture." *Ergonomics* 13, 6 (1970): 625–43.

EDWARDS, RICHARD. *Contested Terrain.* New York: Basic Books, 1979.

EHRENBERG, RONALD G., AND SCHUMANN, PAUL L. *Longer Hours or More Jobs? An Investigation of Amending Hours Legislation to Create Employment.* Ithaca: Cornell University Press, 1982.

EHRENREICH, BARBARA, AND ENGLISH, DEIRDRE. *For Her Own Good: 150 Years of the Experts' Advice to Women.* Garden City, New York: Anchor Press/Doubleday, 1978.

EPSTEIN, GERALD A., AND SCHOR, JULIET B. "Corporate Profitability as a Determinant of Restrictive Monetary Policy: Estimates for the Postwar United States." In Thomas Mayer, ed., *The Political Economy of American Monetary Policy.* Cambridge: Cambridge University Press, 1990.

EWEN, STUART. *Captains of Consciousness: Advertising and the Social Roots of the Consumer Culture.* New York: McGraw-Hill, 1976.

EWEN, STUART, AND EWEN, ELIZABETH. *Channels of Desire: Mass Images and the Shaping of American Consciousness.* New York: McGraw-Hill, 1982.

FAIR, RAY. *Specification, Estimation, and Analysis of Macroeconomic Models.* Cambridge, Mass.: Harvard University Press, 1984.

FISHER, ANNE B. *Wall Street Women: Women in Power on the Street Today.* New York: Knopf, 1990.

FLAIM, PAUL O., AND SEHGAL, ELLEN. "Displaced Workers of 1979–83: How Well Have They Fared?" *Monthly Labor Review* (June 1985): 3–16.

FOGEL, ROBERT W., AND ENGERMAN, STANLEY L. "Explaining the Relative Efficiency of Slave Agriculture in the Antebellum South." *American Economic Review* 67 (1977): 275–95.

FOLBRE, NANCY. "The Unproductive Housewife: Her Evolution in Nineteenth-Century Economic Thought." *Signs* 6 (Spring 1991): 463–84.

FOLBRE, NANCY, AND ABEL, MARJORIE. "Women's Work and Women's Households: Gender Bias in the U.S. Census." *Social Research* 56 (Autumn 1989): 545–69.

FOLBRE, NANCY, AND HARTMANN, HEIDI. "The Rhetoric of Self-interest and the Ideology of Gender." In Arjo Klamer, Donald McCloskey, and Robert Solow, eds., *The Consequences of Economic Rhetoric,* pp. 184–206. Cambridge: Cambridge University Press, 1988.

FRANK, ROBERT H. *Choosing the Right Pond.* New York: Oxford University Press, 1985.

FREEDMAN, JONATHAN. *Happy People.* New York: Harcourt, Brace, Jovanovich, 1978.

FUCHS, VICTOR. "His and Hers: Differences in Work and Income, 1959–79." *Journal of Labor Economics* 4 (1986): S245–72.

———. *Women's Quest for Economic Equality.* Cambridge, Mass.: Harvard University Press, 1988.

FUCHS, VICTOR R., AND JACOBSEN, JOYCE P. "Employee Response to Compulsory Short-Time Work." National Bureau of Economic Research Working Paper 2089, 1986.

GALBRAITH, JOHN KENNETH. *The Affluent Society,* 4th ed. Boston: Houghton Mifflin, 1984.

GALLMAN, ROBERT E. "The Agricultural Sector and the Pace of Economic Growth: U.S. Experience in the Nineteenth-Century." In David C. Klingaman and Richard K. Vedder, eds., *Essays in Nineteenth Century Economic History: The Old Northwest.* Athens, Ohio: Ohio University Press, 1975.

GALLUP, GEORGE H. *The Gallup Poll: Public Opinion.* New York: Random House, 1989.

GIBBS, NANCY. "How America Has Run Out of Time." *Time,* 24 April 1989.

GIEDION, SIEGFRIED. *Mechanization Takes Command: A Contribution to Anonymous History*. New York: Oxford University Press, 1948.

GILMAN, CHARLOTTE PERKINS. "Why Cooperative Housekeeping Fails." *Harper's Bazaar* 41 (July 1907): 629.

GINTIS, HERBERT. "Welfare Criteria with Endogenous Preferences: The Economics of Education." *International Economic Review* 15 (June 1974): 415–30.

———. "The Nature of the Labor Exchange." *Review of Radical Political Economics* 8 (1976): 36–54.

GLOTZ, GUSTAVE. *Ancient Greece at Work: An Economic History of Greece from the Homeric Period to the Roman Conquest*. New York: Knopf, 1927.

GOLDIN, CLAUDIA. *Understanding the Gender Gap: An Economic History of American Women*. New York: Oxford University Press, 1990.

GOLDMARK, JOSEPHINE. *Fatigue and Efficiency: A Study in Industry*. New York: Charities Publication Committee, 1912.

GORZ, ANDRÉ. *A Critique of Economic Reason*. London: Verso, 1989.

GREEN, HARVEY. *The Light of the Home: An Intimate View of the Lives of Women in Victorian America*. New York: Pantheon, 1983.

GREIS, THERESA DISS. *The Decline of Annual Hours Worked in the United States Since 1947*. Philadelphia: Industrial Relations Unit, Wharton, University of Pennsylvania, 1984.

GUREVICH, ARON. *Categories of Medieval Culture*. London: Routledge & Kegan Paul, 1985.

GUSTMANN, ALAN L., AND STEINMEIER, THOMAS L. "Minimum Hours Constraints and Retirement Behavior." *Contemporary Policy Issues* 3 (April 1982): 77–91.

———. "Partial Retirement and the Analysis of Retirement Behavior." *Industrial and Labor Relations Review* 37 (April 1984): 403–15.

GUTMAN, HERBERT. *Work, Culture and Society in Industrializing America: Essays in American Working-Class and Social History*. New York: Vintage, 1977.

HACKER, JONATHAN. "Interpreting the Dual Oppression of Women Workers: The Women's Trade Union League and the Development of the Family Wage Economy." unpublished thesis, Harvard College, April 1990.

HALL, TRISH. "Why All Those People Feel They Never Have Enough Time." *New York Times,* 2 January 1988, p. 1.

———. "The Dinner Party Quietly Bows to More Casual Alternatives." *New York Times,* 24 February 1988, p. C1.

HAM, JOHN. "Estimation of a Labour Supply Model with Censoring Due to Unemployment and Underemployment." *Review of Economic Studies* 49 (1982): 335–54.

HAMBRIDGE, GOVE, AND HAMBRIDGE, DOROTHY COOKE. "Leisure to Live." *Ladies' Home Journal* 46 (May 1930): 30.

HAMERMESH, DANIEL. "Sleep and the Allocation of Time." *Journal of Political Economy* 98 (October 1990): 922–43.

HAMMOND, J. L., AND HAMMOND, BARBARA. *The Town Labourer 1760–1832*. London: Longman, Green, 1919.

HANAWALT, BARBARA A. "Peasant Women's Contribution to the Home Economy in Late Medieval England." In Barbara A. Hanawalt, ed., *Women and Work in Pre-industrial Europe*. Bloomington, Ind.: Indiana University Press, 1986: 3–19.

HARRIMAN, ANN. *The Work/Leisure Trade Off: Reduced Work Time for Managers and Professionals*. New York: Praeger, 1982.

HARRIS, LOUIS. *Inside America*. New York: Vintage, 1987.

———. *Americans and the Arts*, Study 871009. New York: Louis Harris and Associates, January 1988.

HARTMANN, HEIDI. "Capitalism and Women's Work in the Home, 1900–1930." Yale University, 1974.

———. "Capitalism, Patriarchy, and Job Segregation by Sex." *Signs* 1 (Spring 1976): 137–69.

———. "The Family as a Locus of Gender, Class and Political Struggle: The Example of Housework." *Signs* 6 (1981): 366–94.

HAYDEN, DOLORES. *The Grand Domestic Revolution: A History of Feminist Designs for American Homes, Neighborhoods, and Cities*. Cambridge, Mass.: MIT Press, 1981.

HEARN, FRANCIS. *Domination, Legitimation, and Resistance: The Incorporation of the Nineteenth Century English Working Class*. Westport, Conn.: Greenwood Press, 1978.

HEDGES, JANICE, AND TAYLOR, DANIEL E. "Recent Trends in Worktime: Hours Edge Downward." *Monthly Labor Review* 103 (1980): 3–11.

HELSON, HARRY. *Adaptation Level Theory: An Experimental and Systematic Approach to Behavior*. New York: Harper & Row, 1964.

HERSCH, J. L. "Allocation of Time and Human Energy and Its Effects on Productivity." *Applied Economics* 17 (1985): 867–84.

HEWITT, PAUL S. "Something's Gone Terribly Wrong with Being 'Rich'." *Los Angeles Herald Tribune*, 7 January 1989.

HEWLETT, SYLVIA ANN. "Running Hard Just to Keep Up." *Time*, Special Issue entitled *Women: The Road Ahead*, Fall 1990.

———. *When the Bough Breaks: The Cost of Neglecting Our Children*. New York: Basic Books, 1991.

HILL, CHRISTOPHER. *Society and Puritanism in Pre-Revolutionary England*. New York: Schocken Books, 1964.

HINRICHS, KARL; ROCHE, WILLIAM; AND SIRIANNI, CARMEN, eds. *Working Time in Transition: The Political Economy of Working Hours in Industrial Nations*. Philadelphia: Temple University Press, 1991.

HOCHSCHILD, ARLIE. *The Second Shift: Working Parents and the Revolution at Home*. New York: Viking Penguin, 1989.

HOMANS, GEORGE. *English Villagers of the Thirteenth Century*. New York: Russell & Russell, 1960.

HONE, NATHANIEL J. *The Manor and Manorial Records*. New York: E. P. Dutton, 1906.

HOPKINS, ERIC. "Working Hours and Conditions During the Industrial Revolution: A Re-Appraisal." *Economic History Review* 35 (February 1982): 52–66.

HUNNICUTT, BENJAMIN. "The End of Shorter Hours." *Labor History* 25 (Summer 1984): 373–404.

———. *Work Without End: Abandoning Shorter Hours for the Right to Work.* Philadelphia: Temple University Press, 1988.

———. "The Short Life of Kellogg's Six-Hour Day—the Death of a Vision." University of Iowa. Mimeographed.

ILLICK, JOSEPH E. "Child-Rearing in Seventeenth-Century England and America." In Lloyd deMause, ed., *The History of Childhood.* New York: The Psychohistory Press, 1974,

INGLEHART, RONALD. *Culture Shift in Advanced Industrial Society.* Princeton, N.J.: Princeton University Press, 1990.

JONES, GARETH STEDMAN. *Languages of Class: Studies in English Working Class History 1832–1982.* Cambridge: Cambridge University Press, 1983.

JONES, JACQUELINE. *Labor of Love, Labor of Sorrow: Black Women, Work and the Family from Slavery to Present.* New York: Vintage Books, 1985.

JUSTER, F. THOMAS, AND STAFFORD, FRANK P., eds. *Time, Goods, and Well-Being.* Ann Arbor, Michigan: Institute for Social Research, University of Michigan, 1985.

———. "The Allocation of Time: Empirical Findings, Behavioral Models, and Problems of Measurement." Working Paper, Institute for Social Research, University of Michigan, February 1990.

KAHN, SHULAMIT, AND LANG, KEVIN. "Constraints on the Choice of Work Hours: Agency vs. Specific-Capital." National Bureau of Economic Research Working Paper 2238, May 1987.

KALECKI, MICHAL. "Political Aspects of Full Employment." In *Selected Essays on the Dynamics of the Capitalist Economy 1933–1970,* pp. 140–41. Cambridge: Cambridge University Press, 1971.

KANTER, ROSABETH MOSS. *Men and Women of the Corporation.* New York: Basic Books, 1977.

———. *When Giants Learn to Dance: Mastering the Challenge of Strategy, Management and Careers in the 1990s.* New York: Simon & Schuster, 1989.

KARASEK, ROBERT, AND THEÖRELL, TÖRES. *Healthy Work: Stress, Productivity and the Reconstruction of Working Life.* New York: Basic Books, 1990.

KATZMAN, DAVID M. *Seven Days a Week: Women and Domestic Service in Industrializing America.* New York: Oxford University Press, 1978.

KENNEDY, DANA. "Sexes Agree: Women Face Too Much Pressure." *Boston Globe,* 26 October 1990.

KETTERING, CHARLES F. "Keep the Consumer Dissatisfied." *Nation's Business* (January 1929).

KEYNES, JOHN MAYNARD. "Economic Possibilities for Our Grandchildren." In *Essays in Persuasion.* New York: Harcourt, Brace, 1932.

———. *The General Theory of Employment, Interest and Money.* London: Macmillan, 1936.

KILBORN, PETER T. "For Many Women, One Job Just Isn't Enough." *New York Times,* 15 February 1990.

KINGSTON, PAUL WILLIAMS, AND NOCK, STEVEN L. "Time Together Among Dual-Earner Couples." *American Sociological Review* 52 (June 1987): 391–400.

KLEIN, BRUCE W. "Missed Work and Lost Hours, May 1985." *Monthly Labor Review* 109 (November 1986): 26–30.

KNEELAND, HILDEGARDE. "Woman's Economic Contribution in the Home." *The Annals of the American Academy of Political and Social Science* 143 (May 1929): 33–38.

KNOOP, DOUGLAS, AND JONES, G. P. *The Medieval Mason.* New York: Barnes & Noble, 1967.

KOSONEN, KATRI. "Saving and Economic Growth in a Nordic Perspective." In Jukka Pekkarinen, Matti Pohjola, and Bob Rowthorn, *Social Corporatism: A Superior System?* Oxford: Clarendon Press, 1991.

KOWINSKI, W. S. "A Mall Covers the Waterfront." *The New York Times Magazine,* 13 December 1981.

KROEGER, BROOKE. "Feeling Poor on $600,000 a Year." *New York Times,* 26 April 1987.

KUMAR, KRISHNAN. "From Work to Employment and Unemployment: The English Experience." In R. E. Pahl, ed., *On Work: Historical, Comparative and Theoretical Approaches,* pp. 138–64. Oxford: Basil Blackwell, 1988.

LANDERS, ANN. *Boston Globe,* 26 February 1990.

LANDES, DAVID. *Revolution in Time: Clocks and the Making of the Modern World.* Cambridge, Mass.: Harvard University Press, 1983.

LARRABEE, ERIC, AND MEYERSOHN, ROLF, eds. *Mass Leisure.* Glencoe, Ill.: Free Press, 1958.

LEBERGOTT, STANLEY. *The American Economy: Income, Wealth and Want.* Princeton, N.J.: Princeton University Press, 1976.

LEE, RICHARD. "What Hunters Do for a Living or How to Make Out on Scarce Resources." In Richard B. Lee and Irven DeVore, eds., *Man the Hunter,* pp. 30–48. Chicago: Aldine, 1968.

LEETE-GUY, LAURA, AND SCHOR, JULIET B. "Is There a Time Squeeze? Estimates of Market and Non-Market Hours in the United States, 1969–1987." HIER Working Paper 1525, Harvard University, November 1989.

———. "Assessing the Time Squeeze Hypothesis: Estimates of Market and Non-market Hours in the United States, 1969–1987." Harvard University, June 1990 [unpublished mimeo], and forthcoming, *Industrial Relations.*

LE GOFF, JACQUES. *Time, Work and Culture in the Middle Ages.* Chicago: Chicago University Press, 1980.

LEVINE, DAVID I., AND TYSON, LAURA D'ANDREA. "Participation, Productivity, and the Firm's Environment." In Alan Blinder, ed., *Paying for Productivity,* pp. 183–244. Washington, D.C.: Brookings Institution, 1990.

LEVINE, ROBERT. "The Pace of Life." *Psychology Today* (October 1989): 42–46.

LEVITAN, SAR A., AND BELOUS, RICHARD S. *Shorter Hours, Shorter Weeks: Spreading the Work to Reduce Unemployment.* Baltimore: Johns Hopkins University Press, 1977.

LEVY, FRANK. *Dollars and Dreams: The Changing American Income Distribution.* New York: W. W. Norton, 1988.

LEWIS, H. G. "Employer Interests in Employee Hours of Work." 1969, Mimeographed.

LINDER, STAFFAN B. *The Harried Leisure Class.* New York: Columbia University Press, 1970.

LYND, ROBERT S., AND LYND, HELEN MERRELL. *Middletown in Transition: A Study in Cultural Conflicts.* New York: Harcourt, Brace, 1929.

LYNES, RUSSELL. "Time on Our Hands." In Eric Larrabee and Rolf Meyerson, eds., *Mass Leisure,* p. 346. Glencoe, Ill.: Free Press, 1958.

MARCHAND, ROLAND. *Advertising the American Dream: Making Way for Modernity 1920–1940.* Berkeley: University of California Press, 1985.

MARGLIN, STEPHEN A. *Growth, Distribution, and Prices.* Cambridge, Mass.: Harvard University Press, 1984.

————. "Losing Touch: The Cultural Conditions of Worker Accommodation and Resistance." In Frédérique Apffel-Marglin and Stephen A. Marglin, eds., *Dominating Knowledge: Development, Culture, and Resistance.* Oxford: Clarendon Press, 1990.

MARGLIN, STEPHEN A., AND SCHOR, JULIET B., eds. *The Golden Age of Capitalism: Reinterpreting the Postwar Experience.* Oxford: Clarendon Press, 1990.

MARGOLIS, DIANE ROTHBARD. *The Managers: Corporate Life in America.* New York: William Morrow, 1979.

MARGOLIS, MAXINE. "In Hartford, Hannibal, and (New) Hampshire, Heloise Is Hardly Helpful." *Ms.* 9 (June 1976): 28–36.

————. *Mothers and Such: Views of American Women and Why They Changed.* Berkeley: University of California Press, 1984.

MARRUS, MICHAEL R., ed. *The Emergence of Leisure.* New York: Harper Torchbooks, 1974.

MARX, KARL. *Capital.* New York: Vintage, 1976.

MassMutual Family Values Study. Washington, D.C.: Mellman & Lazarus, 1989.

MATTHEWS, GLENNA. *"Just A Housewife": The Rise and Fall of Domesticity in America.* New York: Oxford University Press, 1987.

MCCARTHY, FREDERICK D., AND MCARTHUR, MARGARET. "The Food Quest and the Time Factor in Aboriginal Economic Life." Reprinted from *Records of the American-Australian Scientific Expedition to Arnhem Land,* vol. 2. Melbourne: Melbourne University Press, 1960.

MCCARTHY, MAUREEN E., AND ROSENBERG, GAIL S. *Work Sharing Case Studies.* Kalamazoo, Mich.: W. E. Upjohn Institute, 1981.

MCCRATE, ELAINE. "Trade, Merger, and Employment: Economic Theory on Marriage." *Review of Radical Political Economics* 19 (1987): 73–89.

MCGAUGHEY, WILLIAM, JR. *A Shorter Workweek in the 1980s.* White Bear Lake, Minn.: Thistlerose Publications, 1981.

————. "The International Dimensions of Reduced Hours." *Society for the Reduction of Human Labor Newsletter* 1 (1).

McGuire, Nan, et al. "Survey of Private Sector Work and Family Policy." San Francisco: New Ways to Work, 1986.

McKendrick, Neil; Brewer, John; and Plumb, J. H. *The Birth of a Consumer Society: The Commercialization of Eighteenth-Century England.* London: Europa Publications, 1982.

Meissner, Martin, et al. "No Exit for Wives: Sexual Division of Labour and the Cumulation of Household Demands in Canada." In R. E. Pahl, ed., *On Work: Historical, Comparative and Theoretical Approaches,* pp. 476–95. Oxford: Basil Blackwell, 1988.

Mellor, Earl F., and Haugen, Steven E. "Hourly Paid Workers: Who They Are and What They Earn." *Monthly Labor Review* 109 (February 1986): 20–26.

Mellor, Earl F., and Parks, William II. "A Year's Work: Labor Force Activity from a Different Perspective." *Monthly Labor Review* (September 1988): 13–18.

Mishel, Lawrence, and Frankel, David M. *The State of Working America.* Armonk, N.Y.: M. E. Sharpe, 1990–91 Edition.

Mishel, Lawrence, and Simon, Jacqueline. *The State of Working America.* Washington, D.C.: Economic Policy Institute, 1988.

Moffitt, Robert. "The Tobit Model, Hours of Work, and Institutional Constraints." *Review of Economics and Statistics* 64 (August 1982): 510–15.

Montgomery, David. *Beyond Equality: Labor and Radical Republicans 1862–1872.* New York: Alfred A. Knopf, 1976.

Moody, Fred. "When Work Becomes an Obsession." *Baltimore City Paper,* 23 October 1987.

Moorman, Barbara, and Olmsted, Barney. "V-Time: A New Way to Work." San Francisco: New Ways to Work, 1985.

Morand, Martin J., and Macoy, Ramelle, eds. *Short-time Compensation: A Formula for Work Sharing.* New York: Pergamon Press, 1984.

Niemi, Richard G.; Mueller, John; and Smith, Tom W. *Trends in Public Opinion: A Compendium of Survey Data.* New York: Greenwood Press, 1989.

9to5, *The 9to5 National Survey on Women and Stress.* Cleveland, Ohio: 9to5, 1984.

Norton, Mary Beth. *Liberty's Daughters: The Revolutionary Experience of American Women 1750–1800.* Glenwood, Ill.: Scott, Foresman, 1980.

Nyland, Chris. *Reduced Worktime and the Management of Production.* Cambridge: Cambridge University Press, 1989.

Obelkovich, James. *Religion and Rural Society: South Lindsey 1825–1875.* Oxford: Clarendon Press, 1976.

O'Malley, Michael. *Keeping Watch: A History of American Time.* New York: Viking, 1990.

O'Reilly, Brian. "Is Your Company Asking Too Much?" *Fortune,* 12 March 1990: 38–46.

Owen, John D. *Working Hours: An Economic Analysis.* Lexington, Mass.: Lexington Books, 1979.

————. *Working Lives: The American Work Force Since 1920.* Lexington, Mass.: Lexington Books, 1986.

————. *Reduced Working Hours: Cure for Unemployment or Economic Burden?* Baltimore: Johns Hopkins University Press, 1989.

Oxford English Dictionary. Oxford: Oxford University Press, 1971.

Parents United for Child Care (PUCC). survey comments, Boston, Massachusetts, 1989. Mimeographed.

PARKINSON, C. NORTHCOTE. *Parkinson's Law and Other Studies in Administration.* Boston: Houghton-Mifflin, 1957.

PARSONS, DONALD O. "The Decline in Male Labor Force Participation." *Journal of Political Economy* 88, 11 (1980): 117–34.

PEIXOTTO, JESSICA. *Getting and Spending at the Professional Standard of Living.* New York: Macmillan, 1927.

PEKKARINEN, JUKKA; POHJOLA, MATTI; AND ROWTHORN, BOB, eds. *Social Corporatism: A Superior System?* Oxford: Clarendon Press, 1991.

PERROT, MICHELLE, ed. *A History of Private Life IV: From the Fires of Revolution to the Great War.* Cambridge, Mass.: Belknap Press, Harvard University Press, 1990.

PINCHBECK, IVY. *Women Workers and the Industrial Revolution.* London: Frank Cass, 1930.

PLECK, JOSEPH H. *Working Wives, Working Husbands.* Beverly Hills: Russell Sage, 1985.

POLLARD, SIDNEY. "Factory Discipline in the Industrial Revolution." *Economic History Review* 26 (December 1963): 254–71.

POSPISIL, LEOPOLD. *Kapauku Papuan Economy.* Yale University Publication in Anthropology 67, 1963.

PRESSER, HARRIET. "Shift Work and Child Care Among Young Dual-Earner American Parents." *Journal of Marriage and the Family* 50 (February 1988): 133–48.

————. "Can We Make Time for Children? The Economy, Work Schedules, and Child Care." *Demography* 26 (November 1989): 523–44.

PUBLIC AFFAIRS PRESS. *The Shorter Work Week.* Washington, D.C.: Public Affairs Press, 1957.

PUTNAM, BERTHA HAVEN. *Enforcement of the Statutes of Laborers.* New York: Longmans, Green, 1908.

QUINDLEN, ANNA. "Men at Work, Public and Private." *New York Times,* 18 February 1990, p. 19.

RAFF, DANIEL M. G., AND SUMMERS, LAWRENCE H. "Did Henry Ford Pay Efficiency Wages?" *Journal of Labor Economics* 5 (1987): S57–S86.

————. "Wage Determination Theory and the Five-Dollar Day at Ford." *Journal of Economic History* 48 (June 1988): 387–99.

RAZZELL, P. E., AND WAINWRIGHT, R. W. *The Victorian Working Class: Selections from Letters to the Morning Chronicle.* London: Frank Cass, 1973.

REID, DOUGLAS A. "The Decline of St. Monday; 1766–1876." *Past and Present* 71 (May 1976): 76–101.

REXROAT, CYNTHIA, AND SHEHAN, CONSTANCE. "The Family Life Cycle and Spouses'

Time in Housework." *Journal of Marriage and the Family* 49 (November 1987): 737–50.

RIESMAN, DAVID. "Leisure and Work in Post-Industrial Society." In Eric Larrabee and Rolf Meyersohn, eds., *Mass Leisure*. Glencoe, Ill.: Free Press, 1958.

RIESMAN, DAVID; DENNEY, REUEL; AND GLAZER, NATHAN. *The Lonely Crowd: A Study of the Changing American Character*. New Haven: Yale University Press, 1950.

RIFKIN, JEREMY. *Time Wars*. New York: Henry Holt, 1987.

RITCHIE, NORA. "Labour Conditions in Essex in the Reign of Richard II." In E. M. Carus-Wilson, ed., *Essays in Economic History,* vol. II, pp. 91–107. London: Edward Arnold, 1962.

ROBERT HALF INTERNATIONAL. "Family Time Is More Important Than Rapid Career Advancement: Survey Shows Both Men and Women Support Parent Tracking." San Francisco, 28 June 1989.

ROBINSON, JOHN P. "Household Technology and Household Work." In Sarah Fenstermaker Berk, ed., *Women and Household Labor*. Beverly Hills: Russell Sage, 1980: 53–68.

———. "The Validity and Reliability of Diaries versus Alternative Time Use Measures." In F. Thomas Juster and Frank P. Stafford, eds., *Time, Goods, and Well-Being*. Ann Arbor: Institute for Social Research, University of Michigan, 1985: 63–91.

———. "Trends in Americans' Use of Time: Some Preliminary 1965–1975–1985 Comparisons." University of Maryland Survey Research Center, 1986. Mimeographed.

———. "Who's Doing the Housework?" *American Demographics* 10 (December 1988): 24–28.

———. "Time's Up." *American Demographics* 11 (July 1989): 32–35.

———. "The Time Squeeze." *American Demographics* 12 (February 1990): 30–33.

ROBINSON, JOHN P.; ANDREYENKOV, VLADIMIR G.; AND PATRUSHEV, VASILY D. *The Rhythm of Everyday Life*. Boulder, Colo.: Westview Press, 1988.

RODGERS, DANIEL T. *The Work Ethic in Industrial America 1850–1920*. Chicago: University of Chicago Press, 1978.

RODGERS, EDITH. *Discussion of Holidays in the Later Middle Ages*. New York: Columbia University Press, 1940.

ROEDIGER, DAVID R., AND FONER, PHILIP S. *Our Own Time: A History of American Labor and the Working Class*. London: Verso, 1989.

ROGERS, JAMES E. THOROLD. *Six Centuries of Work and Wages*. London: Allen and Unwin, 1949.

ROJEK, CHRIS. *Capitalism and Leisure Theory*. London: Tavistock Publications, 1985.

ROPER CENTER. *The Public Perspective: A Roper Center Review of Public Opinion Polling*. 1 (May/June 1990).

ROSE, STEPHEN, AND FASENFEST, DAVID. "Family Incomes in the 1980s: New Pressures on Wives, Husbands, and Young Adults." Economic Policy Institute, Working Paper 103, November 1988.

ROTHBERG, DIANNE S., AND COOK, BARBARA ENSOR. *Employee Benefits for Part-Timers*. McLean, Va.: Association of Part-Time Professionals, 1987.

RYBCZYNSKI, WITOLD. "Living Smaller." *Atlantic Monthly* (February 1991): 64–78.

SAHLINS, MARSHALL. *Stone Age Economics*. New York: Aldine, 1972.

SALTZMAN, AMY. *Downshifting: Reinventing Success on a Slower Track*. New York: HarperCollins, 1991.

SANGER, DAVID. "Tokyo Tries to Find Out if 'Salarymen' are Working Themselves to Death." *New York Times*, 19 March 1990.

SCHOR, JULIET B. "The Economics and Politics of Full Employment." *Socialist Review* 81 (May 1985): 65–92.

———. "Does Work Intensity Respond to Macroeconomic Variables? Evidence from British Manufacturing, 1970–1986." Harvard Institute for Economic Research, Discussion Paper 1396, April 1988.

———. "Why I Am No Longer a Progressive." *Zeta* (April 1990).

———. "The Underproduction of Leisure: The Economics of Output Bias." Harvard University, November 1990. Mimeographed.

———. "Working Hours and Global Inequality." *World Development* 19 (January 1991): 73–84.

SCHOR, JULIET B., AND BOWLES, SAMUEL. "Employment Rents and the Incidence of Strikes." *Review of Economics and Statistics* 49 (November 1987): 584–92.

SCHUMACHER, EDWARD F. *Small Is Beautiful: Economics as if People Mattered*. New York: Harper & Row, 1973.

SECCOMBE, WALLY. "Patriarchy Stabilized: The Construction of the Male Breadwinner Wage Norm in Nineteenth-Century Britain." *Social History* 2 (January 1986): 53–76.

SEN, AMARTYA. *Employment, Technology and Development*. Oxford: Clarendon Press, 1975.

SHANK, SUSAN E. "Preferred Hours of Work and Corresponding Earnings." *Monthly Labor Review* (November 1986): 40–44.

SHAPIRO, LAURA. *Perfection Salad: Women and Cooking at the Turn of the Century*. New York: Farrar, Straus & Giroux, 1986.

SHERIDAN, LAURIE. "Interviews on Working Hours." Mimeographed.

SIRIANNI, CARMEN. "Economies of Time in Social Theory: Three Approaches Compared." *Current Perspectives in Social Theory* 8 (1987): 161–95.

SMITH, JAMES P., AND WARD, MICHAEL. "Time-Series Growth in the Labor Force." *Journal of Labor Economics* 3 (January 1985): S59–S90.

SOLO, SALLY. "Stop Whining and Get Back to Work." *Fortune*, 12 March 1990: 49–50.

STANSELL, CHRISTINE. *City of Women: Sex and Class in New York*. New York: Alfred A. Knopf, 1986.

STONE, LAWRENCE. *The Family, Sex, and Marriage in England 1500–1800*. New York: Harper & Row, 1977.

STRASSER, SUSAN. *Never Done: A History of American Housework*. New York: Pantheon, 1982.

SUMNER, HELEN L. "Causes of the Awakening." In John R. Commons, et al., eds. *History of Labor in the United States.* New York: Macmillan, 1918.

SWADOS, HARVEY. "Less Work—Less Leisure." *The Nation,* 22 February 1958, pp. 153–58.

SWEENEY, JOHN J., AND NUSSBAUM, KAREN. *Solutions for the New Work Force.* Washington D.C.: Seven Locks Press, 1989.

SZALAI, ALEXANDER. *The Use of Time: Daily Activities of Urban and Suburban Populations in Twelve Countries.* The Hague: Mouton, 1972.

TAKAHASHI, HIDEO. "The Long Workweek in Japan: Difficult to Reduce." *Japan Economic Institute Report* 11A. Washington, D.C., 1990.

TAYLOR, DANIEL E., AND SEKSCENSKI, EDWARD S. "Workers on Long Schedules, Single and Multiple Jobholders." Research Summary, *Monthly Labor Review* 105 (May 1982): 47–53.

THOMAS, KEITH. "Work and Leisure in Pre-Industrial Society." *Past and Present* 29 (December 1964): 50–66.

THOMPSON, E. P. "Time, Work-Discipline and Industrial Capitalism." *Past and Present* 38 (December 1967): 56–97.

THRIFT, NIGEL. "Owner's Time and Own Time: The Making of a Capitalist Time Consciousness, 1300–1880." *Lund Studies in Human Geography* 48 (1984): 56–84.

TOBIAS, ANDREW. "Getting By on $100,000 a Year." *Esquire,* 23 May 1978.

TREJO, STEPHEN J. "Compensating Differentials and Overtime Pay Regulation." Working Paper 2–89, Department of Economics, University of California Santa Barbara, January 1989.

UNITED STATES CHAMBER OF COMMERCE. *Employee Benefits 1988 Edition: Survey Data from Benefit Year 1987.* Washington, D.C.: U.S. Chamber of Commerce, 1988.

UNITED STATES DEPARTMENT OF COMMERCE. *Statistical Abstract of the United States.* Washington, D.C.: Government Printing Office, 1990.

UNITED STATES DEPARTMENT OF LABOR. *Labor Force Statistics Derived From the Current Population Survey, 1948–1987.* Washington, D.C.: U.S. Department of Labor, August 1988.

———. Press Release 90–96, "Consumer Expenditures in 1988," November 1990.

VAN GINNEKEN, WOUTER, "Employment and the Reduction of the Work Week: A Comparison of Seven European Macro-economic Models." *International Labour Review* 123 (1984): 35–52.

VANEK, JOANN. "Time Spent in Housework." *Scientific American* 231 (November 1974): 116–20.

VICKREY, CLAIR. "The Time-Poor: A New Look at Poverty." *Journal of Human Resources* 12 (1977): 27–48.

WACHTEL, PAUL. *The Poverty of Affluence: A Psychological Portrait of the American Way of Life.* Philadelphia: New Society Publishers, 1989.

WALZER, JOHN F. "A Period of Ambivalence: Eighteenth-Century American Childhood." In deMause, Lloyd, *History of Childhood.* New York: Psychohistory Press, 1974.

WANDERSEE, WINIFRED D. *Women's Work and Family Values, 1920–1940.* Cambridge, Mass.: Harvard University Press, 1981.

WARING, MARILYN. *If Women Counted: A New Feminist Economics.* New York: Harper & Row, 1988.

WEBSTER, HUTTON. *Rest Days: A Study in Early Law and Morality.* New York: Macmillan, 1926.

WELTNER, LINDA. "Once a Shopping Addict, She's Got a Brand New Bag." *Boston Globe,* 16 November 1990, p. 50.

WHAPPLES, ROBERT N. "The Shortening of the American Work Week: An Economic and Historical Analysis of its Context, Causes and Consequences." Ph.D. dissertation, University of Pennsylvania, 1990.

WHITE, MICHAEL. *Case Studies of Shorter Working Time* no. 597. London: Policy Studies Institute, 1981.

WHYTE, WILLIAM FOOTE. *Money and Motivation: An Analysis of Incentives in Industry.* Westport, Conn.: Greenwood Press, 1977.

WILKERSON, ISABEL. "Middle-Class Blacks Try to Grip a Ladder While Lending a Hand." *New York Times,* 26 November 1990.

WILSON, WILLIAM J. *The Truly Disadvantaged: The Inner City, the Underclass, and Public Policy.* Chicago: University of Chicago Press, 1987.

WOLFE, ALAN. *America's Impasse: The Rise and Fall of the Politics of Growth.* New York: Pantheon Books, 1981.

World Development Report. Washington, D.C.: World Bank, published annually.

WORTHY, FRED S. "You're Probably Working Too Hard." *Fortune,* 27 April 1987: 133–39.

WOYTINSKY, W. S. "Hours of Labor." In *Encyclopedia of the Social Sciences,* vol. III. New York: Macmillan, 1935.

YAMADA, NARUMI. "Working Time in Japan: Recent Trends and Issues." *International Labour Review* 124 (November–December 1985): 699–718.

YANKELOVICH, DANIEL. *The World at Work: An International Report on Jobs, Productivity, and Human Values.* New York: Octagon Books, 1985.

ZEISEL, JOSEPH S. "The Workweek in American Industry 1850–1956." *Monthly Labor Review* 81 (1958): 23–29.

ZUBOFF, SHOSHANNA. *In The Age of the Smart Machine.* New York: Basic Books, 1988.

Index

— get reviews_mp4.
— call Irene re Heckscher